Eighteenth-Century Criminal Transportation

Eighteenth-Century Criminal Transportation:

The Formation of the Criminal Atlantic

Gwenda Morgan and Peter Rushton

First published 2004 by
PALGRAVE MACMILLAN
Houndmills, Basingstoke, Hampshire RG21 6XS and 175 Fifth Avenue, New York, N.Y. 10010
Companies and representatives throughout the world

PALGRAVE MACMILLAN is the global academic imprint of the Palgrave Macmillan division of St. Martin's Press, LLC and of Palgrave Macmillan Ltd. Macmillan® is a registered trademark in the United States, United Kingdom and other countries. Palgrave is a registered trademark in the European Union and other countries.

ISBN 0–333–79338–2 hardback

This book is printed on paper suitable for recycling and made from fully managed and sustained forest sources.

A catalogue record for this book is available from the British Library.

Library of Congress Cataloging-in-Publication Data
Morgan, Gwenda.
    Eighteenth-century criminal transportation : the formation of the criminal Atlantic / Gwenda Morgan and Peter Rushton.
        p.   cm.
    Includes bibliographical references and Index.
    ISBN 0–333–79338–2 (cloth)
    1. Penal colonies—Great Britain—Colonies. 2. Penal colonies—Maryland. 3. Penal colonies—Virginia. I. Rushton, Peter. II. Title.
HV8949.M67   2004
365′.34—dc22

                                                                2003060044

10   9   8   7   6   5   4   3   2   1
13   12   11   10   09   08   07   06   05   04

Printed and bound in Great Britain by
Antony Rowe Ltd, Chippenham and Eastbourne

For Gareth and Lesley

Contents

List of Tables

Acknowledgements

We have incurred a great many academic and personal debts during this long project, involving many individuals and institutions in Europe and the United States. Some are indirect – without Roger Ekirch and Peter Wilson Coldham, for example, no one would be in the convict business at all.

Things have changed since the research started. In Virginia, the *Virginia Gazette* is online, and the Virginia Runaways project means that searching for British convicts in eighteenth-century records has become much easier. On the other side of the Atlantic, most English archives and record offices have combined new technology with their traditional role of producing grubby documents for their visitors. The core of the research process, though, remains the text on the desk in front of us.

Consequently: we acknowledge the support of the British Academy for giving us a grant to help with the extensive travelling required to complete this project; and we owe thanks to the staff of the many libraries and archives we have consulted during the work for this project:

In London: the British Library, Euston Road and the newspaper library, Colindale; the Institute of Historical Research; London Record Office; Public Record Office; University of London Library.

In England: Bristol Record Office; Bristol Reference Library; Cumberland Record Office, at Carlisle, Kendal and Whitehaven (Local Studies Centre); County Durham Record Office; Devon Record Office (Exeter); Lancashire Record Office; Northumberland Record Office (Morpeth and Wideopen); Tyne and Wear Archives Service; University of Durham Library; University of Newcastle-upon-Tyne Library; University of Sunderland Library; Westcountry Study Centre, Exeter.

In the United States: John D. Rockfeller Library, Colonial Williamsburg; Library of Congress, Washington D.C.; Maryland State Archives, Annapolis; Maryland Historical Society, Baltimore; Omohundro Institute of Early American History and Culture, Williamsburg; Earl Gregg Swem Library, College of William and Mary.

Many individuals, too, have offered academic help, advice, personal support, encouragement and hospitality during the work, notably Clare Anderson, Bob Barnes, Tony Barrow, John Beattie, Lois Green Carr, Irene

Cassidy, Bill Champion, Margaret Cook, Clive Emsley, Kim Foley, Pat Gibbs, Chris Grasso, Jack Greene, Ann Gross and Bob Gross, Farley Grubb, Joan Hoff, Ron Hoffman, Don and Elizabeth Homsey, Jim Horn, June Jameson, James Kelly, René Lévy, Rob and Jan Lewis, Irene Lewis, Del Moore, Jane Moore, Ken Morgan, Phil and Barbara Morgan, Kay Moyne, Ian Roberts R. J. Rockefeller, Dorothy Rouse-Bottom, Lesley Rushton, Jean Russo, Beverly Smith, Thad Tate, Lorena Walsh, and the participants and audiences of many conferences.

Finally we should mourn the passing of the current Research Assessment Exercise which provided funds to the History Unit of the University of Sunderland, which we were able to draw on. It will be sorely missed.

Abbreviations used in Referencing

BL British Library
BRO Bristol Record Office
DRO County Durham Record Office
NRO Northumberland Record Office
OBSP Old Bailey Sessions Papers
PRO Public Record Office

Coldham, *King's Passengers* – Peter W. Coldham, *The King's Passengers to Maryland and Virginia* (Westminster, MD: Willow Bend Books, 2000).
Morgan and Rushton, *Rogues, Thieves* – Gwenda Morgan and Peter Rushton, *Rogues, Thieves and the Rule of Law: the Problem of Law Enforcement in North-East England, 1718–1800* (London: UCL Press, 1998).

1
Introduction: the Formation of the Criminal Atlantic

In August 1752, a performance of *The Beggar's Opera* was advertised at the New Theatre, Upper Marlborough, by the Company of Comedians from Annapolis, capital of Maryland. Whether there were many convicts eager to be in the audience in what one visitor noted as a 'tobacco-house', is not recorded, but there is a certain irony in the fact that England's best-known dramatic representation of criminals was going to be performed in the colony with the highest proportion of transported convicts in its population. This was not uncommon, for Gay's musical play provided one of the most popular entertainments in the colonies, in Virginia as well Maryland.[1] If British felons did attend, they would only have become prouder of their criminal professions than before, at least so Daniel Defoe asserted (a remark one writer describes as 'pretty rich from the author of *Moll Flanders*').[2] In England, according to apocryphal stories, youthful highwaymen were arrested in London with copies of *The Beggar's Opera* in their pockets, and so influential was the live performance that one seventeen-year-old is supposed to have left the play and immediately spent his last guinea on a brace of pistols in order to emulate his stage hero, the gentleman-highwayman MacHeath.[3] Jenny Diver, one of the women who betrayed MacHeath to the authorities, whom he called his 'dear slut', became virtually real in the figure of Mary Young, alias Jenny Diver, Elizabeth Davis, Catherine wife of Henry Higgins, or Jane Webb alias Murphey, repeatedly transported and successfully returning, who acquired the name and was in fact better known by it in the press than by her various aliases. She achieved national fame as newspapers throughout England reported her return from America in 1738, and the posthumous account of her life after her execution for picking pockets in 1741 became a best-seller.[4]

Reality and fiction become hard to distinguish in this process of inter-weaving literary figures, images and popular reputations. Legendary figures such as the late-seventeenth-century hangman Jack Ketch were turned into generic identities, applicable to anyone who served in the office of executioner. Polly Peachum fears the scene of MacHeath's hanging which she sees in her mind's eye – 'that so comely a Youth should be brought to Disgrace! I see him weep at the tree! The Whole Circle are in Tears! Jack Ketch himself hesitates to perform his duty; he would be glad to lose his fee, by a reprieve'.[5] But the name Ketch was also used in America. In 1756, convict servant man Thomas Poney ran away from Thomas John Hammond in Annapolis: he was 'commonly known by the name of Tom Ketch, having formerly been a Hangman in this County'. In addition, said the advertisement offering ten shillings reward, he 'stutters very much when he speaks hastily, has grey eyes and has a hanging look'. Yet Jack Ketch may not have been a real person either, despite the confidence with which he is attributed to a time and place, given the contradictory accounts of his late-seventeenth-century life.[6] 'When truth becomes legend, print the legend' has long been the maxim of the popular print industry.[7]

The Beggar's Opera had an immediate impact not just because 'crime was topical', but also because there were already so many accounts of crime and corruption in the cheap prints produced for the British public. The conventions of describing the lives of criminals and their underworld were well established, and thoroughly exploited by John Gay, with musical as well as characterful invention.[8] The colonial inter-est, by contrast, was less the outcome of a pre-existing print culture than an unsurprising fascination with the images of British crime and crim-inals: between 1600 and the American Revolution, the colonies were the recipients of many thousands of convicted criminals from Britain and Ireland. Maryland and Virginia in particular made good use of these reluctant migrants as well as many less culpable rejects such as orphans, vagrants and vagabonds emptied from gaols and workhouses. Simulta-neously, British interest in the fate of these migrants once they reached the colonies had been stimulated by satirical representations such as Maryland lawyer Ebenezer Cook's *The Sot-Weed Factor*, and Daniel Defoe's *Moll Flanders*. Both suggested that the colonies were places where criminals could become respectable, the thief turned magistrate, the prostitute a planter's wife, and all previous history forgotten or denied.[9] Moreover, after the 1718 Transportation Act, shipping and receiving convicts became a far larger business than ever before, with hundreds a year leaving Britain for America, going mainly to the

Chesapeake colonies of Virginia and Maryland. With the British government subsidizing the shipments from London and the Home Counties, and investing a great deal of legislative effort into the new direction in penal policy, public debate about the efficacy of the punishment naturally turned to the convicts and their subsequent careers in the colonies. Though convict transportation has been regarded as somewhat anomalous in the development of early modern penal systems, Britain was not entirely alone in seeking colonial solutions to domestic penal problems.[10] Other countries used exile or banishment in their armoury of punishments, though few pursued it so assiduously as a means of avoiding the consequences of so many capital statutes. Transportation, for the British, was both a means of punishing the petty criminal and releasing many more serious offenders from execution at the gallows. Nevertheless, there were similar experiments elsewhere. Portugal had exiled criminals to the mountain regions before adopting banishment to parts of its new empire in the sixteenth century. 'Brazil was populated by penal exiles, people taken from the kingdom to its advantage', said one seventeenth-century soldier, and it is therefore scarcely surprising to hear an early-twentieth-century Portuguese remark that 'penal exile is a traditional sentence among us'. Yet Brazil was also a place where such convicts could prosper, given the availability of so much land and so many Indian slaves. The French, too, attempted settlements of convicts in America, in Lousiana in the early eighteenth century, with variable results. Though it proved unprofitable financially, the experiment did establish that 'transportation was taken very seriously as a punishment, and everyone in France agreed that being sent to Louisiana was about the worst penalty one could suffer'. Later, in the nineteenth and early twentieth centuries, the threat of being sent to the West Indian penal settlement would hang over many French criminals. In contrast to Russia, these were countries which, like Britain, did not possess the option of internal exile for large numbers of criminals.[11]

Nevertheless, it was the British who in the eighteenth century made transportation a key element of their penal policy, and the consequences for some of their colonies were profound, both economically and culturally. The way the punishment was adopted in different regions is dealt with in Chapter 2, but the most striking aspect of transportation is the persistence with which the British authorities resorted to it, from the later Elizabethan period to the Victorian era. One commentator has gone so far as to call this the result of the 'universal appeal of transportation'. In part this was because many local jurisdictions rejected the use of imprisonment for large numbers of petty offenders, at least until the American Revolution, though this was far from uniform in England. Yet there were misgivings about transportation, because it was supposed that the punishment was invisible and thus scarcely a public deterrent: as Samuel Johnson put it, 'the awe of the publick eye is lost, and the power of the law is spent'.[12] In fact, there was great interest in the colonies and the careers of criminals there. Though the new world was unfamiliar and did not have a particularly welcoming reputation – almost everyone agreed that servitude in America was harder, or 'more arduous', there was a considerable public market for news about criminals and others in the colonies.[13] Corresponding to this was an American interest in the nature of the society which produced so many convicts. Crime was therefore one of the links which bound colonies to the 'mother country', however ambivalent the feelings on either side might be. It is one of the central themes of this study that, far from being invisible, punishment of criminals by transportation stimulated cultural and political exchanges between Britain and its colonies, and provided one of the main focuses of news and representations in the two-way traffic in news across the Atlantic.

The criminal and the British Atlantic world

Frequent usage does not guarantee a viable concept, and the 'Atlantic world' may be too vague an idea to permit an accurate and fruitful working definition. Fortunately, as David Armitage has noted, 'Atlantic history has not yet suffered the death by a thousand textbooks that has befallen other fields'.[14] Nevertheless, there are many different ways of approaching the relationships of the early modern Atlantic, and choosing an appropriate way of tracing their growth and development remains problematic. The processes of producing, transporting and then containing British felons in the colonies pose as many difficulties as any other set of economic, political or cultural relations across the British Atlantic. Law enforcement, unlike many forms of economic production such as tobacco, did not generally have as its central focus a transatlantic target for its 'products', but perforce in the seventeenth century came to rely on the colonies as a means of non-capital punishment for many criminals. The business of crime generated its own routes, financial arrangements and administrative processes, just like those links and business routines created by the trades in sugar, tobacco or slaves.[15] It is possible to analyse the convict business like any other in the early modern period, an era which, after all, was characterized by the largest forced migration (of Africans) in history. It has been rightly asserted that migration across the British Atlantic was 'predominantly an African experience'. But within this larger framework, convicts could be included in the history of the compulsory mobility of the unfree organized by many early modern European states.[16]

As a business, shipping convicts and selling them into servitude involved relationships which were typical of much early modern trade. In part, it depended on good personal relationships across the Atlantic, and, with them, good information and local knowledge. Though 'the supply of felons was steady and there was a constant demand for them in Virginia and Maryland', successful exploitation of this market still needed dependable individuals at either end. It was partly a matter of setting up and maintaining a business network.[17] From the American point of view, too, there was a pressing need to explore possibilities of British markets for goods such as iron from the foundries of Maryland and Virginia. The owners of the Baltimore Company, among them the Carroll family of Maryland, naturally turned to the merchants familiar to them in the tobacco and convict trade. They explored with George Buck of Bideford in Devon whether that port offered any opportunities, to be advised that they would be better if they concentrated on Bristol, which was 'to us as London is to ports on the other side of the Land'. By that time Buck had been transporting convicts to Maryland for almost twenty years. In Bristol, the Baltimore Company's contacts were Cheston, Sedgley and Hilhouse – all of them dominant in the convict and servant trade in the West Country in the quarter century before the Revolution (see Chapter 2). Iron exporting may seem a specialized activity, but the iron foundries were the object of investment by tobacco planters seeking to diversify: they were also one of the main employers of convict labour.[18] Networks in one area of business therefore overlapped with networks in other areas, and one link sometimes led to another. In London the agent of the Baltimore Company met the representative of the Crowley ironworks in north-east England, and was able to make a bargain with a company which was looking to replace supplies of Swedish with American iron.[19] Mutual interests tended to reinforce each other in an expanding market for the 'empire of goods' that 'bound together Britain and its American colonies before the War of Independence'. It was therefore common for colonial merchants to build up networks in Britain through personal contact, much as their British colleagues did in the colonies, in order to find export markets.[20]

Economic interests also linked particular people and places around the Atlantic shores. In part, this created similar modes of consumption from London to the colonies, which 'became, in a sense, the outer reaches of an increasingly integrated English economy'.[21] Convicts were just one of the commodities of this British Atlantic economy, and a key source of labour in producing other goods. In the process, they linked places in a common trade. Every county in England had to find a method of transporting convicts to America, and as a result came to know the economic needs of the mid-Atlantic economy. This is what David Armitage has called the focus of 'cis-Atlantic history', which 'studies particular places as unique locations within an Atlantic world and seeks to define that uniqueness as the result of the interaction between local particularity and a wider web of connections (and comparisons)'. By the eighteenth century, many places on the Atlantic coasts of Britain and America were increasingly linked by multiple connections, of which the movement of convict labour was just one. This was a local as well as a regional phenomenon (see Chapter 3).[22] Initially, in the seventeenth century, the movement of free servants created a level of popular awareness of the possibilities of migration to America – something that is evinced by individual actions such as Somerset servants running away to take ship to Virginia, or the welfare difficulties caused to local authorities by the absence of income-earning fathers in Barbados. The images of the colonies were reinforced by cultural representations of American ambitions and settings in plays such as Ben Jonson's *Eastward Ho!* or Aphra Behn's *Oroonoko*.[23] In the eighteenth century, by contrast, the large-scale transportation of convicts created a widespread need among local authorities for information and business structures to ensure their safe export from Britain. Both the communities that lost members to the convict trade, and the county authorities shipping them out, acquired a heightened sense of an immediate relationship with America. A sense of place in Britain or America was increasingly constituted by an awareness of its many connections to other places, in Europe or America. Thus, the creation of an Atlantic economy was not just a matter of finding new markets abroad but of relating local domestic economies through Atlantic exchanges. The convicts, among many other goods, provided the means of linking people at 'the most intimate levels of town, village and even household'.[24] Most analysts of judicial policies of transportation have somewhat neglected the Atlantic aspects of the transportation before the American Revolution, and the role of convicts in the wider world has been studied by only a few, such as Roger Ekirch, Aaron Fogleman and Bernard Bailyn.[25] Yet it is clear that between them, the colonial authorities, the British government and the convicts created a *criminal* Atlantic. The 'criminal Atlantic' is being used here in a very limited way to indicate that through the movement of criminals in both directions across the Atlantic and the publication, communication and exchange of representations of crime in general and transported convicts in particular, a shared concern arose centring on criminal transportation. This was broader than mere administration of the shipping, or the financial advantages derived from the sale of convicts. The criminal Atlantic was also cultural and political. Crime is frequently subject to cultural representation, at least since the invention of cheap printing, and in the early modern period news and crime stories became an important aspect of the publishing industry in both Britain and America (see Chapter 4). Crime is also cultural in another sense, in that the collective experience of being processed by the courts and punished often creates a shared complex of reactions among the convicted. One central question is whether the common experience of *forced* labour migration generated a 'community' of common experience or culture among the transported similar to those of the 'Black Atlantic'. Perhaps convicts and others joined in a wider culture of the dispossessed and exploited, as they moved across the Atlantic and back, providing a counter to the dominant forces of order under British rule.[26] For some of the convicts, there are reports of a kind of collective experience and common culture. In the modes of official reaction, public reporting and discussion, and printed representation, more certainly, there are clear signs of a 'criminal Atlantic', at least in the form of a dialogue between the respectable authorities on both sides. Crime, conviction and servitude provided the links, but crime made the news, and this too was a transatlantic process. A common concern for crime and convicts, however, like other aspects of the shared economy of the Atlantic world, does not necessarily imply consensus, and convict transportation provided one of the underlying themes in the increasingly edgy relationship between Britain and her colonies after 1750.

The focus of this study is the convicts and their representations on both sides of the Atlantic. The convicts themselves provide a key, if not the whole story, and are drawn from the extreme ends of England, from the Borders to Cornwall, including Lancashire and the North West, Bristol and the western circuit of the assizes.[27] This scope encourages the development of a deliberately *regional* perspective which seeks to highlight the roots of diversity among England's felons sent to the colonies – from town and country, north and south, higher and lower courts. It cannot pretend to be a fully national picture – the great suppliers of convicts, London and the Home Counties, are excluded, but the survey might redirect attention to the neglected provinces of England where crime was such that they supplied at least as many transportees as the metropolitan area. Secondly, with the convicts go their representations in many sources and levels, in England and America. They turn up in news stories, published and reprinted in the circulation of prints around the Atlantic, and occasionally in pamphlets and books, as well as in the legal records. The narrative forms of convict stories in England had their own styles and conventions, built up from many individual accounts, and these provide a kind of dominant view of convicts and their fate in the colonies. In the details, particularly in the newspapers, though, there are many different stories, in America as well as England, and when these are put together around the lives of individual criminals, the stereotypes may no longer dominate as they once did. Finally, amidst these representations, there is a serious debate about crime and (effective) punishment, in which colonial and British commentators exchange, at long distance perhaps, but successfully, their opinions, agreements and divergences. This was something that was continued after the Revolution.[28] Before then, however, the more convicts linked the colonies to the 'mother country', the more identities on both sides became more distinct. There is a large literature on the formation of British and American national sentiments and identities in this period, and this study cannot be more than a reflection on one aspect of their development. Conventional views of Britishness stress the conflict with the French as the force which drove the elements of an otherwise disunited Britain together into a largely Protestant national identity.[29] However, it may be that the more links each area and region had with the wider world – the colonies as much as the Continent – the more distinctive they felt. Moreover, economic competition, if fierce, rarely produces solidarity, and the colonies were able to compete effectively in some British markets. Integration into a wider world may of course produce a response of localism rather than internationalism, as twenty-first-century reactions to globalization may remind us. Thus the more convicts had to be shipped by one side, and received by the other, the more different the two felt, rather than united in a common enterprise. This took time to develop, for superficially at least there seems to have been much by way of a common culture between Britain and America. At least one convict was noted for his favourite pastime, when settled on the Eastern Shore of Maryland – 'his relaxation was fox hunting'.[30] In the end, though, as in Australia, the final refusal to receive further shipments of convicts marked the creation of a distinctive American identity.

2
Pedlars in the Outports: Transportation, the Locality and the Atlantic

Adoption by the counties

The varying willingness to adopt transportation as a regular part of the armoury of punishment is most apparent at the county level, where local magistrates responded to the 1718 Act with everything from apparent enthusiasm to complete indifference. While transportation had figured in the seventeenth century as both a political means of dealing with rebellion, and a judicial method of disposing of those reprieved from the gallows, it is unclear to what extent it had been adopted by county authorities before 1718. Transportation of criminals was not new in the eighteenth century, for many individual felons reprieved from the gallows had been transported before 1700. Banishment, together with forms of enslavement and hard labour, had been part of the armoury of penalties directed at rogues and vagabonds by sixteenth-century laws. By the 1590s, after nearly half a century of legislative measures against the uncontrollable poor, 'masterless men', gypsies and vagrants, the final Elizabethan vagrancy statute made transportation a key punishment. The death penalty was still a possibility for gypsies and vagabonds, if they were persistent offenders.[1] With regard to criminals, the initiative was taken by James I who in 1615 gave judges discretion to reprieve felons on condition that they were employed 'in foreign discoveries or other services beyond the seas'. This built on efforts in 1603 both to define vagabondage more clearly, and more importantly to specify the destinations of their exile, which were listed as Newfoundland, the East and West Indies, France, Germany, Spain and the Low Countries.[2] The use of transportation for criminals resolved to some extent the dilemma of the early-seventeenth-century courts which 'faced an uncomfortably extreme choice when they had to decide whether to hang someone, or to brand them and let them go'. In other words, convicted criminals were either guilty without benefit of clergy (resulting in execution), or with benefit, for which only one punishment existed, namely the branding iron. Since James also encouraged the transportation of vagabonds, there is convincing evidence that from the beginning transportation was the outcome of a convergence of policies towards both crime and poverty, 'with significant effects for both'. In the eyes of most contemporaries, idleness and crime were intimately associated, and the search for some way to employ the unemployed or those without masters, and prevent dangerous forms of wandering deviance, concentrated particularly on the young.[3] Yet formal slavery, which had been unacceptable as a punishment for vagrancy in the mid-sixteenth century, became, in the modified form of indentured servitude, the solution to a variety of social ills by the end of the seventeenth, including criminality and idleness. The extreme measure of slavery was still regarded in theory by some educated opinion in the first half of the eighteenth century as an appropriate strategy against poverty, but was never again put into legislation.[4]

The consequences of these developments in practice are, however, none too clear. Scholarly research has established some key aspects of seventeenth-century transportation, and for some counties a rough estimate of the numbers can be achieved.[5] The process of appeal and reprieve has not been subject to systematic scrutiny outside London and the South East, and comparisons with the later situation are therefore difficult. Thus Beattie comments concerning the situation at the Restoration, that 'while it was not available to the courts as a regular punishment in 1660, transportation to the American colonies and to the West Indies had in fact been imposed on a number of convicts over the previous sixty years, principally as a condition of a royal pardon'. The total, he estimates, may not have exceeded a few hundred at best. After the Restoration, a rather more systematic and careful process was introduced, with judges commonly deciding on the eligibility of convicted criminals, and ordering them to be held in gaol awaiting confirmation of royal pardon. This also involved the denial of benefit of clergy to many criminals and substitution of transportation, through judges applying for the first time for centuries the strict literacy test that established an accused's qualification for benefit.[6] This led to allegations that some convicts in the seventeenth century were transported illegally. At Bristol after 1660, it was said, 'where all people . . . trade to the American plantations', the local magistrates transported not only convicted criminals from the assizes and their own quarter sessions, but also 'small rogues and pilferers' who, afraid of being hanged, were induced to 'pray' for their own transportation in ignorance of the law.[7] In some ways this paralleled the contemporary allegations that servants were being seduced or tricked, even kidnapped, into servitude in the colonies. While legal procedures with regard to servants produced some judicial protests and government measures by way of response, the abducted servant seems to have become part of a long-lived mythology.[8] In London at least, there were many stories told in the late seventeenth century of the cheating practices of those 'spiriters' who deceived the young and vulnerable into crossing the Atlantic. The sorrowful accounts of individuals such as a 'poor boy . . . stolen away by spirits, as they call them, who convey such boys to ships for New England or Barbados' became common in the 1660s. Similar accusations in Bristol led to local measures to enforce an official register of emigrating servants as a means of regulating the 'pilgrimage' across the Atlantic.[9] That this was not entirely fiction can be demonstrated from some almost accidental records. Samuel Pepys notes that one of his former servants who had proved unsatisfactory had been equally troublesome to his next master, who had sent him to Barbados. Pepys said this was done 'out of love for the boy; for . . . to keep him here were to bring him to the gallows'. In Somerset in 1654 a fatherless pauper put to an apprenticeship at parish expense complained to the magistrates that his master had ejected him, and 'endeavoured to have transported him to ye Barbados' by having him put on board a ship.[10] There were also Scottish protests at the end of the seventeenth century, concerning the loss of skilled labour to Scottish industry, and the selling of Scots to 'foreigners', while at the same time political campaigners rather contradictorily asserted the rights of Scots to the same privileges as the English in English colonies.[11] These elements of deceit and forceful abduction became essential parts of non-criminal biographies in the eighteenth century – the stories of James Annesley, Scotsman Peter Williamson and the hero of Edward Kimber's novel who was allegedly based on a real person he had met in his American travels, are all examples of the apparently authentic confirmation of an established narrative.[12] The kidnap motif was particularly credible, and occurs in stories of transportation too: Bampfylde Moore Carew produced an 'innocent' narrative, in that he was ordered for transportation as a vagrant (in fact as an incorrigible rogue) rather than as a result of a crime, and could therefore demonstrate his victimhood even more convincingly by telling how his *second* transportation was the outcome of his being kidnapped by his former convict ship's captain. Though no evidence exists that Carew was transported twice, his story may not have been implausible, as in one well-reported case from Northumberland of a ship's captain who allowed one of his convicts to escape soon after arrival in America, and preferred to return to England and recover him himself rather than admit an expensive mistake to the authorities. This suggests that it was essentially more profitable for a captain to return an escaper directly to America than lose the bond for his transportation by having the returned convict prosecuted for being at large. The theme of false imprisonment abroad, or of the wronged hero sold into slavery among foreigners, however, became a useful genre in eighteenth-century stories.[13]

Whether malpractice really pervaded the 'voluntary' process of indentured servitude or not, the pace of transporting convicts increased at the Restoration. Officially, at least, two judicial procedures had been sanctioned by the 1660s, with some convicts being reprieved by the judges at the trial in what Beattie calls 'administrative pardons', in the confident expectation that the courts' leniency would be approved by the king, and others, petitioning for transportation after they had been condemned and were awaiting execution, were reprieved through direct action of the monarchs and their advisers. Some kings took a close interest, while others simply relied on the carefully recorded accounts of trial judges and justices. It is difficult to know whether the same factors influenced the granting of mercy in this process as has been documented for the eighteenth century, such as the youth and relative naivety of the offenders, but it is clear that after 1660 transportation to the colonies developed as a secondary punishment, though without a statutory framework.[14] Every county seems to have experienced the necessity of transportation, as reprieves at the assizes became common. Records suggest that numbers varied between years according to judicial policy, and it is hard to calculate the overall picture, though it has been estimated that 4,500 convicts were sent to the colonies by 1700.[15] Difficulties in persuading colonies to accept convicts in some years in the last quarter of the seventeenth century, however, seem to have led to the granting of more free pardons. Maryland tried to ban the importation of convicts in 1676, following complaints from Virginia in 1670 that 'great danger and disrepute' had resulted from their presence in the colony.[16] The policy at this time was not uniform or very effectively carried out. There were as yet no bureaucratic procedures for ensuring that felons actually left the country and reached their destination. As William Thompson, Recorder of London, recalled in 1736, 'experience has shown that before the Act of Parliament [1718] when felons were usually pardoned on condition of transporting themselves in six months – they never performed that condition but stayed here (even at hazard of their lives) and followed the same wicked courses as before their conviction'.[17]

The surviving records of the assizes in several regions reveal that reprieve was a routine part of the way that judges conducted trials. The sentence was usually contingent on the defendants 'consenting' to be transported. According to one record of the Northumberland assizes in 1674, four consented to transportation, two before they were sentenced, and two afterwards. This was at a time when, in the opinion of Lord North, the Borders were 'obnoxious to thieving'.[18] At least one condemned at Durham assizes, according to an observer, was reprieved in the teeth of the presiding judge's written opposition in 1669. The prisoner, Ralph Jefferson, had been condemned for various crimes seven years before, and was again before the court, on charges of horse stealing and robbery.[19] Transportation orders for counties such as Devon and Lancashire confirm that these practices were widespread at the assizes, mainly as a means of avoiding carrying out the full penalties in the cases of capital charges. In Lancashire in 1685 eight men were pardoned for transportation for Barbados, and in the 1690s there were continual reprieves sometimes explicitly for the plantations in America. At least eleven were reprieved for transportation in 1699 alone. In these records there is also a striking reflection of the search for secondary punishments. Branding was common for grand larceny, and when greater severity became permissible under the law, this became branding on the cheek for a few years. With wartime conditions, some were also sent into the armed forces, while at the same time after the 1706 legislation concerning grand larceny with benefit, some were imprisoned for up to a year in addition to branding.[20] At the local quarter sessions, too, there are a few seventeenth-century cases resulting in transportation. In some instances the convicts had to arrange their own transportation, by order of the court: as in the assizes, the usual phrase attached is that they 'consented' to be transported. Their destinations might be chosen by the county authorities for practical convenience, as when the Continental wars before the Civil War provided a swift outlet. In County Durham Edward Storey, committed to the gaol for sureties for his good behaviour, was discharged and 'committed to Edward Harreson to be carried to Gatesyde [Gateshead] to be shipped in such a shipp as Storyes friends think fitt for him to be sent into the Low Countries'. This seems to have been a kind of pre-trial banishment. By contrast Sarah Brough, after her third conviction for the offence of unlawful assembly, was sentenced to be transported to Jamaica in 1666. A transportation sentence for a third offence of this kind is found elsewhere during the 1660s, in the Hertfordshire quarter sessions in 1664 for example.[21] Other counties made greater use of transportation for removing those responsible for social disorder. The attack on Border gypsies in Northumberland between 1711 and 1717 was the most systematic use of transportation in the period immediately before the 1718 Act, under legislation renewed in 1713. In September 1711, the authorities asserted that

> Whereas severall notorious sturdy vagrants calling themselves by the names of Baleys, Shaws, Falls or ffawes have of late come into this county and keepe themselves together in severall parts thereof – threatening to burne houses and are suspected of burglarys thefts and other evill practices and ride armed to the great terror of her Maj[esty's] subjects. It is therefore ordered by this court that a warrant under the seale of this court issue forth to take and apprehend the said vagrants.

Six pounds was offered for the apprehension of each one above the age of sixteen years, by way of 'incouragement'. At the time, they recorded that there were several vagrants aready held in their gaol, and that the county should obtain 'an order of Councell to transport such of them as next session shall be thought fitt not to be delivered'. Early in 1712 the court, examining the 'Bayleys', decided that they were all incorrigible rogues, and the clerk of the peace was ordered to procure an order 'to banish them according to statute'. This was under the longstanding Elizabethan legislation. However this proved a great deal more difficult to carry out than to order, since it turned out that gaols could not always hold such people.[22] Later the same year the men breached the wall of the Castle Prison in Morpeth and escaped, leaving large numbers of women and children still in captivity, which cost the county considerable sums to repair the damage and keep the abandoned families. In early 1713 four of the women were whipped in Morpeth, and dismissed as vagrants, while at the same time large numbers of indictments for both men and women carrying the surnames Bailey or Carr were sworn out. The men, however, were not yet in custody, as four years later it was reported that 'William Bailey and divers others stand indicted and convicted as vagabonds and incorrigible rogues and do now wander and lurk in divers parts of this county and so affright and terrifie his Maj[esty's] subjects.' More warrants were issued, while at the same time substantial expenditure was incurred in apprenticing the young boys of the families to useful occupations such as a weaver or brickmaker – two or three pounds each, other members of the families often being given two or three shillings a week maintenance. Early in 1717, though, it seems that a number of the group were taken to a ship and transported 'beyond sea', and all that remained was the welfare burden of their families, which went on at least until the early 1720s.[23] This was not entirely the end of the matter, as years later James Spotswood, one of this gang, was reported as a returned transportee, first in 1725 and then again in 1730. In the first, he was mentioned as one of the 'rogues, vagabonds, strowling beggars and other idle and disorderly persons and particularly such as call themselves or go by the names of ffawes Bailey or Gordons' whom the Morpeth Ward High Constable was ordered to search for. In 1730, he was one of two members of the 'gang of the Falls' reported in the *Newcastle Courant* as under arrest in Berwick. Despite this individual failure, the process of banishment mixed with domestic repression seems to have worked, for little was heard of this group again. They had escaped the far more severe measures taken a short distance across the Border in Scotland, where in 1715 one of the gypsies called Patrick Faa had been sentenced to whipping and the pillory (with the loss of both his ears). Eight others, sentenced in Jedburgh, had been dispatched to Virginia from Glasgow.[24] The most important point about this precedent in Northumberland, however, was that it provided the county authorities with recent experience of using transportation, something which they put to good purpose in the 1720s, and later with regard to other 'faws' in the 1750s. The later repression of Border gypsies was under a very different legislative framework, however, as by then the Border Laws, permitting the raising of large amounts of money for rewards and compensation, and for the employment of 'keepers' to patrol and seize offenders in Northumberland and Cumberland, had lapsed. In their pre-1718 policy, it seems, Northumberland's magistrates were mixing some elements of the national framework of laws on vagabonds with the local policy of suppressing uncontrolled wandering.[25]

There are some sentences in the quarter sessions, such as that of Avis Silk in Devon in 1717, which are so close to the 1718 Act to suggest that they must be in some ways anticipatory, though like the cases above she had to 'consent' to the punishment – as it is expressed in the Bridewell calendar, she was 'to be discharged if she transport herself'. The same is true of incorrigible rogue Thomas Curtis in Lancashire, a 'dangerous person' who was sentenced to transportation for 'acts of vagrancy' before the Act came into force: significantly the order authorizing his transportation almost a year later made careful reference to it.[26] Yet the arrival of the judges travelling throughout England in the summer of 1718, armed with the new Act, and willing to sentence to transportation those who were liable to branding in the hand or whipping (in effect those convicted of grand and petty larcenies), posed for many local authorities the dilemma of deciding whether or not to embrace the newly systematized punishment.[27] It is probably reasonable to assume that several factors, rather than any single one, influenced the county magistracy's response to the 1718 Act, and shaped their willingness to adopt the punishment in the courts under their control. A crucial factor was whether there had been any previous local practice of sentencing and transporting offenders at quarter sessions and other local courts. Secondly, counties differed considerably in the ease with which transportation could be carried out. Outside those counties receiving government subsidy after 1718 (London, Middlesex, Buckinghamshire and the Home Counties, Surrey, Essex, Hertfordshire, Kent, Sussex), the punishment's attractions may have depended on its cost relative to the alternatives.[28] This in turn depended on the existence of regular local trade with the Americas, particularly the mid-Atlantic and southern colonies, so that ships were available to take the convicts directly out of the county. In addition, the involvement of local shippers in the voluntary servant trade would also guarantee the final disposal of the convicts within the general structure of unfree labour in indentured servitude. This, together with any transatlantic interests that local gentry and commercial families were developing in the early eighteenth century (which provided a useful source of information and reporting back), would guarantee with some certainty that convicts would be properly transported and settled within the colonial economy.

Local judicial strategies

There were certainly some striking differences in adopting the policy after 1718. Devon's magistrates embarked on a policy of regular transportation from the first, sentencing at the Easter sessions of 1718 two convicts, Ann Osby, alias Asby, and William Lafkey, both guilty of petty larceny. They followed this up in the summer with a sentence for Hugh Woodall who was to be sent to America, and in the autumn Samuel Clapp, who was to be 'transported with his own consent'.[29] In some of these early cases there are hints of negotiation and persuasion, as in the case of Hazell Northcote, who was sentenced to transportation in 1726 after conviction for felony with benefit of clergy, 'at his own request, he choosing to be transported rather than suffer the punishment that the law directs'.[30] In subsequent years, the county was comparatively enthusiastic in its use of transportation, and in part this was the outcome of its quarter sessions trying many of those accused of grand larceny. But in addition to the treatment of theft was the strategy adopted by the local authorities with regard to cases of vagrants and 'rogues'.[31] Although vagabonds were a perpetual problem for Devon's magistrates in the first three decades of the eighteenth century, it was not until 1739 that they finally abandoned their previous policy of applying whipping and periods of incarceration. In that year five male vagrants were transported in a single batch, among them the famous Bampfylde Moore Carew, a middle-class beggar whose embroidered accounts of his transportation and triumphant return have been well known ever since (see Chapter 4). This was exceptional, for transported vagabonds were not numerous in subsequent years, though Devon kept transportation in reserve as a threat in cases of 'rogues', exporting a few every decade between 1750 and the American Revolution, including four women.[32] Devon had a number of small towns in addition to Exeter which possessed sessions of their own, though Exeter also had full powers of gaol delivery in what were in effect its own assizes. These independent jurisdictions probably had a considerable impact on the way law was enforced against certain types of offenders, particularly thieves, since local justices could decide to send larceny cases to the county courts or keep them in the local urban courts. There is evidence that Tiverton and Barnstaple justices sentenced thieves to transportation, though not in large numbers. We know something of the early practices of these towns from colonial records in Kent County, Maryland, where the shipper George Buck delivered them. In the 1730s three female convicts are reported as arriving from sessions in Devon's small towns, two from Tiverton and one from Barnstaple. At least one other woman is known to have been transported by the Tiverton magistrates, Margaret Cradge, wife of Peter, for an unknown crime in 1749.[33] Exeter, by contrast, kept most of its business to itself, and had to organize the transportation of the convicts entirely separately from the county. The city's justices, like those of the county, embraced transportation straightaway, and sentenced men and women to the colonies in 1718 and 1719. They seem to have been sensitive to the problems of some individual prisoners, as Mary Middleton, sentenced in 1719 for stealing 'a serge', was ordered to remain in gaol, 'not being fitt to be transported'. From the middle of the 1720s, the courts of the city, both sessions and gaol delivery, made regular use of the punishment.[34]

In other parts of England, too, transportation quickly became part of the punishments inflicted by quarter sessions. In north-east England both Northumberland and the independent judicial county of Newcastle-upon-Tyne used it in the 1720s, mostly in cases of those convicted of petty larceny. However, in Northumberland there was more variety among the earliest convicts. The first person sentenced to transportation, Charles Morgan, was deemed in 1723 to be an 'idle person and vagabond', who had 'wandered abroad'. Another, Samuel Moor in 1729, had obtained half an anker of brandy by false pretences from a woman at Hexham.[35] More dangerous were two men who in 1723 had broken and entered William Waugh's house at Allendale, and threatened his family with setting fire to it. In that year, too, a parliamentary bye-election in Morpeth seems to have provoked some violence between rival supporters, one of whom, James Chicken, attacked people who had supported William Wrightson from Newcastle (who managed to win the election by a small majority). Though witnesses suggested that he had merely been drunk, Chicken was deemed a rogue and vagabond and sentenced to transportation. In the end, he entered a recognizance for his good behaviour in 1725, and was discharged.[36] Elsewhere in the North East, however, the 1718 Act produced little response. Despite sharing many features with the other counties in the region, and possessing in the Tyne a major river which was already in use for transporting convicts and servants to America, County Durham resolutely refused to adopt the penalty at its quarter sessions before 1750, relying on corporal punishment instead. As in the more rural areas to the south such as the North Riding of Yorkshire, the use of transportation by the visiting assize judges seems to have had no impact on the judicial practices of the Durham magistrates. After 1750, Durham used the penalty systematically, with a consequent decline in the other punishments for minor thefts.[37] In the North West, too, patterns were diverse. Despite their deep involvement in the transatlantic tobacco trade, Cumberland's justices did not inflict transportation at quarter sessions until the 1740s. In 1741 two women accused of robbery, one by picking pockets and the other through assault, were the first to be transported by the magistrates, from the Michaelmas sessions. Careful thought had clearly been given to framing the indictments so that no capital charge was involved. Isobel Martin had 'privately' taken a box containing a shilling from Hannah, wife of the Reverend James Jackson at Brampton, but was charged with stealing only threepence. In the same way, despite the assault and robbery, Margaret, wife of Samuel Likard, was only accused of stealing sixpence.[38] These were the exceptions, for most of the subsequent offenders, as elsewhere, were prosecuted for stealing small quantities of clothes, food, household items or tools, though sometimes the valuation of the goods had been downgraded to ensure a prosecution for petty larceny. Only in cases of fraud did valuable items sometimes change hands. Thomas Sewell acquired a black mare from Joseph Ewing by false pretences in 1765, and was transported for seven years.[39] Westmorland, by contrast, virtually ignored the powers of transportation for the entire period from 1718 to 1776, sentencing only two men, both in 1737. In April 1737, George Routledge was sentenced to be twice whipped and placed in the stocks on successive Saturdays before being ordered for transportation. His crime is unknown, but the other convict, Stephen Nicholson, was a petty thief.[40] Despite having to organize the transportation of dozens of convicts from the assizes, Westmorland's quarter sessions seem to have been uninterested in using the punishment.

These diverse responses to the 1718 Act seem to defy simple classification or interpretation. Some county justices, like those in Northumberland, may have applied to felons those policies that they had previously inflicted on vagabonds and gypsies. Other areas, such as Devon or Newcastle-upon-Tyne, adopted and implemented the new punishment with relative enthusiasm as a useful alternative to the existing penalties. Some counties, however, ignored the new direction in penal practice for many years before making use of it in the 1740s and 1750s. Since many of these contrasting patterns existed *within* the same region, often in neighbouring counties sharing the same maritime outlets, the variations are even more puzzling. One unrecorded factor may be the policies adopted by magistrates in choosing both the court and the level of crime to try accusations. Some counties seem to have sent a far higher proportion of cases to the assizes than others which kept them under the justices' control at the quarter sessions. This was very clearly the case in Newcastle-upon-Tyne, which is why the majority of transported convicts there were sentenced by the town's quarter sessions. This was also the case in Lancashire and Bristol (see Chapter 3).[41] Elsewhere, in counties such as Devon or Northumberland, only about a third of convicts were tried before the justices. This kind of variation suggests that one element of the apparent avoidance of using transportation was the determination to leave the imposition of the new punishment to the judges at assize. There is no obvious explanation for these contrasts, except perhaps that the individual county benches of magistrates could be a law unto themselves in the implementation of statute law which gave so much discretion in handling local criminal cases.

Shipping and administration – the formation of the criminal Atlantic world

In 1700 few places in Britain had thoroughly developed economic or cultural links with the other side of the Atlantic. Connections were dominated largely by ports with specialized interests either in exporting their local goods or in exploiting North American resources such as the fishing grounds of the Newfoundland banks. The export trade from the South, and particularly the South West of England, had familiarized many traders with the transatlantic trade routes.[42] However, the growth of the southern colonies of Virginia and Maryland in the eighteenth century, together with those of the West Indies, and with them the trade in sugar and tobacco, broadened the links across the Atlantic away from a few southern ports to include Ireland, western Scotland and many minor, particularly northern, ports of England. The simultaneous growth of the convict trade after the 1718 Transportation Act was part of these links, as county after county found itself compelled to arrange the shipping of its felons to the colonies. At the same time, the end of the Royal African Company's monopoly in the slave trade in 1712 led many merchants and sea-captains from different parts of the country to experiment with transporting an even more reluctant, and far more dangerous human cargo.[43]

The consequences were that in the first quarter of the eighteenth century the transatlantic trade in people and goods grew in many parts of the country. After 1718 every county was forced to transport those sentenced or reprieved from the assizes, and could, if the local magistrates themselves wished, use transportation as a sentence for petty thieves at the quarter sessions. Although government subsidy encouraged and underwrote the adoption of the punishment in London and the surrounding counties, most of the country had to develop a method of transportation at attractive rates of payment, evolving a system which either stood alone or was designed to fit in with pre-existing trade arrangements.[44] It is because of this intriguing mixture of the need for shipping and the development of greater provincial trade links that the exploration of the place of the convict trade in the context of the growing Atlantic world reflects on so many other aspects of local society.

At first, the impact of the 1718 Act did not result in many local arrangements for transportation. In Cumberland and Northumberland, despite the local authorities' previous experience of organizing transportation, they contracted with London lawyers, John Darley of Gray's

Inn and John Henden of Lincoln's Inn, in 1718 and 1719. In the 1720s and 1730s, however, they turned to local shippers who bid for the contracts.[45] It seems a safe assumption that those merchants who wanted to transport felons were able to make money from the trade, either on its own or at least by using it to supplement other profitable arrangements. The export of servants was already a sizeable business in a number of parts of the country. For example, the north Devon port of Bideford made a brisk trade, not only in fine west-country cloth, but in servants. Although many of them may in fact have been picked up from Irish ports on the way to America, these servants from west-country ships made up a large proportion of emigrants in the later seventeenth and early eighteenth centuries. It was natural that the first contract from Devon should go to a Bideford merchant.[46] In the 1770s Bristol merchants Stevenson and Randolph accused Devon of contractual inconstancy – always in search of a cheaper deal elsewhere. Certainly there are signs in the many surviving contracts for the whole period that Devon justices liked to spread their business between different merchants: a generous view might be that they avoided becoming overdependent on one shipper for their convicts. For most of the 1720s and 1730s the major contractor was George Buck and his brother John and son William, all from Bideford, but from the late 1730s and throughout the 1740s and 1750s Devon also had continual contracts with an Exeter merchant and JP Ethelred Davy, followed by Thomas Benson of Northam, and individual contracts with George Coade of Exeter (1741), and Thomas Kenney and his partners (1750 and 1751). Even when the contract began to go regularly to the Bristol firm of Samuel Sedgley and William Hillhouse from 1756, Kenney and the Bucks were frequently used. In the 1760s, when Sedgley and Hillhouse transported the great majority of convicts, isolated contracts might still be placed locally – to Samuel Follett of Sidmouth, in 1764, for example, and the Bucks again in 1765. Although William Stevenson and William Randolph were under the impression that they had agreed an exclusive deal with Devon in the late 1760s, as they apparently had with other counties, Devon could still find alternative Bristol merchants in William Freeman and George Watson the younger (1768), and again turn to people nearer home such as Edward Cheyney of Teignmouth (1773). One pattern which might imaginatively be reconstructed here is the search for a south-coast shipper to supplement those working out of the Bristol Channel. In this endeavour, the Devon authorities were never entirely successful. The evidence for the City of Exeter is much more incomplete, but what survives suggests that its magistrates also used the Bucks,

Davy, Benson and Sedgley and Hillhouse between the 1720s and 1750s. Only in the 1720s did Exeter use contractors not employed by Devon, apparently local merchants from Exeter or Topsham (which was the highest point ships could in fact land their cargoes on the Exe).[47]

The complaining and somewhat bad-tempered correspondence between the Bristol merchants William Stevenson and William Randolph and the Devon county clerk in the 1770s reflects clearly on the extent to which convict shipping in the West Country, as in London, had become a large-scale business. It also shows how much the merchants expected to get their own way with provincial justices. Although George and John Buck had gathered convicts from most of the western circuit in earlier years and parts of the Midlands including Worcestershire, and Sedgley and Hillhouse did the same for the Bristol area in the mid-century, Stevenson and Randolph operated on a distinctly larger scale. With Devon, however, they seem to have met their match.[48] They thought they had signed a standard exclusive deal with Devon for *all* the county's convicts, to be delivered to them twice a year in spring and autumn, at a fixed price which was three guineas from Bristol. If Devon would prefer it, they would collect the transportees from Exeter for the larger sum of five guineas. Devon's magistrates seem wilfully to have misunderstood this, and sent their gaoler with convicts to Bristol expecting to be paid by Stevenson and Randolph for his trouble, rather than at the county's expense. Moreover, the authorities also tried to find alternative merchants in Bristol, apparently an inexperienced company who offered them a lower price. 'You'll excuse the freedom of my pen when I say how much I have been mistaken in the integrity of your magistrates', wrote William Randolph, 'we have been strangely and cruelly misled in this affair'.[49] The justices had contracted with a Bristol merchant 'who had a chance vessel fitting out and as trade was dull, thought they could make a little freight out by getting your convicts', and in fact Stevenson and Randolph had purchased them from this interloper for twelve guineas for the six.[50] Three years later, there were still problems, as Devon tended to delay sending their felons until all the reprieves had been confirmed by the Secretary of State:

> We are to observe to you, we receive the convicts from 26 different goals in which there will be at least 70 or 80 Transports in the course of a few days and our ship *Isabella* will be at her usual mooring near the hotwells ready to receive them on Monday the 20th Tuesday 21st and Wed 22nd of next month, which is as late in fall as we dare venture to stay for fear of being beat off the coast of America. Under

these circumstances what would the magistrates of other counties think of our conduct were we to alter the time of our sailing to accommodate the County of Devon only . . .[51]

They had complained earlier in the same year of the expense of lodging in Bristol's Newgate Gaol those convicts from Devon who arrived either unscheduled or late, but clearly the message had not been received and understood. Despite these fraught relations, Stevenson and Randolph took pains to reassure their Devon customers in 1771 when Maryland looked likely to forbid the import of any more convicts, and were able to say that 'our Friends advise us' that Lord Baltimore would put a stop to it.[52]

As this correspondence suggests, shippers from south-west England operated on a scale comparable to that of their colleagues in London. Surviving listings document the numbers of convicts involved and the scope of the operation as reflected in the geographic range of their origins. Shiploads of a hundred or more felons were not unusual, particularly after the Lent and autumn assizes. In October 1774, for example, the *William* left the Bristol Channel with ninety-nine convicts, drawn from fifteen counties from as far north as Cheshire and as far east as Northampton, as well as most of the western Midlands, Monmouthshire and the South West. The following spring the *Elizabeth* had 105 convicts on board, drawn from eleven counties. Though a Bristol ship, she carried no convicts from that city. It seems that Bristol's authorities would on occasion ship convicts in small numbers as the need arose. In the summer of 1775, the *Isabella* left with only thirty convicts on board, drawn from the western circuit, the Midlands and Bristol itself. This seems characteristic of some of the smaller shiploads sent in the summer months: the previous year only twenty-five felons had been sent in the July shipment. Sometimes ships were so full that, though they usually 'relieved the city of these unfortunate people twice a year', Bristol's convicts could not be accommodated. Although the data do not confirm Stevenson and Randolph's boast that they regularly emptied twenty-six gaols, it is clear that the larger shiploads were formed by drawing convicts from a very wide area of England and Wales, and bringing them to Bristol for export.[53]

Cumberland merchants, by contrast with their south-western colleagues, were in greater difficulties when trying to find exportable commodities, as the rough woollens and linens of the region, and the pig iron and other goods produced on the back of the local coal industry, were not in much demand in America. Yet ports such as Whitehaven enjoyed some prosperity because of 'the general expansion of British trade with America', primarily through importing and re-exporting of tobacco.[54] As in Devon, moreover, there was a steady trade in servants before 1700, to the extent that Sir John Lowther, developer of both the port of Whitehaven and the Cumberland coalfield, became alarmed at the resulting shortages of workers and attempted to have the 'labour trade' banned. To local merchants, he said, it was the 'most beneficent trade, but borders too much upon kidnapping', and had taken steps to free several people held on board ship, including a nine-year old boy.[55] Yet despite Lowther's efforts there were recurrent labour shortages in the area of Whitehaven and the coalfield, as many people left the region in times of economic depression. It may have been the general shortage of alternative exports that led several of the most powerful merchants in Cumberland first to experiment with, and then to plunge substantial investments in, the slave trade. At the same time, Whitehaven became the natural port through which to export convicts.[56]

Whitehaven, therefore, was unusual in the fact that it dealt in all three types of migrant labour – servants, convicts and slaves. In this it resembled much larger ports such as Liverpool or Bristol. It is scarcely surprising to find some overlap in the shipping agents involved: at least two slave traders, Walter Lutwidge and Peter How, were given contracts for transporting convicts. Walter Lutwidge, of Irish background, was one of a number of nonconformist merchants enticed by Lowther to settle in Whitehaven, and had a chequered career in association with his uncle Thomas, firstly as a privateer in the War of the Spanish Succession, then, with peacetime conditions, in slaving and convict trading for both Cumberland and Westmorland in the 1720s and 1730s.[57] Lutwidge maintained a busy trade between the North West of England and the colonies, as well as Europe, and his business affairs were constantly burdened with debts to Sir James Lowther among others. Though talking about himself modestly as a 'pedlar in the outports', and often short of capital credit, he maintained an agent in Virginia, Alexander Mackenzie, and was close to many businessmen on both sides of the Atlantic.[58] He had useful Newcastle connections, where his son-in-law Isaac Cookson was on the common council. In 1740 it seems he gained from Cookson the contract to transport the convicts from that year's assizes and quarter sessions, which may have included the ordinary felons, excluding the rioters who sacked Newcastle's Guildhall in July. He agreed to take them to Maryland for £5 a head, minus some consideration for the costs of moving them to Whitehaven.[59] Most of the cargoes Lutwidge shipped to the colonies consisted of textiles and, to a lesser extent, the products of the north-western iron industry, as well as servants. Captains seem to have taken up to twenty servants in a shipment, to be disposed of with the rest of the cargo first, before loading up with tobacco for the voyage home. These employees were not necessarily trustworthy: Lutwidge complained bitterly of Captain Patton – 'of all the knaves I ever met with Patton has out done them all', 'the greatest knave I ever knew', because he took the fifteen servants shipped on the voyage for himself. More trustworthy captains reported offloading the servants (at Oxford in one case), before repairing their ships and preparing to load up with tobacco.[60] In bad times in the tobacco business, Lutwidge seems to have turned to slave trading, and in 1740 drew up a model list of provisions for such an expedition based on his experiences of at least four voyages in the 1730s. In 1749, apparently with debts occasioned by over-reaching himself in various ways, including commissioning a ship to be built at Norfolk, Virginia, he offered his ships to Liverpool merchants in the 'Guinea trade'. It would not be 'disagreeable' to him, he remarked.[61] His concern with transporting convicts from the North West was mostly between 1729 and 1737, and he seems to have found other aspects of transatlantic trade more rewarding.[62]

Peter How, a JP and vigorous local tobacco entrepreneur, held the Cumberland contract for about thirty years until his bankruptcy in 1763: even after that, the receivers of his estate still tried to ship convicts. It was a little unusual for a magistrate who had had a hand in trying and convicting people to bid for the contract for their transportation. There is no evidence, however, that he bid for the contract to transport those he sentenced.[63] He had speculated widely in both the slave trade and the French market for re-exported tobacco, as well as in local industries of different kinds. Before his catastrophic fall, How was the 'wealthiest and most powerful' of the coal merchants, and one of Sir John Lowther's best customers at Whitehaven.[64] Certainly he was a busy magistrate, taking evidence in many cases that went to the assizes, and not popular: he could be brutally effective. When he was in receipt of extortion letters in 1753 threatening his properties and businesses with arson, How booby-trapped the place where he was instructed to leave the money, and had little difficulty in tracking down the singed and injured victim of the subsequent explosion, who was 'all over burnt with the gunpowder'.[65] In contrast with Lutwidge, How shipped convicts frequently between the 1730s and 1760s for Cumberland's authorities, and seems to have depended on the trade far more.[66] These two were exceptional businessmen, and remarkably Walter Lutwidge, too, is supposed to have gone bankrupt and died in a debtors' prison, but the evidence is more ancient rumour than precise historical fact.[67]

Westmorland, by contrast to Cumberland, was landlocked and had the choice of only two relatively expensive routes out of the county, and at first alternated between a southern route through Liverpool and a northern exit through the mountains of Cumberland and to the sea from Whitehaven. The shorter northern route eventually became the most used method. Individual factors may have been important: the Liverpool merchant involved in the late 1730s and early 1740s proved unsatisfactory. He let one convict escape, and as a penalty had to transport the next one free. After making one use of Peter How, the county authorities settled in 1744 on another Whitehaven merchant, Joseph Dean, who organized the shipment of the majority of convicts for the county until the 1770s.[68] Nevertheless, the local authorities were not as certain about their chosen method as might appear. In 1753 the quarter sessions investigated the system adopted in the south:

> Ordered that the Clerk of the Peace for this County do write to the Clerk of the Peace for the County of Middlesex to know who is at the Expence of Transporting the Convicts in that County from the respective Courts of Assize and Sessions and who is also at the Expence of their Support from and after their Conviction.[69]

Moreover, Joseph Dean's contract for convict trading was not completely secure from local competition. In Michaelmas 1770, the quarter sessions recorded:

> The Gaoler of this County having proposed to take all the Convicts from the said County at four pounds a man without any Fee for Carrying them to any Port. It is ordered that this Proposal be taken into consideration at a future sessions.

The key promise here was to have a price inclusive of the trip to the nearest port: the trip to Whitehaven could cost more than a pound per head in addition to the usual transportation fee of £4. Land costs were, with convicts as with coal, far higher than for sea transport. However, despite the threat, Dean seems to have been the main shipper for the remaining few years of the Atlantic trade.[70]

The pattern in north-east England was different again: the coal trade to London, and the exchange of goods with the ports of the Baltic and the North Sea, dominated the regional economy for most of the early modern period. The seasonal character of the coal trade was always a difficulty, but what began as only a summer trade rapidly became an all-year round business by the later eighteenth century.[71] As other industries grew up around the supplies of cheap coal, the region, at least until 1750, attracted rather than exported people. American links were relatively few, although (as elsewhere) some of the larger ships in use in the region were built in the northern Atlantic colonies. Some north-east English seamen turned up in America (being executed for piracy, for example), and certainly some efforts were made to develop a more orthodox transatlantic trade.[72] A recent study of the business affairs of Newcastle merchant Ralph Carr, however, suggest that extensive profits were hard to find in trade with New England, even with local allies there, and connections with Amsterdam which provided higher quality goods than the North East could produce. It is significant that only one of the richest businessmen in the region could attempt such an ambitious project.[73] By contrast, the shipping of tobacco from the southern colonies, and the trade with the West Indies, seems to have been the specialist interest of relatively few north-eastern (in fact, nearly all Tyneside) sea-captains and shipowners, and it was on the basis of this small pool of traders that the convict trade was initially developed after the brief flirtation with London lawyers after the Transportation Act. Port Books from 1717 onwards suggest that a handful of specialists from the North East were trading with the mid-Atlantic colonies, whereas there was a growing trade with the West Indies and New England (particularly after 1750).[74] In the 1720s the local tobacco importers, led by Matthias Giles, John Hodgson and John Colville, were contracted to take the convicts from all three counties. Significantly, the price, at £5 per head, was higher than in the North West. In addition, the shippers advertised regularly for servants to accompany them. By timing their voyages after the summer assizes, they could gain the best of both markets. In August 1726, they announced:

> For Maryland directly, the *Esther* of Newcastle . . . any person who has a mind to take passage as a servant, will be well accommodated according to the usage in those cases: any family, particularly those who are skilled in husbandry, or House Carpenters, Joyners, Sawyers, Bricklayers etc., may meet with some Encouragement, and make their terms or conditions there.

They were to contact Captain John Colville, and in his absence Mr Charles Atkinson in Newcastle: Colville was Matthias Giles' brother-in-law, a Newcastle merchant of some standing who became a major landowner in Virginia (see below).[75] In a later advertisement, those who had 'a mind to go as a servant abroad' were guaranteed the 'necessary lodging, diet and apparel as usual' and wages by being employed in Colville's own service.[76] There are signs that, as trade picked up, the annual voyage was replaced by at least two a year, though this seems to have depended on demand. In the 1740s the *Esther* was still the main ship employed, and coopers and husbandmen were still required by Colville for his land in the colonies.[77]

After almost twenty years, the initial contract lapsed, probably because of the loss of the *Esther* in 1745. Every year she had been used to import considerable quantities of 'Maryland leaf tobacco', up to 13,000 pounds weight according to one year's lading. In April 1745, however, Matthias Giles had sent the ship to Maryland with 37.5 chaldrons of coal, 3.75 of 'cynders', four chaldrons of grindstones, ten dozen flagstones and, it transpired, some convicted felons.[78] They soon ran into trouble:

> Advice is come, that the *Esther*, Capt Bowes, who lately sailed from this Port with the Transports for Virginia, and the *Mary*, Capt. Hill, for South Carolina, were taken the 11th May last, by two French Privateers of 30 guns and 250 men each, 12 Leagues off Shutland. Capt. Bowes ransomed his ship for £213, but Capt. Hill was sent to Dunkirk. The above Privateers had taken seven other Prizes since the 8th of the said Month.[79]

After this more news arrived, when a person on the *Esther* wrote to his friends in Newcastle 'that the good usage he has met with from the Captain and officers of the Privateer is almost beyond Expression, being used more like a Relation than a Prisoner of War'.[80] In July, Simon Urling, Recorder of London, reported that some of the contents of the *Esther* had been recovered from the French with a prize seized by the Royal Navy:

> My Lord George Graham having found on board one of the prizes he lately took, four convicted felons, whose names are in the margin, who had been taken by the French in the Ship *Esther*, bound to Maryland and Virginia, which now men are now confined on board His Majesty's ship the *Royal Sovereign* at the Nore, I am commanded by their Lordships to acquaint you therewith, and to desire to know, what is to be done with them.

Matthias Giles, described as a merchant in Newcastle, replied that with regard to the men, 'now confined in Rochester gaol . . . care be taken for their being Transported again according to their former sentence'. There are no further references to the *Esther* which may have been lost to her Newcastle owners.[81]

In the 1750s, perhaps as the consequence of this experience, the local authorities switched to overland transportation to York, subcontracting to the county gaoler there, or to Whitehaven. In the former system the convicts were shipped to Hull, and then taken by wagon to London, sometimes forming part of large-scale convoys going south, a highly visible process of punishment:

> They write from York, that last Thursday se'ennight 50 convicts in that Castle, ordered for transportation, set out for London. There were 33 Men and 17 Women, 23 of whom went from this Town and Durham, viz. 10 Men and 13 Women.[82]

This was also the policy adopted when political necessity made it an urgent matter to rid the region of convicts – as in the trials following the 1740 riots in Newcastle. Then the convicts were shipped directly to London for further transportation.[83] The resumption of direct transportation in the 1760s, using ships leaving the Tyne, may have been the outcome of the development of mass emigration from the region. Bailyn has commented on the numbers arriving in America in the years immediately before the Revolution and certainly there is evidence of a kind of migrant rush from the North East.[84]

There was always some emigration throughout the century, and the few accounts of the breakdown of passengers on local ships suggest that convicts, when sharing a ship, were always outnumbered by voluntary migrants. In 1740, for example, the *Esther*, contained a dozen convicts, but also nineteen servants, sixteen of them women.[85] This was about the average size of convict shipment from the North East, but was probably on the low side for numbers of servants. Other ships, like the *Jenny* in the 1760s, carried at least a dozen or twenty servants in addition to the 'transports'.[86] It is possible that the decision as to the method of transportation depended on waves of demand for servants and their regular shipments. The North East certainly received reports of the high costs of servants and their wages, particularly during the Seven Years' War, which may have stimulated the trade. 'Can't you send us a parcell of good country men: they will find good encouragement and live well', suggested one Baltimore correspondent to a Northumberland family in 1761.[87] When servants were not being exported, or in the face of wartime dangers, a land route may have been preferred.

The relationship of the convict transportation to the other types of trade in both goods and human labour was therefore by no means likely to have been uniform. Each region had its own pattern of developing trade across the Atlantic: the North East, as far as is known, had no involvement in the slave trade. Yet it shared with Cumberland a flexibility among both sea captains and their ships. The tough vessels they used for shipping coal (called 'colliers', a word confusingly also used for the miners themselves) could be adapted for all types of goods, bulk coal and heavy metals as much as humans, free or unfree. Their double-bottomed construction supposedly made them more suitable for the African trade than other ships, and of course it was a Whitby collier that the Yorkshire-born James Cook took around the world. It is possible that one Whitehaven ship, the *William*, was used for both slave and convict transportation. As noted above, there was some overlap between the entrepreneurs involved in both types of trade.[88] This kind of flexibility was also personal. Jonathan Blagdon was both a whaler in the 1750s, and a shipper of servants in the *Jenny* of Newcastle in the 1760s: then, in the 1780s, he became, like Walter Lutwidge of Whitehaven more than half a century before, a privateer.[89]

The convict shippers and the colonies

For those who shipped convicts and other goods to America, trade brought the prospect of long-term relationships and investments in new forms of business. Some convict shippers were well known in the colonies and formed longstanding business relationships with certain areas and partners. Their reputations were established in part through reports in the colonial press advertising their arrival with attractive packages of servants and convicts. The establishment of transatlantic connections and business interests varied considerably. Some, like Walter Lutwidge, had business partners and agents, settling some of his ships' captains in Virginia, or hiring assistance from among the locals. He had an agent in Alexander Mackenzie in Virginia, and a close friend in Henry Lowes of Maryland, for whose cargoes he provided insurance. Moreover, when Edward Chambers, Collector of Port Potomac, decided to return to England, Lutwidge agreed to assist him in acquiring his next post, something that was likely to cost between £200 and £250, 'which is the right way to bring about such things in this degenerate age'. He also furnished letters of recommendation for those going to Virginia, as he did for Dr William Button, a relative of his son-in-law, Isaac Cookson, who was emigrating to 'try his fortune there'.[90] The other important convict shipper from Whitehaven, Peter How, may also have had extensive business interests in the colonies. Certainly he figures occasionally in Virginia county records, for example providing a mortgage for nine slaves to a man in Augusta County. Years after How's death, his executors were still trying to collect the debt. Neither Lutwidge or How, however, seems to have created any permanent holdings in America.[91]

The Buck family from Bideford, by contrast, built a continuous relationship with the local authorities in Kent County, Maryland, on the Eastern Shore of Chesapeake Bay, shipping their convicts there, and investing in some property. From 1719 onwards, they delivered their convicts to the county, and in 1720 appointed a local man as their legal representative. John Buck, George Buck and George Strange of Bideford, decribed as 'merchants for diverse good causes and considerations', appointed Lambert Wilmer of Chester River, Maryland, as their attorney.[92] It seems they also had some property and investments in the area, particularly in Chester Town, for when John Buck died in 1761, his children George and William, still called 'merchants of Bideford', inherited his land there.[93] Some years later, the house was advertised for sale by power of attorney, described as 'completely finished' with eight rooms, 'six of which are richly papered'. Some of the family were still doing business locally in the late 1760s, with debts to be paid to local men by William senior and junior working together.[94]

This was perhaps typical of the involvement of the convict shippers in the colonies. Walter Lutwidge never lived in America, as far as is known, and the Bucks never entirely cut their connections with England or the sea. Others, exceptionally, put down roots and acquired property. The Colville family of Newcastle, substantial merchants in north-east England before 1718, were involved in large-scale landowning in Virginia and Maryland by the 1720s. According to Thomas's will, he was already settled in Virginia when his mother died in 1719, and he may have had the role of handling the family's estates there.[95] Certainly he and his brother prospered, and when John died in 1755, Thomas became the executor of the estates, both those of his own and that left to their cousin the Earl of Tankerville. By that time John, 'late of Newcastle upon Tyne', now of Fairfax County, Virginia, had acquired substantial holdings, and when he claimed in the advertisements in the Newcastle press to be able to find employment for any servants willing to migrate, he was probably merely stating a fact. He left 1,000 acres and a mill in Fairfax County, and to the Earl of Tankerville, 16,000 acres at Catacton Creek, and a further 1,500 acres and interest in a copper mine. In addition he held more than 6,000 acres in Frederick County, Maryland.[96] But the properties were to some extent encumbered by debt, something that became worse under Thomas's management, so that in the 1760s his attempts to dispose of some land were continually thwarted both by legal efforts and forceful newspaper notices taken out by Tankerville's representative in Maryland and Virginia. The gist of this complaint seems be that Thomas attempted to recover some of the unpaid part of his mother's will, which he thought his brother owed him. It does seem that the land was sold in 1768, after Thomas's death in Fairfax, at 'very near 78 years of age' in 1767.[97] However, Thomas himself left an obscure will, granting any surplus to several English families who had been family friends many years earlier, and it was their inquiries about their possible inheritance which led to English lawyers using American colleagues to pester one of the executors of the will, George Washington, in the 1780s and 1790s, even after he had become president. As far as records show, there was no successful outcome, as Washington thought there was little surplus, in part because so many 'pretenders' to the inheritance had sprung up in America. In many ways, therefore, their colonial ventures were a somewhat equivocal achievement for the two brothers, but what success they enjoyed was due in part to the fact they had started out as prosperous merchants, and in great measure to the way that they had migrated to oversee the development of their estates in America personally. Like Harry Piper, the shipping agent for north-western English convicts at the end of the colonial period, they identified with the colonies they had settled in.[98]

3
Cities, Regions and their Criminals

The early eighteenth century was not a period devoted to the collection and publication of statistics on matters of social concern such as crime. Most efforts were, and remained, private, and commentators were frequently more concerned with economic or trade data than crime. State information on criminal matters, by contrast was confined to records of individual cases and their progress. No one attempted to bring together the scattered decisions of the different courts of all the counties into a national picture of crime and punishment in the whole country. Even when this was attempted, at the start of the nineteenth century, the record of convict transportation for the previous ninety years was incomplete. This was because only capital charges at the assizes were included in the survey for all the years of the eighteenth century, and, although reprieves from execution were counted, the consequent sentences were not. Only for the early nineteenth century were transportations included.[1] Some numbers did emerge at the time of the American Revolution when, with transportation blocked, official attention was directed to calculating the number of convicts who would have to be accommodated in the alternatives of the prison hulks or the proposed national penitentiary. Since there was little incentive to explore the criminal records back to 1718, there was no serious retrospective counting of transportees, and only the most general figures emerged of the totals previously shipped to the colonies. Incidental data about this process, such as death rates on voyages, were also provided, though that was not the central focus of debate.

Duncan Campbell, the main shipper of convicts from London, attempted to provide summary data of his own experience to a House of Commons committee anxious about both the burden of incarcerating prisoners in the hulks and their high death rate (about a quarter had died between August 1776 and March 1778, and they wished to check if this had also been the same in the previous system of transportation). Campbell reported that he had transported

> on average of seven years, 473 annually; that he carried from one to two hundred persons in a ship; that the ordinary passage was about two months, during which time, and in the gaol, where they were confined frequently two month before their embarkation, rather more than a seventh part of the felons died, many of the gaol fever, but more of the small pox. He observed, that the number of women who died were only half in proportion to the men, which he imputed to their constitutions being less impaired, and to their sobriety.[2]

Campbell's estimate of a death rate of about one seventh, primarily from diseases such as smallpox and the 'gaol distemper' (probably typhus) entered the official views of the recent past, against which the experience of the prison hulks could be compared. His shipping business accounted for about half the annual number ordered for transportation immediately before the American Revolution, for the committee itself reported that, on the basis of its survey, more than 6,000 convicts that had been transported in the preceding six years or so: 'The Yearly Average of the Felons, who were ordered for Transportation during a Period of Six Years and an Half, from the 1st of November 1769 to the 1st of May 1776, amounts to 960,' of which a quarter were female. This may be an accurate reflection of the national picture, for the committee had requested the figures broken down into the different jurisdictions and levels of court. Certainly the numbers tally fairly well for the North and West Country with those extractable from surviving records.[3] John Howard, whose account of gaols preserves the national statistics, arrived in the counties just as transportation to America ended, and he notes the numbers left in gaols, to be released either on full pardons, in the case of women or, in that of many men, into the armed forces to help prosecute the war.[4]

The provincial picture was not otherwise reported in any detail. Duncan Campbell wrote to Evan Nepean, the under-secretary, that 'he always looked upon the number from the other parts of the kingdom as equal to those transported by himself', which seems plausible.[5] While his ships left from London, however, they were not necessarily filled only with London's transportees. Both Jonathan Forward Sydenham and Campbell himself shipped convicts from the Midlands through London, just as Stevenson and Randolph shipped from Bristol not only convicts from the Western Circuit but also those from counties on the Severn (Cheshire, Shropshire, Worcestershire, Herefordshire and Gloucestershire) and the West Midlands (Staffordshire, Warwickshire and Oxfordshire).[6] The result is that many transportees departing from London could have come from almost anywhere extending from Derbyshire or North Yorkshire southward.[7] In 1766 it was reported in London: 'Thursday upwards of 70 felons, transports, came to town in waggons from Oxford, Northampton, Hertford and Chelmsford, and were shipt on board the Transport ship, lying at Blackwall. The Felons from Oxford had music playing before them.' Within a few weeks, it was reported, 300 were ready to be transported from Blackwall on the *Justitia* under the command of Captain Somerset, drawn from Newgate, New Gaol in Southwark and 'the county gaols' – 'which is the greatest number ever known at one time'. Given the weeks spent awaiting movement to London, and in the city itself, it is not surprising that the paper took pains to reassure the readers that:

> The transports that may, for the future, be confined in any county gaol in England, are to be allowed 2s 6d per week, till the time they embark for America, it having been found that many friendless wretches have perished almost for want, their allowance being but a penny loaf a day.[8]

William Green remembered being brought to London from Nottinghamshire:

> On March the 19th, 1762, it was my lot to share this misfortune. I received my sentence for seven years with Anthony Atkinson. We was [sic] brought from Nottinghamshire on the seventh day of April, in the same year to London, and then carried on board the *Sally* transport, lying at Iron-Gate, near the Tower. There were twenty-six of us unhappy felons, and a most wicked crew as ever went over, most of us did smoak [sic], but all of us did swear.[9]

The colonial papers may not therefore have been disingenuous when they printed notices such as one concerning the *Alexandria* from London arriving in 1771 at Leedstown, Virginia, with forty-five convicts, among them 'an exceedingly good shoemaker', 'an extraordinary good blacksmith', a 'surgeon and apothecary'. 'All the convicts, as well as the servants, are from the Country', the advertisement claimed.[10] This last might well have been true.

If more than 900 a year were being sentenced at the end of the period of American transportation, it would not be unreasonable to suppose that the total number since the 1718 Act would have run into many thousands. Yet no such overall calculation was made in the eighteenth century. Historians have therefore had to turn to their own methods of research to establish likely numbers of convicts transported before 1776. They have struggled with local and central archives of court proceedings and appeals, shipping records, newspaper and journal reports. Early research established that numbers from London in particular were likely to have been large. In 1896 James D. Butler, noting the regular reports in the press at the outset of the 1718 Act, calculated that at least 2,138 were transported in the first ten years, and that the total from the Old Bailey alone must have been at least 10,000 before 1776.[11] London records have proved too intractable for a complete survey over this span of time, so this estimate unfortunately remains untested, though Beattie has shown that between 1714 and 1750 three-quarters of those pleading or being found guilty of non-capital offences at the Old Bailey were transported.[12] Butler noted that, in editions of Samuel Johnson's works, footnotes commenting on his famous remarks that Americans were 'a race of convicts' claimed very high figures for the national picture, of more than 2,000 a year transported nationally, and up to 50,000 in all before the Revolution.[13] However, Butler's own research represents a major shift in interpretation among American historians, not least in that it was the first to attempt to address eighteenth-century sources. Only a decade earlier George Bancroft had denied both the extent and nature of transportation. In print, he preferred to view most indentured servants as either involuntary exiles (royalist supporters for example) or political prisoners. 'Some of them, even, were convicts; but the charges of which they were convicted were chiefly political. The number transported to Virginia for crime was never considerable'.[14] In conversation with him, though, James Butler remembered that Bancroft 'freely admitted that, when speaking of felons among our settlers, he had been very economical in dispensing the truths he had discovered. Having a handful, he had opened only his little finger.' Butler commented that 'he wrote too early to expect that American eyes could bear the light of full disclosures'.[15]

Butler, by trying to examine the legal records of ordinary conviction and transportation, therefore established an unsentimental interpretation of American origins, and this became the dominant tone of twentieth-century work although it met with some resistance in Virginia.[16] Other early scholars, dealing with the local records, found a statistically accurate picture difficult. Basil Sollers, working on Maryland, noted eighteenth-century estimates of 20,000 convicts imported into that colony alone, based on a statement in 1767 that 600 a year had been arriving for the preceding thirty years. But, after careful analysis of entry records for Maryland as well as the Treasury records in England, he concluded that the total was no more than 11,000.[17] The number present at any one time, though, may have been considerable: the only surviving attempt at a Maryland census in the colonial period calculated that there were nearly 2,000 convicts present in 1755.[18] The realistic appraisal of the convict contribution to early colonial society remained one of the tasks of post-war American history. Following Butler and others, Richard B. Morris has remarked of the convicts, 'actually they were criminals, and many had been convicted for serious offences'. Recent radical scholars assert without drama the part played by the various structures of servitude and exploitation in laying the foundation of a 'free' society in America.[19]

The problem of total numbers transported, therefore, remained. Two generations of historians have grappled with the vagaries of the judicial process in order to clarify the issue of precise numbers, mixing eighteenth-century statistical guesses with work on the contemporary records. A. E. Smith pointed to the complex process of condemnation and reprieve, and highlighted the way that no account of eighteenth-century trials alone could lead to accurate numbers of those transported without examination of the subsequent, and often protracted, process of conditional pardon. While he acknowledged that in his time little work had been done on pardons, the execution rate was so low that many of the condemned must have been transported, the process of reprieve thus adding many more to those for whom transportation was the initial sentence on conviction.[20]

Only a few historians have since fought their way systematically through the files of the Secretaries of State dealing with appeals and pardons. The national picture has in fact been made up of a patchwork of counties in England, with little possibility of an overall figure. Ekirch puts overall convict numbers 1718–75 at 50,000: about 700 from Scotland, 13,000 from Ireland and 36,000 from England and Wales.[21] In a wider argument about the role of the American Revolution in transforming social relationships, Aaron Fogleman has recently argued that fully three-quarters of all migrants arrived in North America in the eighteenth century before 1776 'in some state of unfreedom'. Among the non-African peoples of all types, convicts and prisoners of various kinds were at least a sixth of the total, but if only English and Welsh migrants are considered, the proportion rises to a startling three out of every seven. Fogleman's estimate is that more than 30,000 convicts left England and Wales before the Revolution. Much as Richard B. Morris incorporated convicts into the early history of American labour, Fogleman incorporates them not only into the wider history of American unfreedom but also into the annals of American immigration. At the same time he expands the relationship between freedom and the American Revolution since neither convict servitude nor indentured servitude, unlike the larger phenomenon of slavery, survived the aftermath of independence.[22] The current conventional wisdom is still embodied in Fogleman's estimates of free and convict immigrants to the colonies, apparently with little prospect of greater precision.

Types of criminal: Discretion and disorder

The majority of convicts were routine products of the English, Irish and Scottish legal systems; the majority were English. This does not mean, however, that all transportees were convicted felons, or were escaping the gallows. A small number from England, as has been observed in Chapter 2, were vagrants deemed 'incorrigible rogues' and sentenced to transportation. Few of these faced formal indictment and jury trial. As Bampfylde Moore Carew, the most verbose (or well-published) example of this type was wont to boast, he had never been convicted of any crime (see Chapter 4). With these types of legal processes, in which justices dealt summarily with troublesome individuals, the distinction between voluntary and involuntary migration was blurred to the point of abolition. Peter Williamson, equally famous through his printed accounts, managed to establish after his return that the authorities of Aberdeen had connived at his 'kidnap' and transportation to Pennsylvania when he was a young boy.[23] Half of Northumberland's 'gang of the faws' in 1752, essentially the womenfolk, were removed to the colonies by magistrates' order and without trials under the Act of Settlement. In Ireland this was far more common as magistrates transported many paupers and vagrants – 'loose idle vagrants' as a 1735 Act called them, though English authorities seem to have used the practice more sparingly. 'Altogether "vagabonds" accounted for a much higher percentage of Irish than English transportees'.[24] These victims of semi-judicial processes, particularly when their cases were broadcast in published narratives, plausibly perpetuated the myth of the *captive* as contrasted with the *criminal* transportee. It was partly as a result of this kind of story that America continued to feature in a growing literature of captivity narratives – except that it was not the Indians, but Southern plantation owners and English magistrates who figured as villains.[25]

Formal indictment and trial, though, sent the majority of transportees abroad. Yet there was little uniformity across the country: as stressed in the previous chapter, the acquisition of transportation as part of the penal armoury was not greeted with an identical welcome in every county. Variability reflects one of the distinctive features about the English judicial system, namely, the extent of local discretion in the hands of county magistrates. As Peter King has recently argued, the essence of eighteenth-century law enforcement was the discretion exercised at all levels, from the victims making their initial accusation, to the magistrates hearing the complaints, to the jury at the trial, to the Secretary of State deciding the fate of the condemned. The 'long eighteenth century' was 'the golden age of discretionary justice'.[26] Much of this was governed by unwritten rules, which led Max Weber to the much harsher judgement that 'discretion' in fact reflected the arbitrariness of personal decision-making rather than the rationality of a formal system: English law was little more than 'kadi justice', he thought, shaped by the whims of local authorities, as in many Islamic states. It was the worst insult he could contemplate, a sign of the uncodified nature of English law, 'to an extent inconceivable on the Continent'.[27] King's subtle analysis, however, is of a complex interaction of participants in the process of dealing with complaints of offences, with magistrates acting as brokers and mediators in defining the crime and deciding the appropriate court it should be sent to. Many complaints were handled without prosecution, and indeed a large proportion of actions, probably a majority, in which people would initially claim as assaults (even rape) or as thefts were dealt with informally through magistrates.[28]

The regional variations in these patterns, though, suggest that it is necessary to be wary of assuming a clear relationship between the types of crime and the forms of trial and sentence. If a particular county or city had a high proportion of its convicts sent from the quarter sessions rather than the assizes, for example, that may reflect less on the nature and relative triviality of the crimes than on the likelihood that the local authorities wished to keep things under their control (however apparently valuable the goods stolen or threatening the method of theft), rather than risk the lives of the accused in the assize courts. On the other hand, if a high proportion of reprieved convicts derived from those who were tried at the assizes, this may indicate that a county really did face the problem of a particularly large number of non-violent thieves (say, of horses), only a handful of whom were thought to deserve execution. Much of the character of the regions, and indeed of individual counties, therefore emerges in their records of criminal prosecutions, convictions and sentences. The crimes in their courts reflect the priorities of the local authorities, the strong feelings of the victims of criminal actions, and to some degree the nature of their social relationships. To some degree, the interpretation here has to be conjectural, but the striking differences within and between regions suggests that there is still much to be understood about the processes that 'produced' transported convicts.

Each jurisdiction, however small, therefore seems to have been able to develop a separate and distinct judicial culture. In the face of complaints of theft, in particular, the choice of what kind of charge to bring, and at which level of court, and hence the forms of potential punishment, was very wide. Newcastle-upon-Tyne treated most thefts as minor, whatever the value of the stolen goods, trying five times more cases at the quarter sessions than at the assizes. Only the most serious crimes, involving attacks on people or threats to their property (particularly to shops, warehouses and domestic buildings) were tried at the higher court. The rest were dealt with by the town's magistrates, and since the majority of the accused for most of the century were female, the inference is that they wished to keep the judicial outcome of these trials under their control.[29] There are signs that other urban authorities also behaved in this way. In Exeter and Bristol, where there were gaol deliveries of oyer and terminer under a recorder (in Bristol, a visiting judge from London), the local authorities managed things in a distinctive way. In Bristol there was more serious crime, as befits the problems of a much larger city, and more convicted thieves were sentenced to death, whereas in Exeter it was customary for all thefts to be treated as grand larceny, with only the most shocking crimes being classified as a capital charge. The result was that few defendants risked the gallows. This was a matter of careful discrimination, so that for example at the same trial, Thomasine Hose was sentenced to death for house-breaking, while Jeremiah Gordon and Paul Stoneman, for picking pockets, were transported for seven years. Stoneman, of Great Torrington, had been arrested on 12 July 'for picking pockets in St Peter's Cathedral while the Right Reverend the Lord Bishop of this Diocese was confirming the Inhabitants of some of the parishes in the Neighbourhood'. Despite this capital crime, he was found guilty of grand larceny only and transported, while Thomasine Hall or Hose had to wait a year before she was reprieved for seven years' transportation.[30] Unusually, in Exeter, the custom was usually to reprieve for seven years, with few examples of a fourteen-year sentence apart from the receivers of stolen goods for whom this was the statutory (and immediate) sentence. In other areas of the country, it was only shortly before the American Revolution that a seven-year reprieve became common.

In London, as Beattie and others have shown, there was even greater discretion, as it seems that before the early eighteenth century (and rarely even thereafter) petty larceny was never tried by indictment and jury verdict at the quarter sessions or Old Bailey sessions. The long-standing custom, seemingly well-established in Elizabethan times, was to present the petty thieves before the Mayor or individual magistrate who incarcerated them for short periods with corporal punishment in the Bridewell or house of correction. This pattern obtained in both London and the surrounding area of Middlesex. While it is probable that London faced more serious crimes and possessed a far more professional criminal population than any other place in early modern England, many minor offenders were therefore dealt with summarily and locked up in the Bridewell without indictment and trial. This hidden crime wave, treated according to a policy which seems to have had its origins in the sixteenth century, meant that petty larceny was virtually absent from the London courts. Though Beattie does not pursue this, it likely that, without this practice, the proportion of women on trial would have been even higher.[31]

This kind of variability matches what is known from the more rural areas as well. In some areas such as Devon and County Durham, a large majority of convicts were transported from the assizes. In Durham it seems that the local refusal by magistrates to use the punishment at their quarter sessions was accompanied by a determination to send all serious cases before the London judges. This might explain one distinctive character of Durham's assizes, namely, the remarkably low conviction rate compared with assizes elsewhere in the region.[32] It is likely that all juries were aware of the consequences of their decisions, and in these cases, again involving a high proportion of women (particularly in the third quarter of the eighteenth century), various kinds of benefit were being granted by juries anxious to avoid the severest consequences for the convicted. So Durham produced a large number of transportees, but distinctively did so directly from the assizes – three times the number from the quarter sessions, whereas for most rural areas such as Devon, Northumberland and Cumberland, the usual ratio was about twice as many.

In two contrasting types of jurisdiction, the quarter sessions predominated. In Newcastle and Bristol, reflecting the way that urban

Table 3.1   Convicts, courts and counties 1718–75

	Assizes		Quarter Sessions		All
	No:	%	No:	%	
North East					
Co. Durham	152	75.25	50[a]	24.75	202
Newcastle	86	41.15	123	58.85	209
Northumberland	132	63.46	76	36.54	208
North West					
Cumberland	119	70.83	49	29.17	168
Lancashire	206	32.39	430	67.61	636
Westmorland	46	95.83	2	4.17	48
Western Circuit					
Devon	925	67.82	439	32.18	1364
Bristol	277[b]	36.93	473[c]	63.06	750

[a] There are no transportation sentences before 1750.
[b] Data from 1727 onwards.
[c] Data from 1727 onwards.

thefts were directed overwhelmingly at the lower courts, the majority of convicts were transported from the quarter sessions. In Lancashire, too, the sessions were consistently responsible for twice as many transportees as the assizes, a pattern revealed in the 1769–76 survey as well in the surviving archives for the whole period since the 1718 Act (Table 3.1). This does not appear to have been the outcome of a distinctive urban style of managing crime as it was in Newcastle, for the county's urban courts, with the exception of Liverpool, did not produce many convicts. It seems to have been a longstanding policy in the county to deal with most crimes at the peripatetic quarter sessions, which certainly went to major urban centres such as Manchester, but which overwhelmingly dealt with crimes from a widely scattered population.[33]

Categories of criminals

The criminals sentenced for thefts by quarter sessions magistrates were by and large mostly accused of petty larceny or the lesser forms of grand larceny. Those before the assizes faced the possibility of the death penalty, and many had to play what Spierenburg has called the 'game with pardons', either in court or after condemnation: as he puts it, 'the game with pardons was a typical characteristic of British judicial practice. It was less common in the Dutch Republic'. Correspondence between the convicts and the Secretary of State (later the Home Secretary) survives in large quantities, together with judges' reports on the cases, the views of the local justices, support from local dignitaries or petitions of neighbours and even the opinions of the victims.[34] The scale of this evidence might lead to the conclusion that assize convicts were most likely to be serious criminals, and fortunate in being saved from death for transportation. To contemporary protaganists in debates on crime in the middle and latter half of the eighteenth century, particularly those opposed to transportation as a sufficient weapon against apparently inexorably rising levels of serious crime, greater severity was required. A great deal of the discussion centred on how to make the death sentence more draconian and effective – in many ways, how to recover control of the execution drama from the condemned and the unpredictable crowds. The print culture of the time concentrated on the serious and sensational crimes such as murder and highway robbery, and had done so from the earliest period, but the images of punishment associated with serious crimes were not necessarily effective.[35] But, as has been pointed out by modern historians, the pardoned criminals were 'as little as a third' of the total transported to America after the 1718 Act.[36] This might be an overestimate, in fact, even at the assizes.

In no part of the country, as far as evidence is available, were the condemned and reprieved a majority of the transported – with the single exception of Northumberland, where the predominance of horse theft faced the authorities with a dilemma (see Table 3.2). While this was a crime with a long history – mainly because the Scottish border offered opportunities for easy disposal of stolen horses – and had traditionally been dealt the severest treatment in the seventeenth century, which saw horse thieves hanging beside the witches in Newcastle's mass executions in 1650, it was not apparently possible to hang every horse thief after 1700.[37] It has become a truism that while the law became more severe, the execution rate declined in the eighteenth century: in fact much of the transformation in the willingness to countenance large numbers of executions had already occurred in the late seventeenth century.[38] Northumberland therefore executed a few recalcitrants, but generally horse thieves could be reasonably sure that they would be on their way to America on conviction. The result was that more than four out of ten of the men shipped from Northumberland's assizes had been convicted of stealing horses.[39]

Table 3.2   Assize transportees: Directly sentenced and reprieved

	1st Sentence		Reprieved		Total
	No:	%	No:	%	
North East					
Co. Durham	90	59.21	62	40.79	152
Newcastle	62	72.09	24	27.91	86
Northumberland	56	42.42	76	57.58	132
Total	208	56.22	162	43.78	370
North West					
Cumberland	68	57.14	51	42.86	119
Lancashire	117	56.80	89	43.20	206
Westmorland	25	54.35	21	45.65	46
Total	210	56.60	161	43.40	371
Western Circuit					
Cornwall	227	70.94	93	29.06	320
Devon	569	61.51	356	38.49	925
Dorset	188	68.89	81	30.11	269
Hampshire	489	65.64	256	34.36	745
Somerset	539	64.55	296	35.45	835
Wiltshire	335	65.30	178	34.70	513
Total	2347	65.07	1260	34.93	3607
Bristol	194	70.04	83	29.96	277

Elsewhere in the North, the proportion of the reprieved was generally about 45 per cent of the transported. In the West Country, it was significantly lower, little more than a third overall. Reasons for these differences are a little difficult to ascertain, but it seems that west-country criminals were accused, and found guilty, of lesser offences. There were no fewer convictions for threatening burglaries, highway robberies and horse theft, than in the North. Sheep stealing, however, so common in much of Devon and Cornwall, only became a capital offence in the 1740s, and distinctively, the western assizes saw far more accusations of sheep stealing than of horse theft. In other ways, too, the West had its characteristic crimes, particularly in other rural offences such as arson, attacks on toll gates and toll houses, and poaching on places such as Cranborne Chase on the Dorset/Wiltshire border or in the forests and parks in Hampshire.[40] These 'social crimes', though not particularly common in the West, were almost unheard of in the North. There were only twelve transported for crimes under the Black Acts in the western circuit, and two for smuggling, and one for attacking a toll gate.[41] Western riots, too, were more frequent, and more violent, than was general in the North, though the events of Newcastle's Guildhall riots in 1740 were similar, if exceptional. Seven individuals were carried to the American plantations for their role in the Guildhall riots and a further four were sent from County Durham including two women involved in the unrest at Stockton. The politics of food and the 'moral economy' produced their executions and transportations in the west country and the south more frequently than in the far north.[42] However, even well-publicized punishments, such as the execution of seven Hampshire men in 1723, tried before King's Bench and hanged at Tyburn under the new provisions of the Black Acts, made little impression, as E. P. Thompson pointed out.[43] Riots and crimes of rural protest remained endemic in some parts of southern England. In the overall picture, though, they did not figure very largely anywhere. Taking the assize convicts with those from the quarter sessions, the evidence suggests that a large majority of the transported were minor offenders, whose shipment to the colonies was in lieu of non-capital punishments, thus fulfilling the potential of the 1718 Transportation Act which provided an alternative, not just to hanging, but more importantly to the secondary punishments of the whip or branding iron.

Youth might save some from the gallows by consigning them to transportation, thereby not only preserving their lives but also satisfying the constant need for labour in the American colonies, as also envisaged in the Transportation Act of 1718. Many more were propelled across the Atlantic at a relatively youthful age as a consequence of the widely held assumption that criminality began with the commission of lesser offences leading to more audacious crimes. Some newspapers urged that 'the thief takers' catch

> the young fry of pick pockets (for whom there is no reward) who swarm about the Playhouses and other Places and by an early Removal of them to our Plantations, where they may be servicable, prevent their growing up here fit for the Commission of Burglaries and Robberies on the Highways.[44]

A large urban centre such as Bristol provided opportunities for young people to thieve on their own account or at the instigation of others. In one Bristol court in April 1745, a number of young offenders appeared before the judges. Boys as young as Peter Anderson and Robert Bassett, described in the records as 'labourers', one 'about 12', the other 'near 13', faced charges of burglary for having broken into William Price's house in Temple parish, making off with a silver watch, a pair of silver buckles and 14 shillings. Anderson told the court that he had 'several times sold pieces of rope, old iron, brass, buckles and bits of brass' to the same woman. Facing equally serious charges for an unrelated crime was 'labourer' James Coles, described simply as 'a boy'. He was alleged to have stolen 'privately' from a shop over £5 in silver and a guinea, the property of widow Catherine Watkins. Also appearing before the same court was a servant girl Mary Blite, aged sixteen, who being searched by her master confessed to robbing him of £4 in silver which along with a key was found 'all tied up in her hair'. Her master Solomon Phillips, a victualler, had suspected her of earlier thefts to which she confessed. Found guilty of the lesser charge of grand larceny, all four were sentenced to terms of seven years' transportation.[45] How these young convicts viewed their fate we can only imagine but in the case of one fourteen-year-old Matthew MacDonald of County Durham there is no doubt as to his reaction. Found guilty of a minor theft at the quarter sessions in 1757 and sentenced to a spell of seven years in the American plantations, he viewed the prospect with alarm and took drastic measures to avoid his sentence. MacDonald claimed to have witnessed his father and another man burying the body of an unknown person in the ground. When a search yielded nothing, he confessed that he had lied to the authorities in the hope of evading transportation or effecting his escape from the gaol. He managed the first but not the second.[46]

Gender

As the example of Northumberland's horse thieves suggests, those reprieved from the gallows were largely male. It was unusual for women to be convicted of capital crimes in the provinces, and they therefore formed a minor presence among those who had to be saved from execution (Table 3.3). There were some exceptional areas where women were more than a tenth of the reprieved as in counties such as Devon and Durham. Far more exceptional were Newcastle-upon-Tyne where they were a fifth and Bristol where they were between a quarter and a third.

These patterns, though, reflect careful decisions made by victims, magistrates, and juries, in convicting women of lesser offences, through 'partial' verdicts. It does not mean that women were a minor problem in the courts of England. On the contrary, the crimes of which they were accused at the assizes could be serious: more than half of the

Table 3.3   Gender and reprieve at the assizes

	Reprieved		
	Total	**Female**	**%**
North East			
Co. Durham	82	8	12.90
Newcastle	24	5	20.83
Northumberland	76	3	3.95
Total	162	16	9.88
North West			
Cumberland	51	3	5.88
Lancashire	89	2	2.22
Westmorland	21	1	4.76
Total	161	6	4.11
Western Circuit			
Cornwall	93	9	9.68
Devon	356	48	13.48
Dorset	81	8	9.88
Hampshire	256	21	8.20
Somerset	296	15	5.07
Wiltshire	178	13	7.30
Total	1262	114	9.03
Bristol	83	24	28.92

women before the assizes of the North East and North West were initially charged with thefts from houses and buildings or robbery from
the person. Of the 397 females on trial at the assizes for theft in the
Western Circuit 254 were initially charged with stealing from persons
or buildings; yet they too benefited from the unwillingness of judges
and juries to see them committed to the gallows: 64 per cent were the
beneficiaries of partial verdicts. This reinforces the impression that
the partial verdict was vital if women were to escape the threat of the
gallows in these courts.[47] Moreover, the gender patterns of the convicts
transported from different parts of England suggest that there were wide
variations in the proportions of female criminals (Tables 3.4 and 3.5).
In some areas they formed a substantial minority, or even a majority.
In London, for example, Beattie has remarkable evidence of their participation in crimes which led to prosecution at the Old Bailey. Overall,
between 1660 and 1750, 40 per cent of the accused were women, and
in some periods – the 1690s particularly – they were actually the

Table 3.4   Gender distribution at the assizes

	Uncertain gender	Female		Male		Total no:
		No:	%	No:	%	
North East						
Co. Durham		49	32.24	103	67.76	152
Newcastle		20	23.26	66	76.74	86
Northumberland		14	10.61	118	89.39	132
Total		83	22.43	287	77.57	370
North West						
Cumberland		25	21.01	94	78.99	119
Lancashire		16	7.77	190	92.23	206
Westmorland		7	15.22	39	84.78	46
Total		48	12.94	323	87.06	371
Western Circuit						
Cornwall	2	33	10.31	285	89.06	320
Devon	1	160	17.30	764	82.59	925
Dorset		43	15.99	226	84.01	269
Hampshire	2	84	11.24	661	88.49	745
Somerset	1	102	12.22	732	87.66	835
Wiltshire	2	57	11.11	454	88.50	513
Total	8	477	15.34	3122	86.51	3607
Bristol	1	91	32.85	185	66.79	277

Table 3.5   Gender distribution at the quarter sessions

	Uncertain gender	Female		Male		Total no:
		No:	%	No:	%	
North East						
Co. Durham		17	34.00	33	66.00	50
Newcastle		73	59.35	50	40.65	123
Northumberland		25	32.89	51	67.11	76
Total		115	46.18	134	53.82	249
North West						
Cumberland		16	32.65	33	67.35	49
Lancashire		90	20.93	340	79.07	430
Westmorland		0		2	100.00	2
Total		106	22.04	375	77.96	481
Western Circuit						
Devon	4	137	31.21	298	67.88	439
Bristol	8	164	34.67	301	63.64	473

majority. This was a time of great economic depression and poverty, which may have been crucial influences. As Beattie comments, the courts could rarely have had to cope with such numbers of women – defendants who, the established practices of the courts strongly suggest, could not easily be subjected to the terror of the gallows, the only punishment available to the judges in felony cases. The numbers of women on trial gave this period a particular character, and the problems they raised go a long way towards explaining why the late seventeenth and early eighteenth centuries saw so many efforts to make the law and its administration more effective.[48]

Elsewhere, Newcastle-upon-Tyne showed a remarkably high proportion of females among its accused thieves after 1700. This was most obvious at the quarter sessions, where women were in overall majority during the eighteenth century, dominating in the 1750s and 1760s, with males only managing to surpass them in the last quarter of the century. Even allowing for fewer women being accused at the assizes, the town produced an extraordinarily high proportion of female transportees (Tables 3.4 and 3.5). This was also true of other areas of the North East, and, to generalize rather dangerously, women were less of a problem to the courts in the rural South and West. Everywhere, though, proportions were lowest at the level of the assize courts, with the quarter sessions showing a consistently higher proportion. The contrasts between the two levels of courts suggest confirmation of a truism of early modern law, that women figure most prominently at the lower levels, and rarely in the most serious cases.[49]

There are regional differences, too, in the experience of the courts in terms of the gender distribution of convicts over the whole period between 1718 and the American Revolution. In the North East, the proportion of female transportees reached a peak in the twenty-five years before 1776, that is, after 1750. Taking all courts together, nearly 40 per cent of Co. Durham's convicts at this time were female, and more than half of Newcastle's. Even in Northumberland where more than a quarter were female in the quarter-century before the Revolution, the proportion was higher than anything found in the South or North West. But even in the western circuit assizes, most counties showed an increase in the proportion of women after 1750; in only two (Cornwall and Hampshire) was there a slight decrease. Dorset's assizes, for example, had a remarkable increase in the proportion of female convicts, from about 5 per cent before 1750, to nearly a quarter, 24 per cent, after. In Devon, with a large number of quarter sessions cases too, nearly a quarter of the convicts overall were female after 1750. Though this may reflect a

Table 3.6 All transportees: gender distribution before and after 1750

| | All Courts | | | | | | | |
| | Up to 1750 | | | | 1751 Onwards | | | |
	Female	Male	Total	% Female	Female	Male	Total	% Female
North East								
Co. Durham	18	62	80	22.50	48	74	122	39.34
Newcastle	18	47	65	27.69	75	69	144	52.08
Northumberland	13	95	108	12.04	26	74	100	26.00
North West								
Cumberland	17	46	63	26.98	24	81	105	22.86
Lancashire	45	191	236	19.07	61	339	400	15.25
Westmorland	6	22	28	21.43	1	19	20	5.00
Western Circuit								
Devon	169	643	812	20.81	128	419	547	23.40
Bristol	143	223	366	39.07	113	262	375	30.13

Note: these figures include only cases where the gender can be identified.

genuine rise in female criminality, it is more likely that the adoption of transportation as a routine punishment by many quarter sessions benches, and the favourable partial verdicts given by juries to many women at the assizes, led to an increase in female convicts. It may reflect the normalization of the penalty for petty thieves, and the development of effective means of transporting them, as much as any rise in detected criminality (Table 3.6).

In a number of jurisdictions, particularly in the North West, counties experienced a declining proportion of female convicts after the mid-century in both levels of court. The reasons for this must be conjectural, but may indicate either a change in direction of the judicial policies of the local counties, still uninvestigated in the archives for most areas of Britain, or the particular problems of rural crime. For example, the criminalization of sheep stealing, which became a capital offence only in 1741, posed problems for many local authorities where families tended to be involved. Richard Burn noted that the alternative penalty was seven years' transportation for wounding cattle or sheep, and many pleaded to that charge to avoid execution. On the other hand, there were examples of near-professional sheep stealing and dealing in mutton and hides about which local victims and courts felt strongly. It is unclear whether these legislative changes would have had clear consequences for the gender of convicts, though the death penalty might have raised the stakes to the point where prosecutions concentrated mainly on men. Certainly there were examples in the later eighteenth century of judges deciding to make an example of a sheep thief, because there had been no executions for the crime for twenty years. It is perhaps because of this kind of consideration that Hampshire and Cornwall's assize courts shared the decline in female convicts with the North West, though it is difficult to be certain. The problem is made harder by the fact that Bristol also experienced fewer female criminals in the later part of the period than in the earlier (Table 3.6).[50]

The major difference between urban and rural crime lay in this area of animal theft, principally horse stealing and sheep stealing, together with the theft of cattle and farmyard animals. A fifth of all those transported from the western circuit were accused of various kinds of animal theft. Furthermore, since animal theft was almost exclusively male in character, with female participation figuring in barely 3 per cent of the cases, it also impacted on the gender dimension of rural crime as a whole. Only highway robbery had lower female participation rates. Animal theft apart, men and women stole similar items though not necessarily in similar circumstances or for similar reasons.

Newcastle and Bristol

The near total absence of prosecutions for animal theft in the urban centres of Newcastle and Bristol helps to explain why women formed a larger proportion of those accused of theft in cities and towns and the more urbanized counties like Durham and Devon than in rural jurisdictions. In terms of population, their numbers may have also exceeded those of men, as they did in the nineteenth century, especially in seafaring centres with their motley floating populations and recent migrants and widows.[51] Newcastle and Bristol had much in common. Outside London, they were the largest ports in England, engaged heavily in coastal trade and overseas shipping. Newcastle engaged in trade with the Baltic and Continental Europe as well as London while Bristol plied both sides of the Bristol Channel and the Atlantic. As the only town between York and Edinburgh, Newcastle was 'the great Emporium of all the Northern Parts of England and a good share of Scotland'. London depended on it for its supplies of fuel which gave it national importance. In this respect Bristol differed from Newcastle and many other towns in that it lived in, and boasted of, its 'independency' of London. As 'the metropolis of the West', Bristol faced even less competition than Newcastle, drawing into its orbit not only 'much of the social and economic activity of the five largely rural counties of the West Country', but also those of the West Midlands and South Wales. At the beginning of the eighteenth century Bristol was the third-largest city in England, after London and Norwich, with a population of 20,000. In 1730, it was second. According to Latimer, the population of the city and suburbs in 1751 was between 43,000 and 44,000. By 1800, it had reached 60,000, twice the size of Newcastle which grew rather more slowly. Yet both Newcastle and Bristol had declined in rank relative to other metropolitan centres by then.[52]

The assizes were held once a year in Newcastle and, by mid-century, in Bristol too, but while the former was part of the Northern Assize circuit, the latter was an independent jurisdiction with its own recorder. Newcastle courts conformed with those of the rest of the North but in Bristol, at least in 1762, the assizes did not meet at all owing to the indisposition of the Bristol Recorder Sir Michael Foster. Whether this was the only exception is not at all clear for there are no surviving assize records for some years, though from the newspapers it appears that there were meetings of the assize court in some of these years.[53] On the other hand, Bristol's quarter sessions not only met every month, but at times almost weekly (though few of its records have survived). Much information, however, regarding the operation of the lower court, is available from Bristol newspapers, the *Gloucester Journal* and the *Sherborne Mercury*.[54] Records for Newcastle are continuous for most of the century, and after the mid-1720s newspaper reports are detailed. After 1739 there were never fewer than two newspapers in the town, one of which, the *Newcastle Courant*, made something of a speciality of crime news.

In Newcastle women accounted for over half the total number of transportees in the twenty-five-year period before the Revolution; in Bristol, with greater numbers, female transportees were about a third of the total figure for the city. These cases provide a means of exploring the local dimension of what Beattie has called 'the problem of women', which faced some urban authorities in the eighteenth century. Undoubtedly the figures for the Bristol quarter sessions are too low because of incomplete data especially for the period 1754 to 1758 when, following the death of Felix Farley, crime reporting in his *Bristol Journal* under the editorship of his widow was reduced. Yet despite incomplete data for Bristol in some years, the transportation records do not indicate that women ever formed a majority of Bristol transportees. Overall, between 1727 and 1776, a third of all transportees from both quarter sessions and assizes were female. By contrast, in rural Gloucestershire only about one in nine transported convicts was female.[55] Patterns of theft were similar in Newcastle and Bristol with women more likely than men to be accused of stealing clothing, cloth, bed and table linen, and men stealing a greater range of items. Clothing was targeted by substantial numbers of men and pawned by both men and women but, as Lynn Mackay found among women appearing before the Old Bailey, it was women who were more likely to pawn the goods they had taken.[56] Small items of value which might be easily secreted, such as watches, jewellery, silverware and coinage, were sought by both men and women but women's lives, being more circumscribed than those of men, limited their opportunities, especially with regard to work-related theft. Bristol's quays, wharfs, vessels, warehouses, workshops and yards were more accessible to men than women; women found their opportunities where they could, committing serious offences in stealing from people and buildings which could lead to capital indictments and the prospect of the gallows. In particular, Bristol tradesmen and shopkeepers appear to have offered larger opportunities to would-be thieves than those of Newcastle. The City also possessed a prodigious number of taverns. McGarth and Williams suggest that in the middle of the eighteenth century there may have been an inn or alehouse for every 50 inhabitants.[57] Bristol was bigger, richer – *Felix Farley's Bristol Journal* called it 'an opulent city' – and probably better policed than Newcastle which according to Spencer Cowper, dean of Durham, was 'filthy and disagreeable' yet with 'the riches and trade of London in some degree'.[58] Street robberies resulted in harsh punishments such as befell Elizabeth Hind and Ann Brooks. Hearing cries of 'murder', two servants going along the College Green

> went towards the place from whence the Sounds came, and found the sd two Creatures stripping a young Woman of her Gown, and one of them with a large Case knife (which they had just before stole from Mr Rogers at the Bell near the Boar's Head) cutting her Gown off her Back; on which they secured them and on being searched, the above mentioned things together with the Knife were found concealed under one of their petticoats.[59]

Both women were sentenced to death but Ann Brooks, described as a single woman, was reprieved on condition of fourteen years' transportation while Elizabeth Hind, an Irish woman born in County Longford and a widow, was hanged.[60]

Ann Carrill was neither a single woman nor a widow but the wife of Thomas, a tailor of St James parish. When she snatched a six-year-old child from outside the child's home during the daytime, she did not take into account the likely witnesses who would observe her and the numbers of men and women willing to assist in apprehending a suspected thief. When Joseph King, a brightsmith, was called out of his shop 'to assist in apprehending Carrill near St James new square, he saw there a child 'stript of great part of its Cloathes and was informed that the said child was so stript by Ann Carrill who was there present in custody'.[61] The grand jury found a true bill against her for being

> in a certain field & open place near to the Kings Highway therein & upon one Hannah Dools an infant assaulted her & one white holland frock worth 1s 6d, one red stay worth 2s 6d, one skirt worth 2s 6d, one quilted petticoat worth 6d ... did steal and carry away against the peace.[62]

She too was sentenced to death for the crime but was subsequently reprieved on condition of fourteen years' transportation.[63]

Equally transparent were thefts allegedly committed by live-in servants who had come to the city in search of employment and whose place of origin was known to their employers. When Bristol goldsmith and watchmaker William Wady found that his house had been robbed, he suspected his maidservant Elizabeth Sergent and his lodger Sarah Davis, both of whom had fled, 'but being pursued, were overtaken at Newport, and brought back to the City, and having been examined at the Council House, Monday, and the Goods found on them, they were committed to Newgate.'[64] Found guilty of grand larceny, Elizabeth Sergent received a sentence of seven years' transportation but Sarah Davis, regarded as a principal in the case and found guilty of stealing from a house, received sentence of death. The sentence was respited but by the time it was commuted to seven years' transportation and arrangements were made for her passage, she had already spent almost two years in gaol.[65]

Newcastle's thieves were, perhaps, at a disadvantage compared with those of Bristol. The town was smaller, and it was up to ten miles to the nearest small towns such as Sunderland where goods could be disposed of. Most transportees, particularly women, seem to have been easily detected. Some were found out trying to sell goods they had stolen, as happened to Isabel Gross in 1739: the pieces of the stolen silver beaker she was trying to pass in a shop were marked by distinctive initials.

Others, such as young servants, left town and stored the stolen prop- erty at their home and these items were easily traced. In 1736 Jane Swan nearly made her parents complicit in her crime by returning home and hiding her booty in her bedroom in their house in Whittingham (north- ern Northumberland), but they were never prosecuted. Some women committed more serious crimes: labourer's wife Margaret Cockburn forged a promissory note in 1766, for which she was condemned and reprieved. However, since she was illiterate she had some difficulty in executing the crime, and had to persuade a shoemaker to write it for her, and 'afterwards procured a little boy called William Finley' to forge the signatures. She confessed readily on her arrest. The only Newcastle woman executed for a property offence, widow Alice Williamson, was found in the house of her victim, only managing to steal a bagful of clothes – a shirt, two pillowslips, two napkins, a child's frock, apron and petticoat, four caps and some stockings. On the other hand, she had burgled the house, and had three keys upon her person when seized by passers-by. Unfortunately for her, she was also an old offender.[66] What seems to have distinguished Newcastle women from those elsewhere was the larger number of married women appearing before the courts. Although the marital status of accused women in Bristol courts is diffi- cult to establish, especially when surviving cases are derived from the newspapers, Bristol data for 1748 to 1753 accords more closely with the pattern identified by Peter King for London than with that of Newcastle. Mapping female participation in crime to the life cycle King found that nearly three-fifths of offenders appearing before the Old Bailey between 1791 and 1793 were single (58.9 per cent), one third were married (34.4 per cent) with 6.7 per cent widowed. In Newcastle there were roughly equal proportions of single women (41.3 per cent), married (42.8 per cent) and a higher proportion of widows (15 per cent).[67] Not only was Newcastle a poorer town than Bristol, but many male workers such as keelmen, mariners and miners were employed only seasonally.[68] The unreliability of men's incomes may have prompted their wives from hardship or necessity to steal.

The journey over

The sentence to transportation was, for the convicts, just the beginning: the long journey to America had its hazards. Few convict accounts of the voyage over survive outside some of the criminal biographies and the memoirs of voluntary servants, many of which have some details of the experience. Newspapers on both sides of the ocean, however, took an interest. American papers reported the arrivals of human cargo, and advertised the skills of the new workforce. English papers had different purposes. In the North East, they made a particular point of reporting the safe arrival of ships carrying servants or convicts, as though the distance and the hazards were appreciated as threatening their survival. Perhaps the presence of so many women convicts, and the need for local authorities to provide reassurance that transportation was a genuine alternative to execution, and not a secret method of disposal, led to so many careful reassurances. This style of reporting has few equivalents in other regions, not all of which were served by newspapers, but it does suggest a particular sensibility to the fate of convicts in north-east England.

If regions differed in the character of their convicts, as we have already established, there also were different regional experiences of sentencing and transportation. Much depended on the availability of ships and the willingness of shippers. In the 1720s and 1730s in north-east England prisoners might spend years awaiting shipment to the colonies, and shippers were selective about whom they took, being anxious for a quick and easy sale. Women, the sick and the elderly might languish in prison for years, even die there. Two Durham prisoners, part of a group of five young people found guilty of robbing a man on the highway between Gateshead and Sunderland and sentenced to death in 1725 were still in gaol five years later, apparently awaiting transportation, while a third member of the group had died in gaol. Even thirty years later a Durham woman Ann Golightly spent sufficient time in gaol to give birth not just to one but two children while awaiting transportation to the colonies.[69] However, convicts sailing to the Chesapeake directly from the North East did have one advantage. At least until the mid-1740s, they would not be crowded onto ships carrying a hundred or more convicts as was common on vessels leaving London. The courts of the North East seldom generated more than twenty convicts in a single year and shiploads were generally not crowded with passengers. They were usually made up of mixed cargoes of convicts and voluntary servants, and between them they rarely amounted to more than thirty people. The largest reported shipload from the North East was on the ship *Jenny* which arrived in Virginia carrying 'European goods and 41 passengers' in 1766. A rival ship, *Mary*, took about sixteen convicts and fifteen servants later the same year.[70] By contrast, ships from the North West, with the opportunity to pick up more free servants in Ireland on the way out to the Atlantic, often carried more than 100 passengers. Certainly the *Hicks*, which significantly was described as being from both Whitehaven and Dublin, entered the Potomac with 128 passengers, both indentured servants and convicts, as well as fifty-five 'parcels of goods'.[71] Free Irish servants were sometimes likely to feel as suppressed as the convicts. Quaker migrant Elizabeth Ashbridge discovered a plot by Irish-speaking servants to take over the ship while they were still off the western Irish coast which, since she spoke the language, she was able to reveal to the captain. As a result she had to be given protection against her fellow passengers for the rest of the voyage. Since they planned to hurt her, 'several of them were corrected and put in irons for it', she recorded. Irish servants, like those from London and Bristol in the seventeenth century, continued to be associated with forced migration under the appearance of volunteering. As late as the 1770s, the term 'soul-drivers' was being used to describe the activities of ships' captains in the north-ern part of Ireland, who induced large numbers to leave for America. The explanation offered English readers was that, if the servants could not be sold 'at the principal trading towns, they drive them up into the country and dispose of them at the plantations'.[72] Only at the end of the colonial period was large-scale migration a feature of north-eastern England, and there are no reports of convicts accompanying those going to 'the land of freedom'.[73]

Bristol convicts, increasingly combined with those of the West Country, South Wales and the Severn Valley, faced danger at the outset from the treacherous waters of the Bristol Channel and in times of war, from enemy privateers. Some ships came to grief without leaving the coast.[74] In February 1761 it was reported that the *Tyger* of Bristol bound for Virginia had been taken by a Bayonne privateer 'and carried to Vigo'.[75] There were other examples of ships facing threats from enemy action and internal rioting (See Chapter 5) – these incidents contributed to the numbers of people who were sentenced but who never arrived. With these difficulties of weather and warfare, the length of the voyage could vary, depending on the particular route chosen. From the North East, the passage could be as long as eleven weeks, as the *Jenny* found in 1766, which resulted in a shortage of supplies as the captain imposed reduced rations on the passengers. This was only a little longer than usual, as the normal voyage seems to have been between two and two and a half months long.[76] Some ships suffered near-starvation, as bad weather kept them at sea. Few suffered as much as the vessel *Rodney* from London, which, while already in the English Channel, was threat-ened by a conspiracy 'to take away the ship'. Two convicts died as the ship met relentless gales, and there were short rations for 105 people. Because of the storms, they diverted from Virginia to the West Indies, 'and the convicts almost starved for want of food, and almost drowned with water between decks, only two biscuits a day'. More convicts died before in desperation the captain and crew opened some of the cargo, which ironically included cheeses for Charles Carroll of Maryland. By the time they reached Antigua, 'the poor wretches' had 'long ago eaten their leather breeches, and every shoe they found in the vessel'. Even longer voyages are known from some of the servants' memoirs, including up to five months for what seems to have been a very leisurely and incompetently managed trip to the Carolinas in 1728, with scurvy a threat to the point where there were insufficient men to work the ship. Even on shorter voyages, there could be deprivations, particularly of fresh drinking water, as William Moraley remembered.[77]

Disease and death were therefore part of the stories of many voyages involving both convicts and free migrants. The reputation of convict ships arriving in the colonies was summed up when Governor Horatio Sharpe of Maryland wondered 'whether or no the crowding too great a number of poor wretches into a small compass may not be the means of destroying some of them'. The frequency of illness on the voyage led one historian to agree with the statement that 'it has been said that America was built by sick people'.[78] However, as has been strongly argued, 'direct evidence on mortality from passenger ship records for eighteenth-century North Atlantic voyages has been extremely scarce'. Death rates of between 10 and 16 per cent have been suggested, on the basis of losses of troops sent to America or the West Indies, or particularly disastrous experiences of some migrants.[79] Any comparisons are probably misleading, particularly with slave ships which in the early phase in the late seventeenth century could lose as many as a fifth or a quarter of their inmates. Later figures were better, and it seems that things gradually improved for all kinds of transatlantic passengers, however reluctant. Ekirch, on the basis of figures from both London and Bristol at different times of the eighteenth century, suggests that initially the death rate could have been as high as 11 per cent, but fell to below 3 per cent by the 1770s.[80] Nevertheless, the colonies may have had reason to fear the arrival of some convicts with disease – gaol fever, or typhus, was particularly alarming, as there was little of it in America.[81] The colonial newspapers were particularly anxious to provide reassurance that the arriving felons were not diseased, with advertisements that they were 'likely healthy persons', or 'all in good health'. When a rumour spread that a shipload of convicts was carrying illness, 'gaol fever', one captain took out an advertisement by way of denial, and accompanied it with a copy of his statement, sworn under oath, to that effect.[82] Certainly there were scare stories associated with diseased convicts. One in 1767 talked of a 'deplorable havock made in the family of a widow Lady on the Eastern Shore, by that horrid contagous distemper commonly called the Gaol Fever':

> A casual visit, it seems, from one of the felons, sometime since imported in a convict ship, communicated the distemper to the Negroes. It is confidently reported that nearly thirty people in this family, among whom the worthy Lady herself was one, fell victims to the fury of this malignant ravaging pestilence.

The story added that the recent passage of quarantine laws at the last Assembly in Maryland would 'probably give some check to its introduction, and save the lives of thousands'. Whether more than a popular panic or not, it led to images in colonial newspapers of convicts who 'infect our colonies', physically as well as morally.[83] Certainly some ships carried disease. As Harry Piper, agent for Dixon and Littledale in Alexandria, Virginia, who shipped convicts in from Whitehaven and the North West, commented, when one of his captains arrived ill:

> I fear this is something of the Jail Fever, as several of the seamen had it, but not in so bad a manner, be it or, not, the people here are so much afraid of it, that I could not hire persons to nurse, but was obliged to keep some of his own people constantly with him.

This had delayed the departure of the vessel, in addition to bad weather.[84]

The moral dangers of the vessels were also subject to exaggeration, but some sources suggest that the regime on board had to be strict in order to control the bad behaviour of both felons and servants on board. There are records of several incidents of severe discipline by captains in response to drunkenness and complaints about not receiving what the servants had expected. John Harrower remembered two servants were 'put in Irons for wanting other than what was served. But they were soon released on there asking pardon and promising to behave better'. Another, Daniel Turner, a groom from London,

> returned on board from Liberty so drunk that he abused the Capt. Cheif [sic] Mate and Boatswain to a verry high degree, which made to be horse whipt. put in Irons and thumb screwed. An houre after he was unthumbscrewed, taken out of Irons but he then was hand cuffed and gagged all night.

Where water was scarce and drink available on board, thefts were common, and Adam Cunningham recorded two incidents, one in which the convict servants broke open his wine chest and stole wine, 'which was a great loss to us, our water beginning to smell. They were lashed to the pump and whipped with a cat-of-nine tails'. A second incident evoked even harsher treatment, for 'the principal rogue was hanged up at the main yard's arm, and plunged into the sea three or four times successively; the rest were whipped at the main yard'. By this time, the water was 'very loathsome to drink'.[85] An outsider, Goronwy Owen, has left us one of the very few descriptions of conditions on board a vessel carrying convicts. Having accepted the position of master of the grammar school attached to the College of William and Mary, in November 1757 he boarded a Virginia-bound London vessel, *Trial*, along with his wife and three small children. The ship was also carrying convicts. At that time the country was at war with France and when the vessel was riding off Portsmouth on the south coast waiting for a flotilla of ships to gather before sailing in convoy under the escort of five warships he wrote to a friend describing his horror at conditions on board:

> Here we are, through the Providence of the Most High, having come thus far in fine health, without death or illness or sea-sickness or any other mishap overtaking us, despite having a great deal of cold, stormy weather whilst we were in the Downs and from the Downs here. How splendidly resolute my wife and the three little Welshmen have held out without sea-sickness or nausea (apart from a little dizziness the day we came from the Nore to the Downs) whilst the English she-thieves, yes, and the thieves, and a few of the ship's crew were spewing their guts out. Woe to the lot of them! The seamen are a frightfully vile bunch of men. God be my keeper, every one of them has taken to himself a strumpet from amongst the she-thieves and do no work except whoring wantonly in every corner of the ship. Five or six of them have already contracted the pox (dare I mention it) from the women, and there is no doctor here save myself and my little copy of Dr Shaw's book, and it is with its help that I tend them a little with what medicines are to be had in the chest which is here. I fear sometimes lest I should get it myself from being amongst them. I baptised one child (his name was Francis Trial) and buried him later, and a she-thief and thief besides. It was today that I buried the woman. Do you remember how this tadpole of a captain promised that my wife could have one of the she-thieves to serve her whilst

at sea? One of them is here in the cabin, but it was to serve this husband's penis, and not to wait upon my wife, that she was brought here.

This is an exceptionally detailed and vehement narrative.[86] But Harry Piper also gives us some insight into what conditions on board these vessels could be like. Writing from Alexandria in 1767 he said of an Irish cargo of convicts and servants:

> The convicts most deservedly have very infamous characters – One thing I think might be guarded against, that is taking women for four years that pretends to be wives to the convicts, when they come here are commonly with child, and it is with much difficulty I can get quit of them – and they spoil the sale of their pretended husbands – Another thing, I had a boy of about 9 yrs old bound for 4 yrs, another aboutt 12 yrs for same time, also an Idiot bound for 4 yrs – these are no servants; indeed much of the 4 yrs are very indifferent, and I think full as infamous as the Convicts. The women this year are very naked, their cloaths [*inserted above*: espetially their gowns are very scanty] *illeg.*, no handkerchiefs.

Later vessels bound for Australia would be described as little better than 'floating brothels', and perhaps, despite exaggeration, the term could be applied to some of the earlier imprisoned communities on their way to America.[87] Certainly an anonymous letter-writer, 'Pathopoiea', writing in 1774 to *Felix Farley's Bristol Journal* in protest at the sentencing of two sisters to transportation lamented their prospects, especially those of the younger woman 'Banished from all her Friends, an affectionate Mother, and other Ties more tender, to a foreign Country; perhaps to be rudily despoiled of her Virginity and abused at Will by the brutish Seamen'. The plea by the anonymous author that his statement should 'naturally engage the interest of every benevolent reader' with a 'sense of sympathy' promptly provoked a response that the convicts were lucky that the judicial system had spared their lives. They were fortunate that after an impartial trial, an 'act of lenity' mitigated the statutory punishment to transportation. Whatever the difficulties of the passage to America, many would be sentenced, but for a reading public on both sides of the Atlantic, the story would not end with their leaving home.[88]

4
Gangs, Gentlemen and Gypsies: Narratives of Transportation

In August 1752 the *Maryland Gazette* carried a report from Bristol concerning the movement of convicts to Bideford for shipment:

> Last Monday morning a great number of People resorted before Newgate, to see the 11 transports carried away for Bideford. Ten of the Prisoners were mounted two upon a Horse chain'd. People were chiefly concerned to see [Daniel] Bishop who had murdered his sweetheart. They rode them through the crowd who yelled at him and he back etc. They threw dirt and stones at him.

This was part of a much larger story of Daniel Bishop which had run through the west-country papers for more than a year. He had been arrested in March 1751 on suspicion of murdering his fiancée Winifred Jones, who had disappeared. She had last been seen quarrelling with him and pleading with him not to hit her, when, observers reported, he had said 'You B—h of Destruction, I'll use you worse, and kill you this Night'. When her body was later found in a ditch near the river, she had clearly been physically attacked before her death, and Bishop was charged, tried and convicted of murder. However, the newspapers were not entirely unsympathetic, and there was a plea for further information, particularly from Winifred's letters-writer, apparently to provide evidence for appeal. Whatever the reasons, when the reprieve came through the prisoners in the gaol cheered, but, it was reported, 'this has disappointed several Thousand People, both in Town and Country, of their expectations of seeing his execution'. When he was ridden through the town on the way to the ship, people hung nooses or 'halters' from their windows to express their feelings. It was this occasion which was noted in Maryland.[1] However, the news was not only one-way, for Bristol editors kept an eye on any reports of Bishop's fate in the colonies. In 1753, this appeared in the press:

> There is a letter in town from a Captain of Note at New York which was sent to his wife in this city and which divers People have read, giving an account, that *Daniel Bishop*, condemned at a former Assizes in this city for the murder of Winifred Jones, was lately publically whippt at New York, for stealing diverse shirts, [wet?] from a clergyman there – And by other letters we learn, that the murder of his sweatheart is so resented there, that he is become the most despicable Wretch in the Place: – *A Vagabond shalt [thou] be all the Days of thy Life.*

In a sense, readers were reassured, because his reputation had pursued him across the Atlantic.[2] This was not untypical of the two-way traffic in convict news which appeared in English and American newspapers. For example, in 1739 a familiar figure was reported in the Virginia press. London convict Richard Kibble, who had been transported into the colony the previous year in the galley *Forward*, had returned to Virginia: he had 'made his escape home, and was convicted again this year upon six new Indictments'. Shipped to the colony and once more sold into servitude, 'he staid with his master but three days before he went away again'. Significantly, he escaped with several others, one of them also a former convict on the *Forward*, and stole a small boat from the Honourable Thomas Lee to aid their journey northwards.[3] Returning to England, he was no more successful in remaining unknown, for after several years he was caught, convicted and executed for returning from transportation before the expiry of his sentence. At the time of his execution it was reported that he had been transported four or five times.[4]

The detailed knowledge of criminals displayed in these reports shows that by the 1730s the trade in news in both directions across the Atlantic mirrored that in goods. With the people and the cargoes went newspapers, journals and reports, which built up on both sides of the ocean a stock of intelligence by which criminals and their careers were recorded and remembered. As one study puts it:

> News ricocheted by sea and land around the English Atlantic, whether shouted over a gunwhale, exchanged in a tavern, or posted in a captain's mailbag. The emergence of colonial postal services would greatly expand the opportunities for intercolonial correspondence in the eighteenth century, advancing the spread of English, European and colonial news.[5]

Everwhere, there was a hunger for latest news from abroad. The artist Charles Willson Peale remembered during his apprenticeship in Annapolis 'the manly expressive sweetness' of the voice of a ship's captain, just landed from Europe, reading a foreign newspaper to a crowd of people.[6] In part this was the outcome of the way that the British and Irish press took an interest in foreign, and particularly colonial affairs, and the way that the colonial newspapers copied whole sections of domestic (that is, British and Irish) news from them whenever they could. Thus each had a space for each other, and would fill their pages with foreign stories. For the founders of the American press, it was deliberate policy to draw upon the English papers for as much European news as possible, while at the same time seeking markets for items of local interest. William Parks, who established both the *Maryland Gazette* and the *Virginia Gazette*, expressed his intention clearly: 'I made it my particular concern, whilst I was in England, to settle such a correspondence there: by which, upon all occasions I [would] be furnished with the freshest intelligence both from thence, and other parts of Europe.' This was a policy he had adopted when running papers in Ludlow and Reading, before his move to America, and while he cast a 'distinctly American eye' on British news when he settled there, he saw the transatlantic links as central to his editorial policy. In effect, Parks reflected a move that started from London at the end of the seventeenth century, of trained printers going out to English provincial towns to found newspapers, all in their way dependent upon the metropolitan press for much of the news. He was unusual in going from the English countryside to the colonies, and continuing the same policy.[7] The colonial newspapers operated in much the same way, increasingly dependent on each other for additional material, fostering the sense of locality and distinct identity. At the same time, there were some direct imports from Europe: the *Gentleman's Magazine* was available and advertised to the colonists, and each ship arriving carried further newspapers. This kind of news exchange, however, depended on regular deliveries from elsewhere. It is no accident that newspapers tended to be established in seaports, in Britain and Ireland (Newcastle-upon-Tyne, Dublin, Exeter, Bristol or Edinburgh, for example), as much as in America. However, newspapers which had promised to provide 'distant news' could be frustrated and short of copy when shipments were held up. This was just as true of the British as of the colonial press, where the interchange of news depended on the fluent movement of shipping. Despite the increasing prominence of American news in the colonial press, however, European affairs still figured most prominently in newspapers such as the *Pennsylvania Gazette* in terms of both numbers of items and column inches, followed by news from the British Isles, for most of the colonial period.[8]

Crime was a major concern for editors on both sides of the Atlantic. Along with 'plantation news' came reports of crime and criminals in the colonies. Sometimes this provided English readers with satisfying accounts of just deserts, as in the case of Daniel Bishop. In other cases, it seems, where an interesting trial and conviction had been widely reported, the fate of the convict was part of a continuing story. In 1736 the *London Evening Post* reported:

> Letters from Virginia say that Mr Charles Peele, who was some time since transported for robbing the Post Office, having purchased his Liberty was chosen master of a very good school there, in the Room of the Master who died about the Time of his Arrival.

He had pleaded guilty to five charges, in fact, connected with forging a bill of exchange worth £170, and been sentenced to death the previous year. In some ways his reprieve was fortunate, as forgers were among those most likely to be executed. Forty years later his son, Charles Willson Peale, born five years after the transportation, became famous as the primary portrait painter of the American Revolution. His father had certainly worked as schoolteacher and author of educational books in Virginia, before moving to Maryland.[9] This story, for the English press, was a means of noting the personal destiny of one of London's more famous criminals, but the thirst for the 'remarkable and the sensational' often determined the selection of news everywhere, and crime provided a major part of the unusual and exotic items reported.[10] An interest in crime was not the only factor. Stories of crimes and criminals had long been the focus of a large-scale publishing industry in Britain, which by the eighteenth century had grown to be a diverse mix of trial transcripts, criminal biographies, 'last dying speeches' and news reports. This was profitable for many people, from authors and printers to the chaplains of Newgate Gaol, who may have earned up to six times their official salaries by publishing the biographies of notable criminals.[11] Nothing like this arose in the colonies, where New England publishers concentrated on execution sermons and the 'conversion narratives' of spiritual transformations of the condemned as they awaited death. In the other colonies, there was either no market or no interest in local criminals until the end of the eighteenth century.[12] News reports sometimes included gallows confessions if they offered some insight into the criminal career. William Kelsey, for example, who had chosen transportation to America instead of a whipping for his petty thefts, ended up on the gallows in Newcastle, Delaware, providing an outline of his development into sin and crime. Others, like Catherine Smith or Wildman, an Irish convict, simply refused to say anything about their background.[13] Some American editors, however, professed no interest in British criminal affairs. As Samuel Keimer complained in the first edition of the *Pennsylvania Gazette*:

> We have little news of Consequence at present, the *English* Prints being generally stufft with Robberies, Cheats, Fires, Murders, Bankruptcies, Promotions of some, and Hanging of others; nor can we expect much better till Vessels arrive in the spring.[14]

New England publishers did, however, reprint some of London's trial accounts, and this created the model for later American publications. Also, they were not above commenting further on the destiny of English convicts, as one Boston printer did in the case of Elizabeth Canning (who had so preoccupied Henry Fielding), producing a 'circumstantial narrative of her adventures' which was reprinted in London.[15] Crime, therefore, mattered in this period and transportation of felons was part of the solution to that problem. So every evaluation of the efficacy of the law inevitably led to a discussion of transportation and its consequences. If the press on both sides of the Atlantic reported on criminals, the colonial newspapers reported with interest the twists and turns of penological debate in Britain – the parliamentary bill to provide hard labour as an alternative to transportation in the 1750s, or the proposal to send convicts to Florida instead of the Chesapeake. For the British readership, since stories of transportation involved movement to an exotic location in foreign lands, as well as details of crimes committed and well-earned punishments received, such narratives combined both the moral lesson of crime stories with some of the more informative aspects of travel accounts of America. As with much earlier publications on crime, though, transportation stories also took readers in both Europe and America to an alien place of a very different kind – the world of criminals and their friends in a criminal underworld.

Accidental and reluctant narratives

Pictures of transported convicts, like those of criminals in general, emerged from this world of transatlantic print culture. While few stories took criminal transportation as their centre, many accounts of criminals dealt with the experience of transportation and labour in the colonies. It seems that transportation never produced much interest except as a by-product of stories of criminal lives. There are at least four types of transportation narrative. Firstly there are the expert discourses of the increasingly vocal critics of systems of law enforcement and punishment, who used their practical experience to justify their views. Prominent among these was Henry Fielding. A second source of stories was those local accounts of 'old offenders', advertised as arriving in America, running away and returning, found in newspapers and other sources such as letters on both sides of the Atlantic. These are *accidental* narratives. They were often accompaniments to trials of returned convicts which, while they were not numerous, were experienced by every county, and so their stories entered into the perceptions of transportation. Thirdly there is the systematic publication of criminal biographies created with assistance from helpful clergy and printers on the way to the gallows. These were mostly a London phenomenon, as befitted the printing and execution capital of the country, but some were produced elsewhere. In these stories transportation formed part of the experience of the 'hardened' felon who had returned to crime in England: these are *reluctant* narratives. Finally, transportation figured in some literary and fictional narratives, allegedly derived from real experiences. If it is hard to tell fact from fiction in matters of crime in the media in any period, the eighteenth century poses a particular problem. Some criminals occur in several parallel sources – the newspapers in England and America, the trial records, the *Newgate Calendar* and well-marketed entrepreneurial biographies. Other individuals were probably completely invented and perpetuated through repeated endlessly adapted printings. Narratives of transported felons therefore emerge haphazardly in many different forms and with very different purposes, in last dying speeches, criminal biographies, newspaper stories and fragmented reports of individuals on both sides of the Atlantic. It has been said of popular early modern artisan autobiography there was often striking variation in form and content of craftsmen's personal documents.[16] The same is even more true of the stories of transported felons. The process of copying, adding, embroidering and republishing which was the core of the eighteenth-century publishing industry made standardization even less possible.

The unusually frank criminal confession, or last dying speech before execution, frequently confirmed the worst fears of the authorities concerning the insouciance of the hardened criminal and the futility of transportation as a punishment. One of the Northumberland 'Faws', or gypsies, dying penitently at York in 1767 for robbing a house, provided a detailed account of his career over the preceding decade or more. This is an unusually full *reluctant* narrative of transportation from outside London. As the newspapers reproduced it:

> Richard Clark left an account of his life, in his own handwriting, from whence it appears that he was born at Spital, near Berwick upon Tweed, in 1739; that in 1750 his father and mother, along with William Fall, John Fall, and his wife, with some others were committed to Morpeth gaol for breaking into a shop in that town; and [at] the Quarter Sessions they were ordered to be transported for seven years. About a year after he met with a cousin at Richmond Fair, who had returned from transportation before the expiration of the term, and soon after met with his father and mother who had also returned from transportation, and travelled about the country as pedlars, and at different places put him to school. They afterwards went to Ireland where they, with four or five more of the gang, were imprisoned for theft, but discharged for want of evidence. From thence they returned to England, where they continued their old practices of house-breaking, horse-stealing and pocket-picking. About eight years ago he was convicted here of a highway robbery, and transported, but returned in less than a year, and joined his father and mother with the rest of the gang. In 1762 he was convicted of horse-stealing at Shrewsbury, where he received sentence of death, but was reprieved the day before that fixed for his execution, and afterwards transported to Maryland, from whence he also soon returned, and coming to Warrington, in Lancashire, he was informed of his wife's being hanged at Coventry. He then went in quest of his mother, and met with her at Newcastle. A short time after he was committed to Carlisle gaol for house-breaking of which he was convicted and in 1765 transported to Virginia, but soon returned from thence, met with his mother once more at Newcastle, and broke several houses last summer, but got little money or other effects, except for a house near Durham, from whence he took about £13 and what he got in Mark Hattersley's house for which he suffered. Several times, when short of money, he enlisted for a soldier, but always soon deserted.[17]

The early details here are interestingly confused – the shop which the Faws raided was in Rothbury in fact, and the year was 1752: others can be confirmed. Some are new.[18] Under questioning in Cumberland in 1765 Clark had carefully glossed over his previous convictions, claiming to have been pressed into the navy for four years. He had served on board the *Ocean* man-of-war and was discharged in June 1763. The failure of the authorities to connect him with previous sentences meant that he was reprieved for fourteen years' transportation.[19] His wife was part of the Coventry gang, hunted and convicted by Alderman John Hewitt, and described in detail in his self-important memoirs. This kind of published statement, however, confirmed the expert analysis of the professional criminals – the underground society of mobile, apparently uncontrolled gangs, undeterred by transportation which they treated more of an inconvenience than a punishment. John Hewitt later reflected on his experiences of law enforcement:

> In the following narration of my proceedings, I have given the crimes, discovering and apprehending of a notorious gang of villains, called and generally known by the name of the Coventry gang, because of their being apprehended, and receiving so fatal a blow, by my unremitting pains, that ended their family, the most dangerous confederacy. William Fall, and his wife Margaret Clarke, alias Long Peg, were lineally descended from that notorious and ancient gang of vagrant Egyptians, called Faws . . . William Fall, alias Faw, and his numerous gang, became settled in Northumberland. I never heard of one of the name that lived by any other means than that of smuggling and pirating. Under this character I knew one settled as a wine-merchant on the east coast of Scotland, and I have some reason to believe was nearly related to the famous American pirate [John Paul Jones]: and who in the late dispute with the American rebels, did the merchants of this kingdom great injury by his piratical proceedings.

They were traitors as well as criminals, apparently, when the Americans rebelled.[20] Among those hunted down and condemned in 1763 and 1764 was Richard Clark's wife, who is hard to identify among the many aliases of the arrested. Newcastle sources recorded the execution of William Fall's wife, the same year he was tried at Newcastle for returning – at Coventry, it was reported, 'one Jane Smith, alias Fall, the wife of William Fall, formerly transported from this town, was found guilty of felony, and received sentence of death'.[21] Hewitt's account is essentially one of his efforts in tracking down and arresting returned convicts who had been transported from the northern counties such as Cumberland and Northumberland. It was for this reason that he requested the lists of convicts transported from Newcastle and

Northumberland, which he published in his book, and for which the correspondence with Newcastle's town clerk survives.[22] Much attention was paid to William Pallester, a house breaker, and his wife Margaret Brown, for example. Brown, alias Ogden, was twenty-six and a returned transportee: 'she was one of the Foys, and her father and mother both followed the same practices. Her uncle was hanged at Worcester'. On the day of her hanging, 'She swooned away while in church in the morning, and upon the road to the place of execution, and seemed to lament very much her unhappy condition'. She was executed with her husband, and an older Margaret, the infamous 'Long Peg', her aunt who was married to Robert Clark who had been transported with the faws from Northumberland in 1752. Robert and this Margaret Clark were probably Richard's parents. As for William Fall himself, he was returned to Northumberland,

> from whence he was transported; as this man had been at the head of a desperate gang of villains, and who had been such a terror to the northern counties about fourteen years since, I thought it of moment the making an example in that country of the head of the gang, where he formerly had committed so many robberies, and as I know at this time, near one one hundred of these desperadoes are dispersed in parties in the several northern counties.[23]

In fact, at his trial in Newcastle he was again condemned and pardoned for transportation, this time for fourteen years.

This may have been one of the few gangs which really was organized on a national basis, with sufficient resources to guarantee the return of their members from America. Yet the reputation of gangs and the myth of their level of transatlantic organization constituted almost an archetype of transportation narratives. In this network, one of their acquaintances, London criminal Charles Speckman, left an interesting account of his experiences as a convict in America, recording that Pallister and Duplex, 'who called themselves family men, and the heads of a great gang, pressed me violently to go on the highway with them and their companions, but all they could say was in vain'. Speckman's preciousness was disingenuous: he had begun his career with shoplifting and ended it with highway robbery of chaises and coaches around London.[24] The use of the term 'family men' is ironic and yet in many ways truthful. Most of the characters detected in the known gangs were close relatives, with their partners and children of both genders. The word was also used in London and its surrounding area to refer to those who had served together in the privateering squadron the *Royal Family* in the 1740s, and who were known thereafter as the Family Men. Members of this group certainly included some of the Coventry gang, as well as aquaintainces of John Poulter (died 1754), and some individuals in the Mitchell group and the McDaniel gang. The complex relationships between the latter two, which led to some becoming thief-takers, and some their victims on the gallows, have been analysed by Ruth Paley. Together with the prosecutions around the country in the 1750s and 1760s, the convictions of so many members of apparently powerful gangs, inviolable without inside information and treachery, provided much of the grounds for debate about the effectiveness of pardoning hardened criminals for transportation.[25]

This was not a new anxiety. From the first, the Transportation Act had aroused misgivings about the problems of supposedly professional criminals who, with money and influence, could escape the consequences of their crimes. It was not just John Gay's *Beggar's Opera* which linked the returned convict with political corruption, though that became the most famous representation of the connection.[26] After numerous accounts of returning convicts, the *London Evening Post* published a report endorsing the report of eight criminals condemned to death without a hint of possible reprieve:

> This Execution will be of great service to the Public; if all that are condemned every sessions were to be executed, we should not hear of so many Robberies as at present; for *Transportation* does not answer the End proposed, the convicts are continually returning, and are only made more desperate than before. Nothing can put a stop to the great number of robberies, but the Gallows: for every rogue when he sets up for himself looks upon it, that he has several chances to get off, if he should be taken, which, considering the number of ill houses which harbour them, is very difficult.
>
> 1. He'll *whiddle*; that's confess, to be made an Evidence and impeach his Companions
> 2. That the Person robbed can't swear to him, or won't be at charge and trouble of prosecuting; or that he can make it up with the Prosecutor
> 3. That he can get *rapp'd off* by the perjuries of his friends and companions
> 4. That a *weak jury* (if convicted) will recommend him to mercy
> 5. If condemned, he has a cousin married to some Great Man's Pimp, or another relation that is servant to a Man of Quality's kept

mistress, and these are to interceed and get him off, or transported. One of *these* the *Robbers* think seldom fail, and with these Views they start; therefore, if condemned, they should be executed, unless the verdict is apparently against evidence; for the partial Execution of Justice in England is what is cryed out against by all Foreigners, and indeed makes Rogues.

The most interesting thing about this harsh and cynical analysis, apart from its unusual length, is that it was reproduced in its entirety in the *Virginia Gazette* four months later. This kind of opinion had a ready audience on both sides of the Atlantic.[27] These views, published at the end of the 1730s, came after a flurry of reports of insouciant returned convicts, among them several who first made their appearance as 'gentlemen of distinction' at the Old Bailey. One trial that figured as front-page news was that of Henry Justice, barrister, for stealing books from the libraries of both Trinity College, Cambridge, and the University library. It was a difficult prosecution, because the lawyers had to demonstrate that he was not a full fellow of the college, and had no borrowing rights. The accused also encouragingly demonstrated his cooperative spirit by mentioning other books which the searchers of his lodgings had overlooked. The trial was full of examinations and cross-examinations described by the *London Evening Post* as 'very long, curious and particular'. This was partly because Justice took the wise step of employing several lawyers in his defence, so the whole thing lasted six hours, 'the arguments, examinations of witnesses etc, being very long on both sides'. It was judged to be one of the most remarkable to have occurred at the Old Bailey. The case was proved on one charge, however, and Justice pleaded guilty on the other two, and went on to request that he be branded in the hand rather than transported, since he had small children to support in England. However, the Recorder told him that his 'case was greatly aggravated by his education and the profession he was of' and ordered him to be transported.[28] In the end he accepted the sentence, but asked to be able to transport himself, 'or that a worthy Gentleman of the City of York might contract for him'. This was probably a reference to his brother-in-law, Jonas Thompson, former Lord Mayor of York, who had in fact fallen under suspicion of receiving some of the books which had been shipped from London to Bridlington, and who the university authorities had intended to prosecute on that charge. Despite rumours of an intercession on his behalf by the University of Cambridge, Justice was moved to the ship to leave for America:

Yesterday Morning the Transports, to the number of 98, were put on board a lighter at Black-Fryars Stairs, in order to fall down thro' Bridge, and to be put on board a Ship for the Plantations in America; Wreathocke (who is to be transported for Life, with Bird and Ruffhead, his two occasional Evidences), has been in great Confusion for several Days past and vastly angry at some of his Confederates, *who are left at large to follow his Business*, for using him ill; and not making a just account by way of Debtor and Creditor, before he went. Henry Justice Esq, Barrister at Law, convicted for stealing Books of great Value out of Trinity-College Library, who is to be transported for Seven Years, had the Privilege of going two hours after the common transports in a coach to Blackwall; Wreathock went also thither in a coach. 'Tis said that Bird had about £50 collected for him among the Sherrif's Officers etc., he having been a Bailiff himself. This cargo consists of several very eminent Rogues in their Way.[29]

Wreathock was an attorney, tried with Ruffhead and Bird for highway robbery the previous December, and condemned to death. Wreathock had been in such despair of his survival that he gave the printer his last dying speech. The *Gentleman's Magazine* strove for a slightly more satirical note in its report of the journey to the ship, noting that Justice had in fact travelled in convict shipper Jonathan Forward's own coach: 'These five *gentlemen* of distinction were accommodated with the captain's cabin, which they stored with plenty of provisions, for their voyage and travels' . Additional information from the trial was noted in this report, particularly that some of the books had been shipped to Holland, which would be difficult to recover if he was transported.[30] Much of this was repeated with interest in the *Virginia Gazette* later that year, which also noted that on the voyage over:

These five gentlemen were treated with marks of respect and distinction, for the felons of inferior note were all put immediately under the hatches and confined in the hold of the ship, as usual, but these five were conveyed into the cabin which, by agreement, they were to have the use of during their voyage; and, as they pay for their passage, it is supposed that as soon as they land, they will be set at liberty, instead of being sold as felons usually are. Thus, by the wholesome laws of this country, a criminal who has money (which circumstance, in all other countries, would aggravate his guilt and enhance the severity of his punishment) may blunt the edge of justice, and make that his happiness which the law designs as his punishment.

By that autumn, however, there were reports (faithfully followed in Virginia) of Justice's return to England.[31] It was known that after he and his companions had landed in Virginia they had moved swiftly to Pennsylvania, but had caused great consternation by their arrival:

> By Capt. Savage, lately arriv'd from Philadelphia, we have Advice that Mess. Wreathcock, Justice and Bird, who went there in order to settle, were routed out of that Town, and oblig'd to make the best of their way for Newcastle near Philadelphia, from thence they took shipping and were sat on shore at Milfordhaven; but immediately went on board a Vessel design'd for France.

By this time another gentleman-criminal had returned, George 'Lord' Vaughan, brother to Viscount Lisburne, who had also taken up highway robbery and been transported with them on the same ship. Like Justice, Vaughan had tried to persuade the court to permit him to transport himself privately, something that the Recorder of London, Sir William Thompson, had vehemently opposed because the pre-1718 voluntary arrangements had never worked successfully.[32] Vaughan, like the others, had nevertheless returned despite the new compulsory system. At the end of 1736 the government itself had become alarmed at the reports, and sent instructions to the King's Messengers:

> Whereas I have received Information that [blank] Wreathcote an attorney, [blank] Bird, a bailiff, [blank] Chamberlain a butcher, [blank] Roffet and [blank] Justus, a lawyer, Five notorious criminals, that were some time ago convicted of several crimes at the Old Bailey and transported for the same, are returned, from the place to which they were transported, to Holland, and are coming hither, to the great endangering of His Majesty's peace, and the Safety of his Subjects.

They were ordered to take a constable and make a diligent search for them.[33] The next few years were full of stories of this group's presence in London, their haunting of the Dutch ports, and their threat to the public. The newspapers continued to report the misdeeds of Wreathock and, particularly Vaughan, but in the end it was George 'Baby' Bird, the bailiff, who was tried and condemned, in 1739, but he was again reprieved for transportation, this time for life.[34]

Though it was reported in 1737 'that Counsellor Justice has been seen in England since his transportation', there were no allegations of further crimes committed by him, nor any very convincing reports of his presence in London.[35] But as the *Virginia Gazette* reported, copying a story from London in 1739 with regard to Vaughan, this gentleman 'had the Favour of Transportation, along with Messrs. Wreathcote and Justice; but he, as well as his companions, thought fit to return, as indeed many of the Convicts do'.[36] Henry Justice, however, remained active on the Continent where it had been reported so many of the stolen books had been sent. Based in Rotterdam (where he was described as a citizen), he edited a well-known edition of Virgil in several volumes in 1757, and died there in 1763. With superb irony, his assets at his death consisted largely of large numbers of rare and valuable books. These were sold in several advertised auctions between 1763 and 1767 by an agent in The Hague. The introductory biography of the books' owner managed to gloss over the most interesting part of his career. Typically, Justice revived his claim to being a lord of a Yorkshire manor, and claimed to be 'de Rufforth' in all his continental dealings.[37] Nevertheless, he was remembered at his old university, where a copy of the first catalogue was acquired, and at least one librarian wrote some embittered comments on the contents and their former owner.[38]

The story of Henry Justice, barrister of the Middle Temple, is easier to authenticate than any of the previous cases because of the detailed account of his trial published in the Old Bailey sessions papers as well as its detailed reproduction on both sides of the Atlantic. His tale would make fruitful material for an interesting novel, but for the fact that that his estranged wife Elizabeth has already done so. With her work, the *accidental* narrative becomes a deliberately realistic fiction. She turned her marriage to a book thief into a novel entitled *Amelia or the Distressed Wife: A History Founded on Real Circumstances by a Private Gentlewoman* published in London, 1751. The narrative is a thinly disguised account of her life and misfortunes, and forms a part of a literary transformation in the middle of the eighteenth century through which many women published their own stories, and established some degree of control over their own identities through confessional accounts.[39] The story concerns a wife who learnt of her husband's disgrace while employed as a governess in the family of an English merchant in St Petersburg. From Elizabeth's novel, written to support herself, we learn how Mr Johnson [Henry Justice] was obsessed with books. She feared at one point he would become 'bookmad'. He bought books, traded books, conned books out of people and stole books. Old and valuable editions from Trinity College were preferred. The books dominated his life and ruined hers. He spent money – 'for no one could wear finer Cloaths than Mr *Johnson*, both for Velvets, rich Waistcoats, the best of Wigs and Linen, none of which he would appear in before his Mother, that she might not see his Extravagancies'. Her regard for him lessened especially when insulted by his male friends in front of whom she was carefully displayed by her husband. He took all her property, and banned her from seeing her children, and after separation 'Mr Johnson' would not pay her the agreed maintenance.[40] All this mirrored her life precisely, because Elizabeth Justice had written of her troubles some years earlier when she published in 1739 *A Voyage to Russia*, an account of her time working as a governess, and describing the buildings and manners of St Petersburg. This sold a healthy 600 copies, many to subscribers, and went into a second edition in 1746 with some additional material. She had been forced to find work abroad in 1734, she explains in the introduction, because, while estranged from her husband, the annuity of £25 he was supposed to pay her was not forthcoming, and he threatened her with expensive litigation if she tried to go to law. So, 'contrary to my inclination', she says, she had sought work with an English family in St Petersburg. She worked there about three years, and heard of Henry's difficulties by accident when it was mentioned to a gentleman in correspondence from London, though her employers tried to conceal it from her. In May 1736 she wrote in a letter:

> Bad news never wants for carrying, for there is a gentleman in *England* who has wrote his correspondent here that Mr Justice is under confinement, and charged with the robbery of the Library at Cambridge. . . . I was from the unwelcome news much disordered, and not willing to believe to be true, but there was in three newspapers, immediately following, some circumstances that agreed with it.

The papers followed the English to Russia as well as America, it seems.[41] This has been noted as one of the first travel accounts by any English-woman, and was apparently successful, to judge from the numbers sold.[42] By contrast, *Amelia* had the same title as a novel by Henry Fielding published the same year – and on a similar theme of wifely distress, and may not have been very profitable. Certainly it has attracted little attention, though more recently literary scholars have begun to address the different worldviews of male and female writers on the same topic. Perhaps the most important thing to notice is that real *personal* experiences provided the basis for the novel, something which for writers like Defoe in his *Moll Flanders* were only available secondhand through artful syntheses of the reported lives of criminals.[43] In reporting in fictional form almost twenty years of misfortunes in marriage to a known convict, the novel is unique. Elizabeth Justice, however, attracted little public attention in reports of her husband's activities. By contrast, it was reported before the trial that Henry's mother had died of 'Grief for her Son's Misfortunes'.[44]

Elizabeth Justice's account is one of the few provided by those left behind by convicts. Apart from scant records in the local archives of the costs of maintaining convicts' families, and some general folksongs concerning the cruelties of loss through transportation, there is nothing comparable. Accounts of the convict experience rarely made their way into popular fiction, remaining mostly as incidents in the supposedly factual criminal biographies. One deserted wife in Northumberland, married to James Johnson, transported for seven years by the Hexham quarter sessions, reacted in a very different way to Elizabeth Justice's response. 'After sentence Johnson's Wife went to him, and told him that she was sorry at his Fate, but that she would be married again in a Month, having another ready'.[45] The interplay of experience and fiction figures, however, in the works of Edward Kimber, who turned his travels in America in 1742 and 1743 into a later novel which purports to be a realistic fiction. He had taken part in James Oglethorpe's unremarkable expedition to Florida in 1743, and also kept a journal of his journey from New York southward.[46] Though a 'hack' writer, Kimber produced a large number of pieces for his father's *London Magazine*, where his travel narrative was first published in 1745 and 1746, and several novels, some of which drew on his American experiences.[47] His criticisms of slavery, and his account of the situation of transported felons and servants have been influential. About the latter, he said:

> The Convicts that are transported here, sometimes prove very worthy Creatures, and entirely forsake their former Follies; but the Trade has for some Time run in another Channel; and so many Volunteer Servants come over, especially the *Irish*, that the other is a commodity pretty much blown upon. Several of the best Planters, or their Ancestors, have, in the two Colonies, been originally of the Convict-Class, and therefore, are much to be prais'd and esteem'd for forsaking their old Courses.

He goes on to tell one such tale of redemption, of a gentleman who, years before, was kidnapped as a six-year-old in London by a ship's captain, and shipped from Bristol into fourteen years' servitude. He nevertheless endeared himself to his master and made a success of his life, in part by marrying his master's daughter. However, he lost contact with his parents, and not even a later vengeful reunion with the captain, whom he bought from a ship as a convict servant, helped, as the miscreant killed himself before giving him any information. Thus Kimber manages to put together in a couple of pages most of the clichés of convict stories – the convicts turned gentlemen planters (satirized in Defoe's *Moll Flanders*, but drawn with apparently serious intent by Kimber), the wrongful capture, the innocent young man (who, like the industrious apprentice in Hogarth's story of *Industry and Idleness*, married his master's daughter), and the final just desserts of the oppressor.[48] All this would have remained enough for one account, but less than ten years later Kimber created a novel based on this legendary colonial character published anonymously in London and Dublin. Here, in *The History of the Life and Adventures of Mr Anderson* the story is, like the brief earlier account, one of virtue finally rewarded in the face of hostile conspiracies and repeated cruelties. He set the initial kidnap in 1697, and followed the earlier account by portraying a particularly brutal Bristol ship's captain. Naturally the subsequent story in the colonies included many kindnesses, reversals of fortune, time spent among the Indians and other melodramatic events. Despite these hackneyed contents, the colonial scenes in the novel have been described as accurate.[49] The theme was hardly original: captive narratives had been in vogue since the days of the 'spiriting' scandals of the late seventeenth century, and had been revived by notorious cases such as the alleged sufferings of James Annesley, who asserted that his legitimate claim to fortune and title had been the cause of his kidnap and 'slavery' in the colonies. His eloquent account of hard labour in America set the tone for many of the subsequent representations of colonial life.[50]

Gentlemen and gypsies

Other representations of transportation, derived from 'life', were even more successful. Bampfylde Moore Carew is perhaps the best-known Englishman transported to America, because of both the length of his two biographies, and the repeated printings. He also provided graphic details of the vagrant life, of the experiences of transportation, and the convicts' society in America, which attracted attention from his contemporaries, and have been used by historians ever since. The story of his life and adventures in America is, like the accounts by Edward Kimber, a semi-fictional text, but one which continues to be used extensively by modern historians of criminal transportation as if there was no question about its authenticity. There have been many editions of his life story and even a play in 1830, *Bampfylde Moore Carew, or the Gypsey of the Glen: a romatic melodrama in three acts.*[51] All are within the tradition of the picaresque, defined by Gladfelder usefully as characterized by

> an episodic structure, usually organized around a succession of journeys and chance encounters; a satiric presentation of diverse social levels and milieus; a lingering over scenes of brutality, trickery, and humiliation; the exposure of pretense; and a protagonist struggling to survive.

The picaresque presents as an accident of fate what were really the commercial necessities of a uncertain life in early modern society.[52] Bamfylde Moore Carew's stories certainly fit this pattern. He was born in 1693 into a prominent Devonshire family at Bickleigh near Tiverton, where his father was the vicar (and relatives owned the castle). By his own account when he was still at school in Tiverton, as a consequence of a prank, he ran away with a party of gypsies. In 1739 when he was in his forties Carew was ordered to be transported from Exeter by magistrates at the Devon quarter sessions on a charge of vagrancy. Reaching the Chesapeake, he escaped but was retaken by the Maryland authorities, an iron collar was put around his neck and he found himself in a gaol containing other men from the West Country whose speech was familiar to him. He escaped again, taking refuge among the Indians, and when he grew tired of their mode of existence moved on, first to Pennsylvania where, pretending to be a Quaker, he visited Philadelphia where he was made welcome, then on to New York and from thence to New London. From there he sailed for England where, when approaching the port of Bristol, he managed to evade being pressed into the navy by feigning smallpox. Recaptured in Devon, and taken to America a second time, he escaped once more and returned via Rhode Island.

There were two editions of his life, a version of 1745 which ends with him going on board ship to America, *The Life and Adventures of Bampfylde-Moore Carew,*[53] and the second, *An Apology for the Life of Bampfylde-Moore Carew*, with not one but *two* shipments to America, followed by two equally dramatic escapes from captivity and return trips to England. These firmly cement his place as the subject of most prominent transportation narrative in the eighteenth century. The second, much longer, edition of Carew's tale created a more diffuse and less credible narrative. It lifted material from other publications and found fault with Henry Fielding's novel *Tom Jones* so that what began as a cautionary moral tale about an ill-spent life was turned into a literary phenomenon.[54] The *Apology* was sold in many editions during the 1750s and 1760s. At the outset, unlike its predecessor, it was advertised widely across the West Country. In Bristol in November 1749, the *Apology* was publicized in a large panel in the *Bristol Weekly Intelligencer* as the only authentic account: no other except this published by Robert Goadby would be genuine, readers were informed. Moreover, 'though the book has now been published but one month, there are only 60 books left out of the whole impression, which consisted of above a thousand copies, it having been so well received in London, that some hundreds were sold in the city within two days after the publication'. The copyright issue may have worried Goadby, for in other newspaper notices he threatened to prosecute rival publishers.[55] Subsequent editions were sold for their quality, one a 'pocket volume' advertised in 1754 being 'bound in calf cost three shillings'. This was a steep increase on the sixpenny edition of earlier years.[56] The story reached an even wider audience as subsequent editions stretched over nearly two centuries. Almost from the beginning, there was debate about the truthfulness of the accounts, their authorship, and the fate of the man himself.[57] The first of several American editions was published in Philadelphia in 1773.[58] An English critic reviewing the second edition of *The Apology* in the *Gentleman's Magazine* in 1750 thought that '[H]is adventures among the Gypsies, till he was transported to *Virginia*, have nothing very surprising: but his escape from his Capt. and his travels among the wild Indians, are full of the *marvellous*.' An American audience would have probably reached the opposite conclusion.[59]

It is hard to evaluate the Bamfylde Moore Carew story in detail. Devon's local records certainly confirm his career as a vagabond, incarcerated repeatedly in the 1720s: on one occasion he was arrested for being an army deserter as well.[60] At Easter 1730, when he was again in the workhouse, he was ordered 'to be delivered to his Sister Mrs Dorothy Rogers next Monday in order to go to Bideford and from thence to Newfoundland on a Voyage'. He records several voyages or fishing expeditions to Newfoundland in the published stories.[61] There is then a hiatus for nearly nine years in the local records. The central event in his own account is the 1735 naval expedition to the Baltic, which is described in graphic detail, particularly the execution of an Englishman in the Russian service who was pulled apart by horses.[62] The *Life and Adventures* ends with his transportation after many adventures and misfortunes. He was probably sent abroad because he was a known vagrant who had already received severe punishment. In his own account, he had returned to Devon after his travels, but got into a quarrel with one of Squire Blagden's men in Chard and had to 'stand the flog', that is, be whipped in public, through the streets of the town – this was for the second time in his career. After several examinations he came up against Justice Lethbridge, who had him imprisoned and after two months in St Thomas Bridewell, Exeter, he was sentenced to seven years' transportation. His own account is boastful:

> The Chairman then told him, He must proceed to a hotter Country; he enquired in what Climate, and being told Merryland, he with great Composure made a critical Observation on the Pronounciation of that Word, implying that he apprehended it ought to be pronounced Maryland, and added, it would save him Five Pounds for his Passage, as he was very desirous of seeing that Country; but, notwithstanding, with great Resolution, desired to know by what Law they acted, as he was not accused of any Crime: However, Sentence of Banishment was passed upon him for seven Years; but his Fate was not singular, for he had the Comfort of having Fellow Companions enough in his Sufferings, as out of 35 Prisoners, 32 were ordered into the like Banishment.[63]

He was put on the *Juliana* commanded by Captain Froade, from Topsham, and stuck in Falmouth for two weeks, and then spent eleven weeks in travelling to Maryland. In his own view, he was not convicted of any crime – the 1745 account ends, 'he stole *only* dogs, and did no *real* mischief to any Man'.[64] The legal record is more prosaic, but indicative of the magistrates' attitudes. At the Easter sessions of 1739, the quarter sessions files record:

> Whereas Bampfylde Moore Carew a most Notorious common Vagrant having been apprehended and Committed to the Common Workhouse of this County and being Brought before this Court and having Confessed that he was ordered by Richard Beavis Esq to be committed by order under his hand and seale to the Custody of Ethelred Davy merchant who was willing to receive him as his Apprentice or Servant for the space of seven years.

Carew confessed to having been a 'beggar or vagabond for the space of two years past', and was judged to be a 'dangerous and incorrigible rogue'. He was not alone in that fate. At the same time, three other men, Abraham Hart, Edward Brown and John Smith – 'notorious common vagrants' were apprehended because they

> pretended to have been sailors and to have been taken by the Algerines And ... by thrusting their Tongues down their Throats pretended by Answers in writing on oath that their Tongues were cut out by the Algerines and that they were actually dumb.

They joined Carew on the same ship to America in a group of what the transportation bond describes as 'felons and vagrants'.[65]

Carew's fate in the colonies is graphically described in the *Apology*, for he recounts his arrival and escape. The ship anchored at Talbot County, Maryland

> when the Captain ordered a Gun to be fired as a Signal for the Planters to come down, and then went ashore; he soon after sent on board a Hogshead of Rum, and ordered all the Men Prisoners to be close shav'd against the next Morning, and the Women to have their best Head Dresses put on, which occasioned no little Hurry on board, for between the triming of Beards, and putting on of Caps, all the Captain order'd publick Notice to be given of a Day of Sale, and the Prisoners, who were pretty near a Hundred, were all order'd upon Deck, where a large Bowl of Punch was made, and the Planters flock'd on board; their first Enquiry was for Letters and News from Old England, what Passage he had, how their Friends did, and the like. The Captain informed them of War being declared against Spain, and that it was expected it would soon be declared against France; that he had been eleven Weeks and four Days in his Passage. Their next Enquiry was if the Captain had brought them good Store of Joiners, Carpenters, Blacksmiths, Weavers, and Taylors; upon which the Captain call'd out one Griffy, a Taylor, who had lived at Chumleigh, in the County of Devon, and was obliged to take a Voyage to Mary-land, for making too free with his Neighbours Sheep; two Planters who were Parson Nichols and Mr. Rolles, ask'd him If he was sound [of] Wind and Limb, and told him, It would be worse for him, if he told them an Untruth; and at last purchased him of the Captain. The poor Taylor cry'd and bellow'd like a Bell-Weather, cursing his Wife who had betray'd him.

This scene was recounted in other stories of transportation, though eye-witness accounts do not necessarily report that the felons made a good appearance. Carew himself reacted to the scenery of Maryland favourably, describing it as a 'fine glorious country'.[66] There were a number of inquiries about him by planters, who were told by the captain that he would make an excellent schoolmaster, but since Carew himself explained he was 'Rat-catcher, a Mendicant and a Dog-Merchant', he remained unsold. Eventually he went on shore and made his escape from some drinking companions. Recaptured and imprisoned, he found the gaol 'well peopled', and his ears confused 'with almost as many Dialects as put a stop to the Building of Babel': some were 'of Kilkenny, some Limerick, some Dublin, others of Somerset, Dorset, Devon and Cornwall'.[67] In the harbour here, at New Town, he saw ships belonging to Mr Buck of Bideford, 'to whom most of the town belonged'. The ship's captain reclaimed him, had him flogged and had an iron collar put on him 'which in Maryland they call a Pot-Hook, and is usually put about the necks of runaway slaves'. He was threatened with labour in the iron works if he continued to misbehave. Eventually, two friendly Devon captains gave him advice as to how to run away, providing him with a compass, by which he means he fled northwards to Pennsylvania via Newcastle (Delaware).[68] Long detailed descriptions of Philadelphia and New York are included in the escape narrative; in the latter

> he was surprized at the Sight of a great Number of Gibbets, with Blacks hanging upon them; but, on enquiring, he found the Negroes had, not long before entered into a Conspiracy of burning the whole City; but the Plot being timely discovered, great Numbers were executed, and hung up to terrify the others.

This was the outcome of the New York Conspiracy in which repeated acts of arson had terrified the city in the spring of 1741. Many of those subsequently found guilty of the conspiracy were black, and some were executed by burning. It was there that he took ship, and returned to the Bristol Channel.[69] However, 'Merchant Davy' recognized him at Topsham Key (downriver from Exeter on the River Exe), and without officially arresting or charging him, had him put on board ship where he was 'ironed down with the convicts', and found himself in America again, this time in Annapolis. So, he says, he was 'dragg'ed to slavery by the lawless Hand of Power, without the Mandate of sovereign Justice'. Here he met a man called Hildrop, transported three years earlier, who had married a currier's widow in the town, and wanted to purchase him, but failed to agree a price. Samuel Hildrup, also known as Samuel

Groves, was sentenced to transportation when he was reprieved from the death sentence for horse stealing in Devon in 1740. Carew, then, was sent to Miles's River, where the planters recognized him as having arrived the previous year. Again, he escaped, this time in a canoe, and headed north to Rhode Island, when again a friendly captain arranged his passage home.[70]

The colonial experiences in the story are as difficult to evaluate as the preceding English episodes. There is an authentic tone to some of the American parts of the story – the auction of the convicts for example, and some of the basic geography. Clearly he knew the Buck family, and Samuel Hildrup was genuine. But two escapes sound overdone. However, some aspects can be confirmed from other sources. It is likely that Carew had returned by 1744. In Bridgwater (Somerset), widow Sarah Leakey reported to one of the aldermen, a local justice, that a lodger in her common alehouse, 'one Bampfyld Moore Carew', had 'come into her house very drunk and greatly intoxicated with liquor'. He had with him a woman, whom he called his wife, and a daughter. 'She believed the said Carew to be a common stroller, and had nothing to subsist on but what gentlemen gave him'. A few years later he made his last official appearance in the Devon records. He was yet again in the Bridewell, in Michaelmas 1747, with many others 'to be confined according to their former commitments', eventually being discharged shortly after Christmas.[71] By that time his story was in print, published by the Farleys in Exeter, yet this account ends with his transportation. In 1749, the much enlarged and embellished version *An Apology* was published by Robert Goadby, editor of the *Sherborne Mercury*, and printer of several exciting accounts of crime and travel. Indeed, he specialized in exploiting West Country subjects for the London market. Significantly, with his London outlet run by W. Owen with whom he also published the account of John Poulter, executed in Ilchester in 1754 (and who also printed Edward Kimber's novel *Mr Anderson* the same year as Poulter's execution), Goadby continued to make money from the Carew story well into the 1760s, after the man himself was dead.[72] The impact of the *Apology* seems to have been to make Carew a national figure, his death reported in the *Gentleman's Magazine*, and his life becoming part of the local history of his county.[73] Locally, the word he uses for fraudsters operating in disguise passed into the language of law enforcement. In 1751 a report was published that Somerset was beset with 'mumpers' or 'rather sharpers who, under the appearance of distressed gentlemen, attended by a servant, and in other artful disguises, have imposed upon several worthy person by writing to them to borrow small sums of money'.[74] Carew may have had his imitators.

Well-known felons: Myths and fancy stories

Other narratives leave even more to the imagination, if only because so little truth can be demonstrated by later research. Sarah Wilson, described by Ekirch as ingenious in her technique of adopting a false identity after running away from her American master, is one such.[75] The story first appeared in a somewhat cryptic form in the *South Carolina Gazette* in 1773 which implied that the arrest of a female trickster was imminent:

> Last Thursday Night the Extraordinary FEMALE TRAVELLER, who lately excited so much curiosity here, and in the Northern Colonies, returned to this Town, by Land, from North Carolina, and is at Lodgings in King St – 'Tis affirmed, that she is no longer *unknown*.[76]

Many more details then appeared in a New York paper, *Rivington's Gazeteer*, concerning a mysterious traveller in the southern colonies:

> Some time ago, one SARAH WILSON, who attended upon the Hon Miss Vernon, sister to Lady Grosvenor, and Maid of Honour to the Queen, having found means to be admitted into one of the royal apartments, took occasion to break open a cabinet, and rifled it of many valuable jewels, for which she was apprehended, tried, and condemned to die, but through the gracious interposition of her mistress, the sentence was softened to transportation, she accordingly in the fall of 1771, was landed in Maryland, where she was exposed to sale, and purchased by Mr W. Devall, of Bush-Creek, Frederick County.
>
> After a short residence in that place, she very secretly decamped, and escaped into Virginia, travelled through that colony, and through North, to South Carolina, where, at a prudent distance from Mr Devall, she had assumed the title of the Princess Susanna Carolina Matilda, pronouncing herself to be an own sister to our sovereign lady the Queen. She had carried with her clothes that served to favour the deception, had secured a part of the jewels, together with her Majesty's picture, which had proved so fatal to her. She travelled from one gentleman's house to another under these preten-

sions, and made astonishing impressions in many places, affecting the mode of royalty so inimitable that many had to honour to kiss her hand. To some she promised governments, to others regiments, with promotions of all kinds, in the Treasury, Army and in the Royal Navy. In short, she acted her part so plausibly as to persuade the generality she was no imposter. In vain did many exert themselves to detect and make a proper example of her, for she had levied heavy contributions upon some persons of the highest rank in the Southern colonies but at length appeared the underwritten advertisement, together with Mr Michael Dalton at Charlestown, raising a hue and cry for her serene highness. But the lady had made an excursion a few miles to a neighbouring plantation, for which place the messenger set out, when the gentleman who had brought us this information left Charlestown. How distressing to behold a lady of exalted digree [sic] and pretensions, thus surprized into the hands of her inexorable enemies.

This was followed by a reprinted advertisement headed 'Bush Creek, Frederick County, Maryland October 11 1771', for the runaway servant, describing her as having a 'blemish in her right eye, black roll'd hair, stoops in the shoulders, makes a common practice of writing and marking her cloaths with a crown and a B'.[77] The story spread south and north through the colonial newspapers, appearing in the *Pennsylvania Gazette* and the *Boston Evening Post* in May and the *Virginia Gazette* in June 1773, but not, curiously, in the *Maryland Gazette*.[78] It then crossed the Atlantic, appearing in the *London Magazine* for June 1773 – datelined New York, 13 May, which ended that 'there is no doubt but her highness will soon be stripped of her royalty, and suffer the punishment due to her crimes'. It also appeared in the *Gentleman's Magazine* under the headline 'American News', which noted that in 1771 she was 'transported for robbing the Royal apartments at St. James's', reported her deceits in America, and concluded that she was however, soon detected in her frauds, and 'reduced to her former slavery'.[79]

As with the story of Bamfylde Moore Carew, historians have picked up the tale – it is after all a good one – and related it without comment, the most recent being Michael Zuckerman in a discussion of class and social relations in the colonies. In past years other, more popular accounts have become equally prevalent.[80] However, despite the tale being often repeated, it has proved remarkably difficult to demonstrate that there was such a convicted felon transported. Some clues were connected together at the time by contemporaries, for Sarah Wilson, or someone remarkably like her, had had an earlier career in England. A few years before the American reports, a 'letter from Coventry' appeared in the *London Evening Post* in July 1766, telling the story of a young woman called Miss Wilbraham, who

> said [she] was of a considerable family in the North, who were Roman Catholick; and that she had been obliged to leave her friends being a Protestant, and that she was in great distress. Under these pretences, she visited (and solicited for money and assistance) most of the principle families near this city and the town of Warwick, but on visiting Lady Denbigh, they had a strong suspicion of her being an imposter, and immediately sent over to Mr Alderman Hewitt, of this city, desiring he would, on her return to her inn, take her under his notice, and examine into the truth of her relations; accordingly the Alderman gave her the meeting when she gave him the following account. That her name was Wilbrahammon, and daughter of a gentleman who lived at Corby Castle, near Carlisle, who was a Roman Catholick; that her mother was a Protestant, and had brought her up in that religion; but she being dead, from the ill treatment she had received from her father, she was obliged to leave home; had been some time at Sigerhall near Kendall, at Lord Mullineaux's, and Lord Derby's on a visit; that she was going to the Duke of Leeds, being very intimate with his family. That she was married at Great Budworth in Cheshire to a person she called the Honourable Mr Irving, but did not know where he was at that time.

Her papers revealed she had travelled 'most of the north country' as well as the Midlands and the West, and that 'she had taken upon herself the title of Lady Viscountess Wilbrahammon; likewise of the Hon Miss Mullineaux alias the Hon Mrs Irving, pretending to be the daughter of Lord Mullineaux'. Found upon were her two certificates of marriage, one suggesting that she was married by the name of Sarah Charlotte Lewissearn Wilbrowsom, at Frensham in Surrey, and another with the name of Wilbrahammon. When questioned, she gave George Jackson, of the Navy Office, as her 'particular friend' and had a letter directed to her at Lord Strange's in Grosvenor Square.

The correspondent, almost certainly Alderman John Hewitt himself, asserted that a glance at the handwriting demonstrated that:

> there is great reason to believe she is connected with some very bad person, who makes a trade of being an agent for such purposes. This

notorious vagrant and impostress made her escape from Coventry and went to Banbury. The following description of her is given to the public by way of caution, and to prevent her farther success, viz., a short slender made woman, of a pale or sallow complexion, a little deformed, a speck or kell over one eye, had a light coloured riding habit, white hat, blue feather and cockade, with gold tassels, and said she was about 20 years of age.

The style and the physical description of the deformity of the eye are strikingly similar to those of the American Sarah Wilson.[81]

Later reports from the north described her skill in practising 'her usual arts' there after escaping from Coventry, and remarked that:

She has bad nerves, and seems to be great Disordered Mind which she pretends to be owing to the ill Usage of her Father. She went to Kendal in May last, in a Post Chaise and Four, and was short of Money, but the Day after her arrival had a considerable Sum brought her by a man of beggarly appearance. She attempts to borrow Money of Waiters, Servants and Chaise Boys . . . Her name is supposed to be Sarah Wilson.

This person – 'the notorious Vagrant and Imposter, mentioned in the London papers' was described to be 'a short slender Woman, of a pale or sallow Complexion, a little deformed with a speck on her right eye, which she conceals for some Time by excessive Winking'. She skillfully adapted her story to 'move the compassion' of those she visited.[82] Years later, John Hewitt made the connection with the American stories, and reinforced the impression of himself as the sharpest detector of fraudulent practices outside London. The woman was 'the greatest impostress of the present age', he asserted, going on to recount her deceptions around the country, quoting extensively from his own correspondence. She was imprisoned in the house of correction in St Albans in 1767, he notes, because she could not properly identify herself, but was still vague as to how she ended up in America:

She was a menial servant in the kitchen of George-Lewis Scott Esq. after the adventure at St. Alban's, and other places, was transported to America, where she imposed on the credulous, and pretended to be allied to the Royal Family, calling herself the Princess Louisa, producing some valuables as jewels, supposedly taken from one of the royal palaces.

Thus ended the 'comedy of errors', he claims. In fact, she was also in that year incarcerated in the Bridewell in Devizes, as Sarah Wilson alias Nixon, 'a notorious cheat and impostor', who styled herself the Countess of Normandy, 'supposed to be the same woman who lately played many Pranks at Lichfield, Coventry and places adjacent'. After that, the trail goes cold until the American stories in 1773.[83] However, the narrative offered different possible interpretations, according to taste and prejudice. Sarah Wilson's story spoke to different audiences, providing evidence which confirmed impressions as well as providing inherent fascination. New York readers may have read it as simply poking fun at the social pretensions of South Carolina planters but to British readers, less sensitive to geographical and social distinctions, it may have demonstrated the credulity of all colonial Americans. To John Hewitt, it probably demonstrated his own acuity, and the naivety of others who were taken in. For him, susceptible snobbish colonials were no better than the numerous respectable inhabitants of England taken in by a young woman with a plausible tale.

The unhappy transport

A much more detailed account, complete with a great many details of the journey across the Atlantic and the hard labour in the colonies, is the long poem supposedly by James Revel of London, though also by John Lauson of Bristol. The Revel version has achieved the status of being an authentic record of early America, reprinted in student collections of vivid texts. *The Poor Unhappy Transported Felon's Account of his Fourteen Years Transportation at Virginia in America . . . being a remarkable and succinct history of the life of James Revel* has almost iconic standing among stories of transportation, ever since it was discovered and given some publicity by John Melville Jennings in 1948. The publishing history at the time was obscure, though it seemed that most of the printed editions were from the mid-eighteenth century. On the basis of a diagnostic reading of the text in which he noted that the poem refers to a Rappahannock County which was abolished in 1692, Jennings concluded that the 'real' person must have been transported in the late seventeenth century.[84] This has been followed in several scholarly collections of early American texts, and many other historical studies of servant experiences in the 'the land of the living dead'.[85] In fact *The Poor Unhappy Transported Felon* demonstrated remarkable flexibility in a long publishing career, being born in two different cities under two entirely different names, and being transported to both America and

Australia. Whereas James Revel seems to have been a Londoner, born near Temple-Bar, and apprenticed to a 'tin-man' in Moorfields, a rival version, John Lauson, was born in Bristol, and apprenticed to a cooper in Broad Street. In all other respects, the two versions of the poem are the same, a long, rather doggerel, verse in six parts.[86] James Revel seems to have won the competition for dominant identity, for his version was reprinted until the early nineteenth century in both London and Dublin, though in the latter his name had become Ruel.[87] By the 1820s, however, the story had been rewritten with a new destination, namely Botany Bay, though the victim of the story still contrived to return successfully to London. Even then, the tale of the 'unhappy transport' was told under at least two names, and 'James Revel' was claimed as the publisher of a third. As has been remarked, it would seem that a thorough study of broadsides dealing with transportation could turn up even more versions of the life of the ubiquitous 'James Revel'.[88]

This complex publishing history does not necessarily lead to the conclusion that the story of the 'American' James Revel is inauthentic, for some of the details sound as though they were based on realistic reports of the transportation process and the work in the colonies. It forms a dramatic story of an apprentice led astray through bad friends: the following extracts give some idea of the tone of all the versions:

> Part I
> Strong liquor banished the thought of fear,
> But justice stopped us in our career,
> One night was taken up one of our gang
> who five impeach and three of them were hanged
>
> I was one of the five that was tried and cast,
> Yet transportation did I get at last,
> a just reward for my vile actions base,
> So justice overtook me at last
>
> Part II
> In a few days we left the river quite,
> And in short time of the land we lost the sight,
> The Captain and the Sailors used us well
> But kept us under lest we should rebel
> We were in number much about threescore,
> A wicked lousy crew as e'er went o'er
> Oaths and Tobacco with us plenty were,
> For most did smoak, and all did curse and swear.

> Five of our number in our passage died
> Which were thrown into the Ocean wide,
> After sailing seven weeks and more,
> We at Virginia all were put on shore.[89]

After being cleaned up and shaved for presentation to the planters, he is sold to a 'a grim old man' who takes him to 'Rappahannock County', one hundred miles up river, and he is dressed in canvas and set to work in the fields with a hoe.

> My Fellow slaves were just five Transports more
> With eighteen Negroes, which is twenty-four
> Besides four transport women in the house
> To wait upon his daughter and his Spouse

Escaping was hardly worth it, the story goes on, because for every hour away 'we must serve a day, for every day a week', for every week a month – 'they are so severe'. Eventually, after twelve years, he is transferred to a better master in James Town, who promises to return him home at the end of his service, and he lives 'in plenty and ease'.[90] He returns home, and is reconciled to his distressed parents. The moral lesson is read at the end:

> My countrymen take warning e'er too late,
> Least you should share my late unhappy fate,
> Altho' but little crime you here have done,
> Consider seven or fourteen years to come.
> Forc'd from your friends and country for to go
> Amongst the Negroes to work at the hoe,
> In distant countries void of all relief,
> Sold for a slave because you prov'd a thief.[91]

The account of the ship could easily have been drawn from many other stories, and the description of hard labour in the colonies – particularly working with the hoe in tobacco fields – is well attested. The legal details of penalties from running away were commonplace in criminals' biographies giving accounts of the Maryland and Virginia.[92] Other details sound a false note, particularly the idea of four female house servants: very few houses in the colonies were that grand. Other twists in the plot are traditional, the bad master compared with the good, the virtue in the end rewarded, and so on. The date of the story remains problematic, but the it sounds like one derived from many eighteenth-century accounts of mass transportation of convicts from London and Bristol, and from a period when the idea of servants' 'slavery' in the colonies had been well established. The temptation to break into verse is found in other narratives, as William Green does when he describes his companions on a London ship in the 1760s: 'A wretched crew as e'er was seen Our cloths ragged, and our bodies lean.' However, no other story seems to have been entirely in verse.[93] All that can be concluded is that 'Revel' was a fictional figure turned into a Tin Pan Alley poem with strikingly authentic details, to be sung, say most printed editions, to the well-known tune of 'Death and the Lady'. As one editor has commented,

> There is some evidence that James Revel was not only a convicted felon, but also a complete fabrication, perhaps dreamed up by an enterprising writer hoping to cash in on Daniel Defoe's success with the lurid adventures of Moll Flanders and Captain Jack, the most notorious felons, fictional or otherwise, to be transported to Virginia.[94]

In that sense, James Revel fits into an established pattern of composition by anonymous authors, striving to meet a need for dramatic and entertaining reflections on themes of public interest, set to familiar tunes so that purchasers could easily perform them themselves if they wished.[95]

Folk representations

Less artful, perhaps, and more reflective of a genuinely popular culture, are the few surviving folksongs about transportation. Some of these, too, were probably carefully written by semi-professional composers and printed in broadsheet form for public purchase, while others were collected by later folklorists seeking authentic voices of a threatened culture. Exactly how much was truly 'folk', and how much the product of a burgeoning popular music industry, remains contentious.[96] Transportation to the colonies, though, was a firm favourite of many nineteenth-century singers, for there were well-known versions of songs such as 'Botany Bay', and many other songs featured the threat of transportation, all reflecting popular fears.[97] Transportation to America, however, either did not figure largely among eighteenth-century songwriters, or their products have not been remembered.

One apparently authentic folksong is 'Virginny'. Significantly the song is also known as 'Australia' in a far longer version collected from traditional singers in the early twentieth century. This suggests that the American experience may have been subsumed under later versions concerning Australian transportation. Only three verses survive in the oral tradition:

> Now come all you young fellers where'er you may be
> Come listen a while and I'll tell you
> It's many's the young man myself I have seen
> More fitting to serve than to die on a string
> But how off were the judges how cruel they have been
> For to send us poor lads to Virginny.
>
> Now when we come to Virginny that cold shameful place
> Which I now recall in my story
> Our captain did stand with his whip and his cane
> To bargain for us poor souls out of hand
> Like horses they yoked us that had plowed the salt main
> How hard was my fate in Virginny.
>
> O England sweet England I fear I'll never see you more
> And if I do it's 10,000 to 20
> For me fingers they are rotting and me bones they are sore
> I wander about I'm right down to death's door
> But if I can just live to see seven years more I will soon bid
>   farewell to Virginny.

This is curiously ambivalent, for the young men are not portrayed as deservedly escaping the gallows. Moreover, some of the details are remote from the careful authenticity of the 'Revel' poem, as Virginia is oddly deemed a cold place. Moreover, the convicts are yoked to a plough, which was the standard story of the fate of those sent to Australia.[98]

The Virginia Maid's Lament

Another song concerned with Virginia, though not obviously involving convicts, is from Scotland, 'The Virginia Maid's Lament', recorded in the early nineteenth century by Peter Buchan, who linked it to the custom of kidnapping children for the colonies, and the longstanding contention over Scottish migration.[99]

Hearken, and I'll tell
You a story that befell,
In the lands of Virginia, O;
How a pretty maid
For a slave she was betray'd,
And O but I'm weary, weary, O.

Seven lang years I serv'd
To Captain Welsh, a laird,
In the lands of Virginia, O;
And he so cruelly
Sold me to Madam Guy,
And O but I'm weary, weary, O.

We are yoked in a plough,
And wearied sair enough,
In the lands of Virginia, O;
With the yoke upon our neck,
Till our hearts are like to break,
And O but I'm weary, weary, O.

When we're called home to meat,
There's little there to eat,
In the lands of Virginia, O;
We're whipt at every meal,
And our backs are never heal,
And O but I'm weary, weary, O.

When our madam she does walk,
We must all be at her back,
In the lands of Virginia; O;
When our baby it does weep,
We must lull it o'er sleep,
And O but I'm weary, weary, O.

At mid time of the day,
When our master goes to play,
In the lands of Virginia, O;
Our factor stands near by,
With his rod below his thigh,
And O but I'm weary weary, O.

But if I had the chance,
Fair Scotland to advance,

> From the lands of Virginia, O;
> Never more should I
> Be a slave to Madam Guy,
> And O but I'm weary, weary, O.

Like 'Virginny', this too reproduces the image of humans treated like plough animals, of poor food and savage discipline. The narrative could in some ways be the verse counterpart of the stories of James Annesley or Edward Kimber, who had established the themes of hard labour and cruelty in colonial 'slavery' by the middle of the eighteenth century.

Conclusion

Reality and fiction are intertwined, particularly with regard to crime. As has been noted, 'the fact/fiction boundary has always been particularly fluid in crime narratives. Crime and criminal justice have always been sources of popular spectacle and entertainment, even before the rise of the mass media'.[100] From the time of the *Beggar's Opera* to modern-day film and television, fictional narratives drawn from 'life' have been accused of creating more crime, if they appear authentic, or criticized as misleading, if seeming fanciful. Many fictions in the past were influenced by published information such as the Old Bailey Sessions Papers or the Newgate Calendar. Some fictions coexisted with a more sober account, as Edward Kimber's did, and Elizabeth Justice's, if you cared to look at the newspapers. In others, the fiction and the marvellous or sensational were combined. 'It seems evident that "truth" was not only stranger than fiction, but more lucrative as well. It allowed the writer considerable latitude in terms of recounting the more lurid highlights of a criminal's career.'[101] In such a competitive market, there was also scope for many versions of the same tale. For a long time crime has been the subject of both expert and popular publications, which have coexisted uneasily, often in conflict with each other, offering rival interpretations of characters and events.[102] With borrowings and copyings so frequent, it may be pointless to search for the *original* text, but it might repay great effort to seek out the most *factual*. With some, as we have seen with Sarah Wilson, that remains a remote possibility. Separating the 'real' convict from the fictional or semi-fictional one is complicated by a number of factors. Historians have to contend with works of fiction which have coloured the historical landscape for generations: this is not to suggest that all works of fiction are misleading, but historians must now recognize that autobiographical works of different types, once regarded as authentic accounts, can be a snare and delusion because, unfamiliar with the literary conventions of the eighteenth or even the nineteenth century, we have lacked the scholarly apparatus to 'read' them knowingly, to recognize what parts might be genuine, what invented and what 'lifted' from other writers (a polite way of saying 'stolen'), a practice common among many popular writers. Some narratives were 'true' stories which became almost mythical, such as those of Sarah Wilson and Bampfylde Moore Carew, while others, though supposedly true, became the basis for fictional representation, such as Edward Kimber's stories. Carew, the fictional gypsy, is far better known that the real gypsies transported to the colonies, whose complexions, described as 'swarthy mulatto in colour' caused some confusion.[103] The process of creating these kinds of semi-fictional accounts, or semi-factual fictions, was continued when Australian convict narratives were produced in the nineteenth century, and modern historians are still trying to address the distinction between the truthful and the invented.[104]

Some narrative elements of American convict stories were of great antiquity, already in print by the earliest years of the eighteenth century, as the satiric representation of convicts and servants in Ebenezer Cook's *The Sot-Weed Factor; or a Voyage to Maryland*, printed in London in 1708, shows. A picture is drawn of a society of felons and servants, many bound as a 'slave for twice two year', working at the hoe, all with excuses for how they washed up in the colonies. Cook was particularly harsh on the women, as they pretended they were fleeing unwelcome marriages or had been deceived and kidnapped, hiding their real background in prostitution. But all of the 'detested race' of convicts disguised their lucky reprieve from the gallows, the 'triple tree'. Planters greeted strangers, 'whether you are come from gaol or colledge, you're welcome to my certain knowledge'. Some women gain advantage, becoming planters' wives, while others work barefoot in the fields. Though written by a Maryland lawyer and merchant, this provided a cynical view of a place where 'no man's faithful and no woman chast'.[105] It also offered another twist on the representation of the servant's life as a harsh, amoral world of survival, much like that of the criminal and corrupt society they had left. This kind of product added to the diverse market on both sides of the Atlantic, resulting in images of transportation in eighteenth-century print culture that were varied and sometimes contradictory. If the best-known news stories and criminal biographies, with their accounts of returned convicts, suggested that, for organized criminals, transportation was easily evaded because they could return home without difficulty, a rather different tone was created by some of the more popular accounts. Many felons like Charles Speckman and William Green told stories which indicated that, once trapped into indentured servitude, convicts found labour in the colonies hard and the discipline relentless. In the ballads and the many verse stories of 'James Revel', this image of harsh exploitation was deeply entrenched. Although convict servitude in America did not achieve the fearful reputation later attached to the penal colonies of Australia in folksong and criminal stories, it was certainly portrayed as harsher than anything experienced in England or Scotland – hence the increasing use of 'slavery' to describe it. Narratives of transportation therefore offered different opportunities for interpretation. On the one hand, some readers might conclude that harsher penalties were needed because so many convicts returned, while others might argue that popular fear of transportation (evinced by the few petitions by criminals who preferred execution to the alternative, and the tales of hard labour) indicated that it was having the desired deterrent effect. Between these two versions, however, there was hardly an equal competition. The overwhelming power of the London print industry meant that the returned convict, privileged by class, degree of organization, or level of depravity, dominated the imagery of transportation. Unchallenged, the preamble to the Hard Labour Bill of 1752 put the official view that transportation had been a failure because so many escaped and returned home before the expiry of their sentences. This became almost the official ideology of the time, and has been one of the central questions of historical investigation.[106]

5
Flight, Escape and Return

When John Poulter and an accomplice held up a post-chaise belonging to Dr William Hancock on Claverton Down near Bath one Wednesday evening in March 1753, he set in motion a chain of events which led not only to his own execution and a nationwide hunt for his former accomplices, but also to the publication of *The Discoveries of John Poulter, alias Baxter*, one of the best-known and most remarkable of eighteenth-century criminal biographies.[1] *The Discoveries of John Poulter, alias Baxter* purported to reveal, as nothing had before, the existence of a complex network of professional criminals who operated at will across the length and breadth of England. Published by the same West Country printer as *An Apology for the Life of Bamfylde Moore Carew*, Poulter's *Discoveries* catered to the seemingly insatiable public appetite for criminal narratives. In notices placed in the Bristol and London press in January and February 1754, Robert Goadby informed the reading public that Poulter was 'expected to receive a pardon on account of the great discoveries he has made' and that, though the press had been kept constantly busy, he was unable to satisfy the demand for orders. He promised a 'proper supply for the future'.[2] If Goadby's claim was merely a shrewd marketing strategy to boost demand, it was hugely successful for in May and June 1754 he was advertising the eleventh and twelfth editions of the work, by which time Poulter was dead.[3]

In *The Discoveries of John Poulter, alias Baxter*, not only did Poulter expound upon his extensive career as a thief, horse stealer, burglar and highwayman, name accomplices, supply dates and locations and list goods stolen and the methods employed in acquiring them, but, more importantly, he gave credence to the suspicion that transportees found it easy to return home from the colonies, explained the method by which this was effected, and, in identifying the men and women who had allegedly subverted their sentences, implied that escape could be accomplished with impunity and by large numbers of men and women eager to return. In the section entitled 'The WAY that Convicts return from Transportation, and the only way to prevent it', Poulter observed:

> The general Way is this:
> Just before they go on board a Ship, their Friend or Accomplices purchase their Freedom from the Merchant or Captain that belongs to the said Ship, for about ten Pounds Sterling; some gives more and some less: Then the Friend of the Convict or Convicts, gets a Note from the Merchant, or Captain, that the Person is free to go unmolested when the Ship arrives between the Capes of *Virginia* where they please. But I never heard of any Convict that came back again in the same Ship they went over in; for the Merchant or Captain gives a Bond to the Sheriff of the County where such Convicts go from, to leave them in *America*, and they get a Receipt from the Custom there; but as there are Ships coming Home every Week, if they can pay their Passage they are refused in no Ship. Some men will work their Passage back again, and them that cannot free themselves, take an Opportunity of running away from their Master, and lay in the Woods by Day, and travel by Night for *Philadelphia*, *New York*, or *Boston*; in which Places no Questions are asked them. This encourages a great many to commit Robberies more than they would, because they say they do not mind Transportation, it being but four or five Months Pleasure, for they can get their Freedom and come Home again . . .[4]

At no point in his account did Poulter disclose that he was himself a returned transportee. *The Discoveries of John Poulter, alias Baxter* was not a last dying speech or a narrative constructed on the eve of execution. It is therefore not a full and frank confession and plea for forgiveness in the hope of winning salvation, nor is it the tale of a misspent youth whose origins lay in the rejection of parental authority, bad company and lewd women. It covered only the last five years of Poulter's life and was written in the hope of advancing his claims for a pardon on the basis of his volunary informations and future testimony. Poulter had begun talking to the authorities, to play the 'game' of pardons, as Spierenburg has termed it, almost as soon as he was apprehended in Exeter less than a week after the robbery on Claverton Down. His 'Voluntary Information, Examination, and Confession', dated 28 March 1753 was concerned with revealing the names and activities of a vast criminal network of which he had been a part.[5] More details followed in the 'The further Information, Examination and Confession', dated June 1753. Poulter pleaded guilty at his trial in August, 'being Conscious of the Fact and unwilling to trouble the Court', thereby ensuring that no evidence was presented against him at this time. When asked by the Earl of Holdernesse, then Secretary of State, for his opinion on the case, the trial judge Sydney Stafford Smythe was broadly sympathetic, for Poulter, it seems, had now disclosed further information. He had 'likewise discovered the Manner, in which Persons, order'd for Transportation, procure their Liberty, and return to this Kingdom; From which Discovery, Regulations may be made to prevent that great Evil'.[6]

In 1746 Poulter had been tried at the Old Bailey for receiving and given the statutory sentence of fourteen years' transportation; he was carried to the Chesapeake aboard the *George William* (Captain James Dobbins) in January 1747.[7] As to what he did between that date and 1749 when his narrative begins, and how he himself returned from transportation, he is silent. Poulter's claims are misleading not because they were advanced in order to save his own skin, nor because the method outlined was defective, but rather because so few in fact did return.

The obstacles were indeed formidable. William Moraley, a Newcastle man who was a servant in Philadelphia in the early 1730s, declared that it was nearly impossible to escape:

> there being a reward for taking up any person who travels without a pass, which is extended overall the British colonies, their masters immediately issue out a reward for the apprehending them, from thirty shillings to five pound, as they think proper, and this generally brings them back again. Printed and written advertisements are also set up against the Trees and publick places in the town, besides those in the news-papers.

Hotly pursued and brought back, 'a Justice settles the expences, and the servant is oblig'd to serve a longer time'.[8] When he became free, Moraley himself was mistaken for a runaway after he got hopelessly lost in the crossroads of New Jersey.[9] Convict servants who returned to England to resume their criminal careers, only to end their lives on the gallows, had similar and worse experiences. James Dalton, 'the noted street robber', met with mixed fortunes in the colonies. Sold to an Irishman,

> who not agreeing with my Temper, I run away from him; but he soon took me again. There was no way of helping myself, so I was con-

tented, and continued with him some time, and then thought of an Expedient to quit myself of his Service, which I effected by running away with a Long-Boat that lay in the River with Masts and Sails in her. When I got on the other side the River; I bore several Holes in the Long Boat with an Augur, and sunk her. Then I went and stole a Horse, upon which I travelled about the Country several Days, till I arrived at a Place call'd *Portomock River*, where I continued about three Weeks, and then enter'd myself on board a Ship bound for *Bristol*, and had 10*l.* paid me for my Service in this Voyage.[10]

On his return Dalton did not dare to go to London but remained in Bristol, a city which offered him plenty of scope to practise his old trade until his luck ran out and he was committted to Bristol's Newgate Gaol on a charge of burglary. Though found guilty on a reduced charge, once again Dalton was sentenced to transportation. Back in Virginia but 'not being fixed to stay', he plotted to run away with two others. They struggled to survive:

When we had got clear of the inhabited Country, we were oblig'd to live very hard, having no Provision with us. We took Fire-Arms with us and kill'd Deer, and liv'd mostly upon that and the Moss of Trees. At length we met a Horse without either Bridle or Saddle, which we laid hold of; and having made a Briddle of our Garters, we got all three upon him: Coming to a River that we were oblig'd to cross, the Current run so strong that we could not pass it for three Days, whereupon we kill'd our Horse the second day and lived upon that. When we had passed the River we made our Way for *North Carolina*, where we no sooner arrived, but were discover'd, and sent back again to our Masters.[11]

Charles Speckman was a petty thief and confidence trickster who was transported to Virginia on the *Trial* in 1751. His servitude 'being very intollerable', he determined to escape but 'not considering the expence, the danger in crossing the rivers, and having no pass from a magistrate', he was soon taken up and returned to his master. His master beat him mercilessly. ['H]e fleed me from neck to rump, so that I was obliged to lie on my belly for several days and nights; [and] when I was well enough to walk, he sold me into the back settlements of Virginia. . . .' Located in the backcountry, he was hundreds of miles inland when General Braddock and his troops passed through on their way to the Ohio in 1755. Following Braddock's defeat and the flight of his master and family, Speckman followed the army to Philadelphia where 'being bare of cloathing, and in want of money, being withal very hungry', he took up his 'London trade'. Moving on to New York, he began to practise in his 'usual way' but was apprehended, brought to trial and 'sentenced to be whipped behind a cart, at the corner of every street in the city'. Ordered out of New York on pain of having his punishment repeated, he was 'passed twenty miles by constables', then released.[12]

The convicts' new world was not essentially different from that encountered by those leaving London for Virginia in 1635, who entered upon 'a world laced with rivers, streams, runs, and swampy waterways' unlike the 'ancient footpaths and thoroughfares' with which they were familiar and where, engaged in the production of tobacco, 'a crop foreign to English husbandmen', they found themselves 'laboriously tending tobacco seeds and removing insects by hand'.[13] Arriving in Virginia in 1759 over a hundred years later, the Rev. Andrew Burnaby reported that not a tenth of the land 'is yet cultivated: and that which is cultivated, is far from being so in the most advantageous manner'. He hesitated to describe Virginia as 'flourishing' because 'though it produces great quantities of tobacco and grain, yet there seem to be very few improvements carrying on in it. Great part of Virginia is a wilderness, and as many of the gentleman are in possession of immense tracts of land, it is likely to continue so'. Maryland was less problematic; it resembled Virginia, wrote Burnaby, in its 'climate, soil, and natural productions', it was 'watered by many fine rivers, and almost innumerable creeks; but it is far from being well cultivated, and is capable of much improvement'.[14] Burnaby's travels took him beyond Chesapeake Bay across the Blue Ridge and into the Shenandoah Valley. Servants might cover such distances before reaching their final destinations, travelling 'by foot or by wagon, river boat, or raft'. And 'even highly skilled artisans' were committed to years of manual labour . . .'.[15]

England's Chesapeake colonies, like its Caribbean colonies, had rapidly acquired the reputation for harsh punitive labour.[16] While contracts in Europe between masters and craft apprentices and servants-in-husbandry, from which indentured servitude derived, were designed to be self-enforcing, the conditions that made this a reality on one side of the Atlantic were absent on the other with the result that '[t]he customary norms of behaviour changed'. 'What would become common and acceptable treatment of immigrant servants in America', writes Farley Grubb, 'would have been considered shocking if applied to bound labour in England or to apprentices in either place'.[17] In Europe, the costs incurred at the beginning of the master-servant relationship were borne by servants and their families. If the master failed to abide by the terms of the contract his reputation was damaged and his ability to recruit more servants was seriously impaired but if the servant deserted the master, he not the master suffered the financial loss. In the colonies, however, the master assumed the costs from the start because of the need to compensate contractors for the passage of servants across the Atlantic. The servant, however, had little to lose if he or she deserted the employer, hence they were 'exposed to more legal and extra-legal coercion.[18] Convict servants according to Grubb were much like other indentured servants though they served longer. They did the same work and cost the same to maintain but their price was negotiable in a way that that of other indentured servants was not.[19]

The use of advertisements in colonial newspapers to recover runaways was a powerful but recent addition in the second quarter of the eighteenth century to the already considerable panoply of powers enjoyed by the state and masters of labour in the Chesapeake (and elsewhere). These powers were created initially to harness large numbers of young English people to the tobacco economy by the extension of service and, augmented with the advent of slavery, to curb the mobility of all unfree labourers. Through the use of outlawry, the introduction of passes when off the plantation, the employment of patrols, the selective use of irons and by a system of public and private rewards, Virginia legislators sought to police their society and bind small planters to the support of the planter class and slavocracy.[20] With the integration of the colonies into the British consumer economy in the 1740s, there came 'an increase in the importation and resale of unfree labor, white and black in the mid-Atlantic', all of which was reflected 'in the number of advertisements for goods, for the sale of servants and slaves, and for the recapture of runaways in the newspapers . . .'.[21] But the print culture of runaways varied according the forms of contract and employment in Britain and the colonies. In the latter, runaway notices appeared in the press with far greater frequency and runaways of every sort were pursued with greater rigour and over far more extensive geographical areas than in contemporary England.[22]

British uses of the press

In England, the papers took note in their news reports of a wide range of people, mostly those under arrest or witnessed as behaving in publicly threatening ways. Personal losses, of property such as horses and stolen goods, of spouses, apprentices and, more rarely, servants, were advertised at private expense as well as listed in crime reports. There were more advertisements for stolen horses than escaping servants or apprentices.[23] Nevertheless, this too was a society alert to the wandering, threatening elements which appeared at times to be out of control. The poor might be arrested and interrogated, returned to their places of original settlement by 'pass' – literally returned by being passed from constable to constable and parish to parish across the country, with a certificate giving their destination. The more dangerous, as we have seen, the 'incorrigible rogues and vagabonds', might find themselves transported.[24] Complaints by employers about deserting servants and apprentices were more commonly directed at the parish magistrates as a means of enforcing their contracts, and this suggests that few went very far. Indeed, the overwhelming impression given by most of these is of a breakdown of relationships in a small community. Above all, there were few financial incentives for detecting and returning those who ran away, as official rewards were not legally established. The laws against servants and apprentices, however, could involve imprisonment and other punishments, though that continued the workers' absence from their employment.[25]

Advertisements in England for runaway servants did on occasion match the levels of detail shown in the American newspapers:

> whereas the three following persons who had indentured themselves a few days since to Mr Nicodemus Ridout, of the City of Bristol, linen-draper, in order to serve him and his assigns in Maryland, beyond the seas, for a certain number of years, have absconded: – *this is to give notice*, that if they will voluntarily return to the said Mr Ridout, on or before the 30th Inst, they shall be kindly received.

This is strikingly similar to the language of the advertisements in the colonial papers, and it may be significant that the servants were destined for Maryland. The runaways were two West Country men, Thomas James, of Newland, Gloucestershire, aged twenty-five, a carpenter and millwright, and William Brimble, of Tiverton, Devon, aged nineteen, a carpenter, while the third came from further away – William Atkinson, from Orbafield in Yorkshire, aged twenty-six, a stone-cutter and brick-maker. Each man was described in detail, with their heights, appearances and clothing. Significantly, a reward of two guineas was offered.[26] Most attention, however, was devoted to crime and suspects in criminal cases, and with this area of anxiety the English press developed a national system of criminal intelligence under the guidance of Sir John

Fielding of Bow Street, London. In the autumn of 1763, as London criminals were reported to have been escaping from the city into the countryside, he wrote to the county authorities, 'inclosing his plan for the more speedy detection and apprehending of offenders, which was unanimously approved of by all the Justices', and from that time on descriptions of those under arrest in gaol were sent to him as well as being fixed on local church doors and market crosses.[27] This was not an entirely original idea, and local debate was often devoted to the best methods of inspecting and describing prisoners and suspects. As one anonymous author put it, in a letter to the printer of *Felix Farley's Bristol Journal*,

> The desperate Gang now in Custody at Coventry, the greatest Part of which are suppos'd to have returned from Transportation, will greatly puzzle the Magistrates of that City, for want of a proper Description of their Persons, and as there is not in any of the Gaols in this Kingdom any Description Book kept, consequently many of them will escape that punishment justly due ...

The writer suggested that the county sheriffs in charge of the gaols should keep a 'description book' of all those convicted of any crimes from the highest felony to petty larceny,

> and to enter therein all the Features and particular Marks (if any) of the Body, Arms and Leggs, by searching them to the Skin: Could such a Description now be had, the Villains at Coventry would soon meet with their Deserts.[28]

The author may have been Alderman John Hewitt, the scourge of the so-called 'Coventry gang' though the letter was signed 'T', or at least someone familiar with the problems of running down and prosecuting so mobile and amorphous a group. In this kind of proposal, therefore, local and national anxieties came together. Fielding was certainly effective in subsequent decades, as Bow Street served as a clearing house for criminal intelligence from far away. To take one example, in 1774 it was reported in north-east England that:

> this week John Dick, who, by the vigilance of Sir John Fielding was lately apprehended in London, for uttering in this town, a counterfeit bank note of the banking company of Aberdeen, was brought hither and examined and is now in custody for further examination.

This system required constant vigilance and personal prodding from Fielding who, missing intelligence from the north wrote to the gaolers of Newcastle upon Tyne asking why they had not sent in their *weekly* account of the names and descriptions of the prisoners committed to their custody, 'as it is a circumstance of great service to the community'.[29] Characteristically, perhaps, Britain was evolving an embryonic national system of central intelligence, albeit one still reliant on the volunteer services of local constables, sheriffs, and magistrates as much as the salaried gaolers.

The convict in the colonies

Why some convicts took flight but most stayed put is a matter of speculation. Direct testimony of convicts is very rare. It may be that those who fled sought to escape an alien enviroment, a brutal master or unfamiliar work patterns, or some combination of these factors. Convicts were seldom employed in large-scale enterprises with one singular exception – the ironworks. Skaggs has described these and the shipyards as 'the least desirable places to work', and from these flight was endemic.[30] Escape may have been dependent on location, requiring access to the Bay or the large rivers penetrating the interior, and the availability of small craft with which to flee the vicinity and larger vessels to secure egress from the region. Some stole horses, others left on foot. Although fleeing alone was probably more effective, some left in pairs, others in groups of three, usually linked by place of origin or workplace. Some had come over on the same vessel or else were from the same county. Some quit remarkably quickly with little time to recover from the Atlantic voyage or adjust to new circumstances. Others responded to the prospect of war and sought out recruiting agents.[31]

One hundred and twenty-five male and female convicts from northern England and the West Country were advertised as runaways in the newspapers of Virginia, Maryland and Pennsylvania between 1736 and 1776. This is a minimum figure, for not all runaways were advertised, and others who may have been from one or other of the two regions cannot be positively identified and for Virginia, in particular, issues of the *Virginia Gazette*, especially before 1766, are incomplete. Of the 125 who can be positively identified, only two are known to have returned to England. William Moraley's claim that servants in the colonies were 'perpetually running away but seldom escape[d]' may have been closer to the truth than Poulter's boast that many returned and did so with impunity.[32] On the basis of advertisements for 993 separate Maryland convicts between 1746 and 1775, an average of thirty-three per year, and estimating that a minimum of 12,000 convicts entered Maryland during this period, Ekirch has tentatively suggested that 9 per cent of convicts may have appeared in runaway notices.[33] Taking his total of 1,401 for Virginia and Maryland (for whom gender is known), the runaways in this study from northern England and the West Country might have represented 8.4 per cent of the total. If Maryland alone were taken, the proportion of west-country runaways could have been between 10 and 12 per cent. Ekirch takes the view that chances of escape were good, and that most 'probably' returned to England. Morgan, on the other hand, citing William Eddis, argues that they did not.[34]

Regional differences

There were distinct regional differences in the propensity to run away, suggesting that the trade networks from their region, and the presence of many ships returning there, enticed some to try to escape (see Table 5.1). West Country men were most likely to run away, followed by those from the North East. Convicts from north-west England were the least likely of all to be advertised in the newspapers. For men from all regions,

Table 5.1 Male runaways advertised in the colonies 1745–76

	Runaway	Transported	% Runaways
Western Circuit			
Cornwall	7	163	4.29
Devon	19	382	4.97
Dorset	14	133	10.53
Hampshire	21	461	4.55
Somerset	14	427	3.28
Wiltshire	14	242	5.78
Total	89	1808	4.92
North-east England			
Co. Durham	3	88	3.41
Newcastle	1	75	1.33
Northumberland	4	88	4.55
Total	8	251	3.18
North-west England			
Cumberland	3	94	3.19
Lancashire	8	383	2.09
Total	11	477	2.31

running away was only for a small minority, with just under 5 per cent overall in the western circuit recorded, with a maximum of 10.5 per cent for the men from the county of Dorset, but there were far fewer from elsewhere.[35]

The struggle of convicts for survival in the colonies is not to be found in criminal biographies or last dying speeches, nor as depicted in sensationalist reports in colonial newspapers which beg the question why some men who were relatively minor offenders at home turned murderous in the colonies, but rather in the runaway notices that proliferated in colonial newspapers from the 1720s onwards. Though the historical moment they capture was brief, and the portraits they draw are unflattering, they provide access to the convict's old and new world.[36] Flight was a phenomenon among all categories of unfree labour throughout the colonial and revolutionary periods; indentured servants, slaves and convicts all ran away, and some absconded together, though Ekirch believes this to be rare.[37] Just as advertisements for runaway slaves can be read as the 'first slave narratives' and the better-known published slave narratives reclassified as 'counter-narratives', so advertisements for runaway convicts, some of them astonishingly detailed, can be read as convict narratives, though written by masters, their agents, contractors or gaolers, while criminal biographies and last dying speeches, limited to capital offenders but in which convicts may have had a hand, can be viewed as counter-narratives.[38] The convict narratives connect these men, though seldom the women among them, to the world they have lost, providing information on their place of birth, age and occupation, details often missing from English court records, especially at quarter sessions.[39]

Edward Billingham was one convict whose odyssey began after he was convicted of petty larceny for stealing two geese at the Durham quarter sessions and ordered for transportation.[40] One of twenty unnamed felons sent from the gaols of north-east England, he was despatched to Virginia aboard the *Jenny*, formerly a whaling vessel under Captain Thomas Blagdon, along with twenty-six 'volunteer passengers of different trades' whose departure from Newcastle was recorded in the *Newcastle Courant* in January 1766.[41] The voyage was long, taking eleven weeks, forcing the crew and passengers onto short rations before they reached Virginia. The *Jenny* was at Burwell's Ferry on the James River in the week of 18 April when the sale of its cargo at Bermuda Hundred, 'a common place for the sale for servants and slaves', was advertised in the *Virginia Gazette*.[42] It is only from the runaway notice placed in the *Virginia Gazette* that we learn that Billingham was purchased by

Sampson Matthews, the twenty-five-year-old son of an Irish immigrant who had settled on the 'Borden tract' in the late 1730s, where he and his brother George had been born. '[A]s partners in a variety of money-making ventures', the brothers lived in Staunton, a frontier community in Augusta County where they owned a store and tavern.[43] Indentured servants had been coming to the Shenandoah Valley since the 1730s. If Matthews acquired Billingham at Staunton rather than Bermuda Hundred, it would indicate that he had not been bought up quickly but herded westward along the lower of the three circuits used by so-called 'soul drivers' to dispose of those who remained unsold.[44] Billingham had worked for Matthews for a few months at most when he boldly asserted his autonomy and absconded. As it was so early in his contract, Matthews valued Billingham enough to advertise for him but not sufficiently to offer a substantial reward so he could 'get him again'. The fugitive notice identifying Billingham as a convict runaway appeared on 17 October 1766 in Purdie and Dixon's *Virginia Gazette*.[45]

RUN away from the subscriber at Staunton, in *Augusta* county, *Virginia*, a convict man named EDWARD BILLINGHAM, born in the north of *England*, and speaks like a *Scotchman*, or those born in the borders, about 5 feet 2 inches high, thick made, has a blemish on one of his eyes, down look, dark coloured hair, about 30 years old, is a chimney sweeper and labourer, and makes but an ordinary appearance; had on when he went away a light coloured broadcloth half worn coat, a dark coloured jacket with a white stripe down the back, an old hat, coarse shirt and trousers, and old shoes. Whoever takes up and secures said servant, so that I get him again, shall have 20 s. reward, if taken in this county, and if taken in any other county or colony 40 s. besides what the law allows.

SAMPSON MATTHEWS.

Billingham was a convict 'of the common sort' or 'inferior note', distinguished as most convicts were from that small minority of gentlemen such as Henry Justice, William Wreathhock and George Vaughan who merited the label 'felons of distinction'.[46] In describing him, Matthews who was already part of Augusta County's governing political structure, provided details not only of his height and age, the most frequently cited physical attributes found in well over half of runaway notices in the second half of the eighteenth century, but also those of build and hair colour and, rarer still, those of speech and posture. Reference to his 'ordinary appearance' and 'down look' fitted 'the polite conviction that plebian types should neither stand erect or stare back'. The 'blemish' on one eye was useful as a 'peculiar mark' of identification but according to Prude, it was clothing more than any physical attributes by which runaways were most 'consistently depicted'.[47] Billingham's clothing was old and worn and coarse and probably English. Although Billingham refused to accept his allotted role, we do not know whether he escaped. The advertisement, unlike that for William Webster and Thomas Spears, penned by George Washington, contains no indication of how and when Billingham fled or what he might do next. If running away was intended to claim or reclaim one's liberty, where did freedom lie? In which direction and among whom? Returning to England before one's time was up was a capital offence. Billingham's best chance of escape was probably to head either north or south, for Staunton was well situated, being located on the route from Pennsylvania to Georgia. To the north were Philadelphia and New York, large, growing and anonymous seaports; to the south was the turbulent backcountry of the Carolinas and the infant colony of Georgia, already filling up with newly arrived Scots-Irish, Scots and German immigrants.[48]

The advertisement placed in the hope of recovering William Webster and Thomas Spears was more knowingly drawn. Spears does not appear to have been a convict and Webster, who most certainly was, was not identified as such.[49] Webster had been transported from the County of Northumberland in 1773, having been found guilty of breaking into a house occupied by a widow and sentenced to seven years' transportation at quarter sessions.[50] Purchased in Annapolis, Maryland, by William McGaughen on behalf of George Washington, of Fairfax County, Virginia, Webster's indenture was dated from 26 February 1774, the date on which the brig *The Swift*, carrying him to Maryland, arrived in the colony.[51] Webster was one of a batch of four felons bought on behalf of Washington, along with four indentured servants and a husband and wife. McGaughen thought the £110 paid for the convicts was a little high but as they were 'country likely people', the deal was quite sound.[52] Webster had been in Washington's employment for just over a year when he ran off with fellow-servant Thomas Spears, though not for the first time. Washington waited five days before writing the runaway notice, which appeared three weeks after the men had run off. The information Washington supplied was fuller and more detailed than that used by Matthews in a number of respects. Physical attributes were quite precise. One man was 5 feet 6 inches high, the other 5 feet $6\frac{1}{2}$ inches high. Additional details were supplied such as the shape of Webster's face, the colour of Spears's eyes and how he wore his hair. Born in Scotland, Webster, 'rather turned of 30' talked 'pretty broad' while Spears, Bristol-born, had a voice that was 'coarse and somewhat drauling'. Spears departed with eleven items of clothing, Webster with six. The men left at night making off 'in a small yaul, with turpentine sides and bottom, the insides painted with a mixture of tar and red lead'. A reward of twenty dollars was offered for each man; both were skilled, Webster was a brickmaker and Spears a joiner. Anticipating that the men would try to escape by sea, Washington warned all 'masters of vessels' not to receive them. The men were recovered by two servant-catchers employed by Washington for the purpose, who pursued the two men across the Potomac to Maryland, then back to Virginia to Najemoy, Boyd's Hole, Stafford Court House and Dumfries.[53]

The advertisement placed by James Duncanson of Fredericksburg, Virginia, in 1770 in an effort to recover John Booker aged 31 and John Libiter (alias Leadbetter) aged 35 traces the men, convicted at the Lancashire quarter sessions and 'just arrived' from Liverpool in the *Nassau*, to Port Royal on the Rappahannock River. Duncanson, who had only recently acquired them, described them as 'brought up to farming and country business, and Leadbetter pretends to understand dying colours' but the Lancashire records described them as weavers. Duncanson was fully alert to the possibilities of escape. The runaways did not carry a change of clothes with them but they did have some money. He had followed their movements on the Rappahannock River.

> They were at Port Royal last Saturday last, and were observed Sunday morning on the bank hailing two schooners bound down the river, one to Baltimore, the other to Norfolk; and as they could be traced no lower by land, it is supposed got on board one of the said vessels, where it is probable they will endeavour to pass for sailors, as they have a little of that appearance. All masters of vessels are forbid to carry them out of the country.[54]

Though running away was largely a male phenomenon, five women from northern England and the West Country were among those advertised as running away in the colonial press.[55] The law regarded these women, with the exception of Ann Wilson, as relatively serious offenders because despite their gender, the authorities had seen fit to try them at the assizes rather than the quarter sessions. Two of the women faced charges of burglary, one of breaking and entering and two of theft. Elizabeth Hawkins and Elizabeth Tizard were both transported from Dorset where the former had been prosecuted on a charge of burglary in 1750 but, benefiting from a partial verdict despite stealing silverware, received a sentence of seven years' transportation, as did the latter in 1753. Purchased by Rachel Pottinger of Queen Anne County, Maryland, Elizabeth Hawkins waited three years before running away.[56] Elizabeth Tizard, found guilty of stealing two holland aprons valued at five shillings, did not tarry long with her new master Thomas Pecker of Annapolis. Arriving in Maryland on 22 May 1755 aboard the *Falcon*, she ran off before the end of August with a fellow passenger and convict servant Robert Pearce, also from Dorset. It was reported that they would 'probably' pass for man and wife. A ship's carpenter, Pearce had been bought by Patrick Creagh, also of Annapolis.[57] Elizabeth Loyd, found guilty of burglary and stealing a quantity of bread and bacon when much of the population was still recovering from famine conditions, had been sentenced to death at the Wiltshire assizes in 1767 but reprieved on condition of serving fourteen years in the American plantations. Within a year, she too had absconded, fleeing from Thomas Johnson of Chestertown, Kent County, Maryland, with Thomas Moore, a Surrey quarter sessions transportee.[58] Ann Wilson, a married woman who came from the small Lancashire town of Ulverston, was forty-five years of age when sentenced by the quarter sessions to seven years' transportation in January 1775. She could not have been in Maryland more than a few months before she too deserted her master James Braddock in Talbot County, Maryland, fleeing with fellow servant (but not a convict) William Manly, 'a well made fellow', also from Lancashire, whose age was given as between twenty-five and thirty. Ann Wilson 'who calles herself the said Manly's wife' was described as 'handy at doing housework and speaks the same dialect as Manly'.[59] Possibly the most resourceful of the women and certainly the most colourful was Sarah Knox, alias Sarah Howard, alias Sarah Wilson, alias Charles Hamilton. Born in Yorkshire, she was transported from Whitehaven aboard the *Duke of Cumberland* in 1750, having been tried for breaking and entering but found guilty only of theft and given a seven-year sentence. By all accounts she had been a camp follower with the army in Flanders, she was present at the battle of Culloden where her husband was killed, she was a cross-dresser and confidence trickster who posed as a doctor and pretended to be a dancing mistress. She claimed to be twenty-eight years of age but her master David Currie, Anglican minister in Lancaster County, Virginia, thought it more likely she was forty.[60]

Table 5.2 Dates of running away, north-east and north-west England and Western Circuit

Years after the year of transportation order*	No.	%
0	22	17.60
1	48	38.40
2–3	34	27.20
4–6	16	12.80
7+	2	1.60
Unknown	3	2.40
Total	125	100.00

* '0' indicates the same year, 1 the next year etc.

Thus two of these women acted alone but three ran with a male partner, so reversing the pattern to be found among male runaways.

These cases are typical in that the convicts ran relatively quickly after their arrival in the colonies. From our evidence, more than half (56 per cent) ran either in the same year they were transported or in the following year (Table 5.2). In escaping and being advertised, these English criminals were asserting their independence, but also revealing many aspects of their appearance and character.

The advertisements

The descriptions of runaways in both Britain and America concentrated mostly on the visible aspects of appearance – hair, clothes, shoes, facial expressions and marks. Nevertheless, as the correspondent to *Felix Farley's Bristol Journal* recognized, these could be changed or disguised by enterprising people trying to avoid identification. The hidden aspects of the body could provide a more secure means of proving identity, particularly scars, tattoos and other ineradicable marks. However, the conditions in eighteenth-century Britain and its American colonies were not designed for the total surveillance achieved in later years. Prison records were sketchy, advertisements a private or individual matter, the level of scrutiny haphazard. No one could achieve the level of description common in the convict records of those sent to Australia in the nineteenth century, when both British officialdom and those in the penal colonies kept detailed records of every personal and bodily aspect of convicts. In one survey of descriptions of bodily tattooing the records of more than 1,000 convict descriptions were studied. The tattoo – described as 'the closest to the "convict voice" that it is now possible to attain' was visible to unavoidable official inspection. Similarly, in her analysis of the descriptions of Indian convicts sent to Mauritius, Clare Anderson refers to the repeated documentation available, the result of them being constantly surveyed and disciplined, 'as subjects of the colonial panopticon eye'.[61] As in the eighteenth century, these were largely descriptions of working-class criminals under conditions of servitude. There are parallels in the individuality achieved by those described, even under adverse conditions of their servile state. As with slaves, the minute descriptions of suspected and actual criminals in the British and American press in the eighteenth century describe the distinctive marks of individuals, and accidentally reveal their distinctiveness and individuality. Only those who were, literally, nondescript, would escape such careful inspection, and perhaps enjoy greater chances of escape.

Waldstreicher identifies four attributes: clothing, trades or skills, linguistic ability and usage, and ethnic or racial identity. Owners of convict labour may have been particularly aware of the appearance of their workers but they were also attuned (or convey the impression that they were) to their accents, dialects and the quality of their voices. West Country and northern English runaways do not appear to have differed in the physical descriptions given of them from those from elsewhere though there was a slightly greater emphasis placed on the way they spoke. John Baker, transported to Maryland from Hampshire in 1759, was described as 'born in the west of England, and speaks much in that Dialect'. William Kneller, transported from Wiltshire, 'speaks pretty much in the West-Country dialect'. William Springate, a gardener, born in Wales but bred in Bristol, 'speaks in that dialect' yet George Browning, a shoemaker by trade, who was born in Bristol spoke 'good English'. Abraham Matthews was also born in the west of England 'but speaks pretty good English' and despite her West Country birth, Elizabeth Tizard spoke 'plain'.[62] Some West Country and northern transports were natives of other regions, such as John Sergentson, who spoke the Yorkshire dialect but had been sentenced to transportation in Northumberland, and John Bishop who though transported from Dorset spoke 'in the Shropshire accent'. Sentenced in Somerset in 1762 was Richard Stevens; he was described as 'Prussian born' and spoke 'broken English'.[63] Some north-eastern men were taken for Scotsmen or 'those born on the borders'.[64] Other features also elicited comment.

John Hardy, a Lancashire transportee, talked 'very hoarse', Joseph Loveday, a West Country-man had 'a very squeaking voice' while his fellow runaway Tynie Roach possessed 'a smoothe insinuating tongue'.[65]

References to physical infirmities suggest that many convicts had suffered injuries when young or in fights or at work. Matthew Gallop, arriving from Dorset only six weeks previously, was described as having 'a crack under the tip of his nose'. Thomas Dyer had 'a large scar on inside of one of his legs'. John Crayton who ran away from Patapsco Neck in 1766 had 'a large scar upon his right leg, a little below the knee'; William James had a 'large scar on one of his knees'. George Browning was 'lame in one knee', the advertisement maintained, 'which makes him walk with a stick'.[66] George Newton walked 'clumsily' but Joseph Loveday had his knee disjointed 'when he was a boy'.[67] Edward Rose has 'a sore on the outside of his leg occasioned by a cut with a reep hook'.[68] William Boyce or Boyle's 'middle finger of his right hand [was] straight'. John Bishop, who ran off with Edward Hooper (who was wearing an iron collar), had 'a remarkable scar on his left hand'. John Blandford had 'the first joint of the forefinger of [the] left hand just lately cut off'.[69] Abraham Matthews 'had lost [the] end of one finger'.[70] Other 'peculiar marks' were also noted. William Kneller, it was reported 'has a remarkably large Knot on the Joint of one of his great Toes'. John Williams had 'a great blemish in one of his eyes' while Richard Williams had 'two small scars just above one of his eyes'.[71] Other distinctive features though not abnormalities were noted such as Rees Price's 'very long nose' and William Snow's 'very hooked nose'.[72] There was no reference, however, to Bristol convict Jeremiah Jones of whom it was noted at his trial that he had one leg.[73] Numerous advertisements noted that a convict servant had suffered from smallpox. John Wrigley imported into Virginia on the *Litchfield* in 1748, a transportee from Hampshire, was described as 'pock fretten'. George Browning was described as 'pitted with the Smallpox', Andrew Young, a Northumberland transport was 'pock pitted' but John Booker from Lancashire was only 'a little marked with the smallpox'; John Libiter alias Leadbetter with whom he ran away was 'marked with the smallpox'.[74]

Convict servants could best express their individuality in the use of personal adornments and how they dressed their hair. Only one man, John Monroe, who had been transported from Northumberland, wore a wig, presumably to keep alive his claims to status as an apothecary. Thomas Lamprey, a woolcomber from Somerset, wore his own hair, that was 'if not taken off since he went away'. His hair was 'of a fair colour, and [he] took great pride in it'.[75] Most men were clean shaven but Robert

Mills who arrived from Wiltshire was described as having a 'full black beard and very hairy on the breast'. John Ansell, transported from Hampshire, had a 'large black beard and black eyes'. Samuel Watts from Somerset had 'very red hair' and a beard. Daniel Unthank had 'little or no beard' but did possess 'fine shirts'. Daniel Peters, it was remarked, had 'one good white shirt and an old felt hat'.[76] Few went so far as Elisha Bond, transported from Devon in 1746, who had 'GB' marked 'with gunpowder on his right hand'.[77]

Demeanour and character were crudely assessed. Elizabeth Tizard had a 'stooping walk' whereas Elizabeth Loyd 'stoops very much in her walking'.[78] George Gale brought over from Dorset in 1756 was credited with 'a heavy clownish look', John Sergentson was 'a bold impudent sly fellow', Robert Pearce 'a sly roguish fellow', William Kneller 'a pert saucy fellow', Robert Mills 'a pert talkative fellow' and Andrew Young 'was an impudent fellow'.[79] John Wrigley, on the other hand, was 'a great rogue', John Bishop, a Dorset transportee, it was supposed, was 'a great villain' though James Sartain who ran away from Richard Croxall's iron works at Elk Ridge had 'a down look and a lubberly walk'.[80] Anthony Densley who ran away from Frederick Town was 'pretty much addicted to drinking and swearing'. Some were literate like George Browning who could write 'a blotched hand' and many were skilled.[81]

Returning and being at large

Only two of the 125 convicts advertised as running away in the colonies from northern England and the West Country are known to have returned to England. Yet, in the regions of northern England and the West Country which sent more than 5,000 convicts to the colonies, at least a further thirty-five men and women were prosecuted at the assize courts for infringing the terms of their sentences. They had either returned prematurely from transportation, not left at all or, in a small number of cases, had left but never arrived. Of these thirty-five prosecutions, twenty were for 'returning' and a further fifteen were for 'being at large' within the period for which they were transported (see Table 5.3). None of these people were ever advertised as running away in the colonies, which raises the question of whether they escaped before they could be sold in the manner described by Poulter.

John Hockaday, found guilty of petty larceny at Devon quarter sessions in January 1765 and sentenced to seven years in the American plantations, does not fit Poulter's model.[82] He was in the colonies long enough to acquire a master, Michael Earle of Sassafrass Neck, Cecil

Table 5.3 Prosecutions for transportation offences
1718–76

	'At Large'	'Returned'	Total
Western Circuit	8	5	13
Bristol	0	2	2
Lancashire	3	3	6
North East	4	5	9
North West	0	5	5
Total	15	20	35

County, Maryland, in whose employ he seems to have remained for
about a year. Earle wanted him back. The man identified in the advertisements was no longer a young man, his age was given as forty.
In appearance, he was described as a 'low squat fellow' with a 'fair
complexion' and bald.[83] Hockaday must have worked his passage back
or secured the funds by some means or other to pay for his passage.
Convicts returning to England found it difficult to get work and Hockaday, it appears, turned to robbery.[84] He was apprehended in Bristol in
1767 for the theft of a sacrificial silver flaggon valued at £10 from the
church of Newton St Cyres, thus becoming answerable on two capital
charges. Brought to Exeter by a writ of *habeas corpus*, Hockaday was condemned to death and quickly executed.[85] He was no John Poulter. At
his execution, it was reported in the *Exeter Flying Post*, 'he seemed sen-
sible of his unhappy situation, but would make no confession either of
his accomplices or manner of returning from transportation'.[86] William
Elliott, a Cumberland horse thief transported in March 1772, was the
only other known example of a runaway advertised in the colonial press
who returned. Judged by the interval between his transportation and
the appearance and nature of this runaway advertisement in the *Virginia Gazette*, Elliott's escape and return may be the only one that comes
close to matching the method identified by Poulter in his *Discoveries*.
Along with fellow Cumberland transportee John Usher, Elliott fled from
a snow at Port Royal, Virginia, on the Rappahannock River, quite possibly before he had been delivered to his prospective owner.[87] Poulter's
claim that successful returners entered port, transferred to another
vessel and sailed back again across the Atlantic required resources and
may be truer of members of well-organized gangs, especially those
leaving from and returning to London (as in the case of Mary Young,

alias Jane Webb, alias Jenny Diver), from where complaints about returners were most vocal.[88] Something similar may also have occurred in the case of one north-east gang (in effect, married couples, their children and partners) who were transported and successfully returned, though not to the north of England.[89]

Returning from transportation before one's time had expired was a capital offence and for those already reprieved from the gallows once, a second gift of mercy was problematic.[90] But prosecuting an individual for allegedly returning from transportation required certain legal niceties to be observed.[91] Evidence had to be produced that the person before the court had been transported and that he or she had been found guilty of the crime for which they were supposedly transported. Evidence from a contractor or ship's captain, and a landing certificate from a naval officer in the plantations were sufficient for the first and from gaolers, victims and witnesses for the second.[92] Apart from William Elliott, two other men on trial in our regions are known to have returned after serving a portion of their sentence in servitude and their accounts of their arrival are quite different from Poulter's. On the eve of his execution, William Cudmore, transported from Devon in 1749, related how

> the Captain who carried him to Maryland, kept him on board and never let him land, but sold him to another Captain belonging to Boston, whose ship being sold, he was set at Liberty. He made several Trips to and from Bristol, but was unfortunately apprehended by an intimate Acquaintance who pretended Friendship to him; which treacherous Action, he said, had been a great Grief to his Soul, and the Loss of his Life.[93]

Samuel Drayton, removed from Gloucestershire in 1773, told a different story. Having set sail, the Captain and Surgeon

> seeing my good behaviour, indulged me with my liberty; and said as the time of my banishment was not specified, there could be no danger in my returning again to *England*. With this encouragement I returned with them to *New York*, where the merchants gave me three dollars and I wrought for my passage home.[94]

Of those sentenced to transportation or reprieved on condition of transportation, four categories of convicts were at risk in eighteenth-century England. There were those like John Poulter and John Hockaday who having returned, offended again and were bought before the assizes on capital charges. Then there were those who were picked up and prosecuted as returned transportees who had not, at least as far as we can tell, committed further offences. A third group were not technically returners at all but men and women who had succeeded in temporarily escaping from custody and continued to evade their punishment by remaining 'at large'. A final group comprised those who, having embarked for the colonies, encountered difficulties at sea which frustrated, at least temporarily, the purpose for which they had embarked.

In the first group, known transportees who had returned prematurely and reoffended, three of the four, John Poulter at Ilchester (Somerset), John Hockaday at Exeter (Devon) and Daniel Haynes at Bristol were hanged, but the fourth, William Elliott, mentioned above, escaped execution though initially condemned to death. Of the four, Poulter had previously been sentenced to fourteen years' transportation at the Old Bailey for receiving, and Hockaday was given a seven-year sentence for petty larceny; but Elliott and Haynes, both younger men, had received the death penalty for their original crimes of horse stealing and house breaking only to be pardoned on condition of transportation for fourteen years.[95] Elliott returned to the area where his father lived and moved among people with whom he was familiar, but when yeoman Robert Walters lost a chestnut gelding from his stable in December 1772, he suspected Elliott, whom he described as 'a person of a loose and disorderly way of life', was responsible. Recovering the animal from Northumberland, Walters refused Elliott's offer of payment for 'riding' the gelding, preferring instead to prosecute. In his examination Elliott admitted that 'he made free to take the said gelding out of the said Robert Walters stable', Walters 'being his relation' and having occasion 'to fetch some Cloaths from Newcastle'. Sentenced to death for a second time in 1773, Elliott was again reprieved on condition of transportation. Presumably some favourable circumstances were demonstrated on his behalf.[96]

Daniel Haynes, otherwise known as Thomas Stephens, was not so lucky. He was executed on the gallows at St Michael's Hill in 1775 for burgling a dwelling house in Bristol belonging to Levi Ames Esq. in Bristol. In the light of his execution, *Felix Farley's Bristol Journal* furnished the public with his biography. '[T]hough young, now but 21 years of age', it was reported, 'he was old in iniquity'. He was a native of Worcester, 'and of reputable parents' and a sadler by trade. Together with an accomplice, he had broken into twenty-one houses before justice caught up with him. He was sentenced to death but reprieved for fourteen years' transportation. In America he pursued the same wicked course of life. He was convicted of a robbery in Philadelphia, sentenced to death but reprieved owing to some disclosure he made on condition he would leave the province. Meeting up with his old accomplice, they agreed to return to England by the first ship. Shortly after their arrival, Haynes came alone to Bristol where he committed the robbery for which he suffered the death sentence. His execution attracted large crowds:

> He was attended to the place of execution by two clergymen, where he prayed very devoutly, acknowledged the justness of his sentence, and met his fate with a becoming resignation. An incredible number of spectators were assembled on this melancholy occasion, whom he earnestly exorted to take warning by his unhappy exit, and to shun bad company, particularly that of lewd women.[97]

Even if they did not reoffend, those prosecuted for returning from transportation were liable to be condemned to death. Between 1749 and 1771 there were thirty-one people sentenced to death at the Old Bailey and between 1755 and 1775 six death sentences were handed down in the Midland Circuit and seventeen in the Home Circuit. These figures, however, do not indicate the numbers actually hanged.[98] It may have been easier to condemn those who were taken up for returning in a jurisdiction other than the one from which they were transported, where they were less well known or not known at all. Certainly this was true of two of the men hanged in Bristol for returning. One of these men, William Curtis, was a former hangman whose death sentence in 1740 at Gloucester assizes, for stealing goods valued at £8 from a Scottish pedlar, was commuted to transportation for fourteen years.[99] Having returned before his time, Curtis was passing Bristol's Newgate gaol when

> seeing his Prosecutor at the Debtors Grate, began to upbraid him in a very opprobious Manner, telling him, *You are in the Inside, but I am Without*; upon which the said Andrew bid him go away, otherwise he would be taken up, upon which he went away. But on Monday last the infatuated Transport repeated his Visit, and gave Three Half-Pence to Andrew to drink; but on going off, Andrew called to him and said, *Will you not shake Hands?* to which Curtis readily complied. Upon shak [ing] Hands, Andrew kept him fast to the Grate, and Assist [ance] coming up, he was secured and clapt into Prison . . . [100]

The peddlar was well revenged. Committed to Newgate, Curtis was sentenced to death by the Bristol court 'for feloniously returning from Transportation' and duly executed.[101]

While Curtis, it might be argued, was foolhardy, William Cudmore was betrayed. At his trial in Bristol for returning early from transportation, Cudmore declared that both he and his father were innocent of the crime for which they had been condemned at Exeter assizes in August 1749 – stealing a roan mare. His father 'suffer'd death for the same at Heavy-Tree Gallows' but his own sentence was respited 'on account of his Youth' and he was sent for transportation.[102] Cudmore sought desperately to cheat the hangman. It was reported in the *Bristol Weekly Intelligencer* that he was unlikely to survive until the day appointed for his execution. Feigning illness, Cudmore sawed off his irons and made a hole in the wall of the condemned room, but the scheme came to nought when, visited by one of the debtors, his irons were found 'conceal'd in his Bed'.[103] Samuel Drayton, like Cudmore and Curtis, was tried as a returned transportee in a jurisdiction other than the one where he had been convicted and sentenced, but unlike Cudmore, he confessed to the crime, committed in Gloucestershire, that had led to his transportation two years earlier.[104] Drayton appears to have survived his return without recourse to theft until he was picked up in Sherborne. With half a crown from the captain with whom he sailed into Liverpool, he had travelled to Wolverhampton where 'with what cash he had', he laid out 19 shillings for the purchase of a quantity of buckles. At Bristol he acquired a quantity of linen goods from his 'old dealer', and travelled about the country visiting markets and fairs. When taken up in Sherborne, he was found with a pistol in his possession, which he claimed to carry for self-defence but which probably did him no good despite his protestations that he had 'neither robbed, nor designed to rob any person since my return from sea'. And although 'an ill-natured world' might magnify his faults, his violations of the laws of his country were 'but few and small'.[105]

Similarly, William Brown was sentenced to transportation in one county, and condemned to death and executed for returning in a neighbouring one. Commonly known as 'Sir' William Brown, he had been convicted of sheep stealing in County Durham in 1741 but was back by January 1743. Expecting to be transported again at his trial in Northumberland, no one was more surprised than he when he was sentenced to death. His outburst in court, if not his family connections which were viewed as extensive and menacing, probably denied him all possibilty of a reprieve. On learning of his sentence, he earnestly begged to be transported again but when the judge failed to heed his plea, 'he broke out into all the opprobrious language he could think of against both the judge and the whole court, and wished that G-d Almighty might d-m their Souls to H-ll'.[106] Little time elapsed between sentencing and execution. Clearly the authorities wanted rid of Brown. Not only did they allow little time to elapse between sentencing and execution, but fearful lest his criminal family mount an attempt to rescue him, they called on the military for assistance. The *Newcastle Courant* recorded how

> On Monday Morning, the noted Sir William Brown was executed at the Westgate, near this Place, by the Judge's Order. Notwithstanding his former obstinate and harden'd Temper, the short Warning he had to prepare for Death, occasion'd in him a sudden Remorse, which was very visible in all his Actions; and, being attended by the Vicar, at the Place of Execution, he express'd a great Concern for his past wicked Life, and seem'd very penitent, ask'd Pardon for his rude Behaviour after he receiv'd his Sentence, and told the Vicar that he was very sorry for it, declar'd he died a Member of the Church of England, and desir'd the Prayers of all Spectators. The two Companies of Col. Price's (late General Clayton's) Regiment, quarter'd here, guarded him from the Castle, and were likewise drawn out at the Place of Execution, for fear of his being rescued.[107]

John Morris alias Hambledon also fits the pattern of the hanged transport. Convicted in Middlesex in May 1769 and sentenced to transportation, he was shipped out in August aboard the *Douglas*. Picked up in Wiltshire, he was sentenced to death as a returned transportee in 1771.[108]

Most of those prosecuted for returning, though initially sentenced to death, were usually reprieved on condition of being transported again, this time for fourteen years or for life. Of six known returners in Lancashire, not one was executed. William Mordue was prosecuted as a returned transportee in 1750, sentenced to death at the Lancashire assizes and reprieved for fourteen years.[109] Jonathan Darbyshire, a weaver from Flixton in Lancashire, had been sentenced to a term of seven years' transportation at the quarter sessions in 1761. How long he spent in Virginia or Maryland is not known, but in 1764 he appeared before the Lancashire assizes charged with returning before his term had expired. He was sentenced to death but reprieved on condition of being retransported for a period of fourteen years.[110] In the autumn of 1764 he was back in the Chesapeake and employed by Enoch Magruder in

Prince George County, Maryland, from whom he ran away after a short period.[111] Peter Parr, a Warrington weaver, received the death sentence for returning but was reprieved and transported for life.[112] Edmund Cooper, a weaver of Middleton, was sentenced to seven years' transportation at the Lancashire quarter sessions in March 1767 and indicted at the Lancashire assizes for returning from transportation in the summer of 1768. There was insufficient evidence to convict him of the offence and he was ordered to remain in gaol until he could be transported according to his former sentence.[113]

Those prosecuted for 'being at large' were likely to have escaped from gaol or evaded their punishment by some other means. Awaiting transportation in Newgate, Bristol, John Cope escaped. John Poulter, under sentence of death, broke out of the gaol in Ilchester. Mary Low, cast for transportation in Durham, got out of Durham gaol. John Gibson sawed off his chains and fled the vessel that had carried him from Berwick to London while the master of the vessel was at Grays Inn finalizing arrangements for his voyage to the plantations.[114] Mass breakouts also occurred in some gaols among those awaiting transportation, but few seem to have escaped permanently. John Cope's original offence was neither highway robbery nor animal theft but grand larceny, yet he was hanged, in his case, for being at large before the expiration of the term for which he was ordered transported. Cope had been convicted at the Bristol assizes held in May 1761 of stealing three mahogany boards and given a seven-year sentence.[115] While awaiting transportation, Cope along with two other transportees, Abraham Smith and William Hicks, 'by forcing the Staple on the Door of the Apartment where they were confined and by the Assistance of Files and a Scaling Ladder, that they had found Means to procure the Day before' contrived their escape from Newgate. Cope alone was retaken a few days later at Bath 'and in the Evening brought back to his old Lodgings'.[116] Presumably, Cope's failed attempt to evade his lawful punishment for his former offence precluded his reprieve for the latter. For women desperate to avoid transportation, escaping from gaol was preferable to flight from the plantations. A Newcastle hawker Mary Low, convicted of picking the pocket of a local farmer in the market place in Durham, escaped from Durham gaol with the help of her husband only to be taken up again and condemned to death. In a rare expression of sympathy, the *Newcastle Courant* lamented her fate. '[S]he is the mother of six children the oldest not 14, and the rest under nine years of age which are left to the charge of her disconsolate husband'.[117] But Mary Low, it turned out, was no first-time offender succumbing to a sudden impulse or driven by necessity, being identified by Alderman Hewitt as a key member of a network of thieves and robbers who were active across large parts of the three kingdoms.[118] Eleanor Connor had similar credentials. Found guilty of pickpocketing in Bristol, she had been initially sentenced to death and reprieved for transportation in 1748. Having saved her life as a result of one appeal, it was unlikely she would overturn the order for her transportation by making another to the same quarter. Consequently, she wrote to the Archbishop of Canterbury pleading that 'should she be transported into a strange Country', never seeing her children again would be 'next to Death itself'.[119] When this failed, according to Poulter, she 'bribed some of the Ship's Crew lying in the Transport Hole, Bristol'.[120]

Then there were those whose ships encountered disaster at sea, mutiny on board or else were intercepted en route by privateers. The *Esther* was one of two vessels taken by two French privateers 'of 30 guns and 250 men each, 12 Leagues off Shutland' in 1745, having taken the northern route to the American plantations (see Chapter 3).[121] *Felix Farley's Bristol Journal* reported in 1761 that the *Atlas* sailing from Bristol to Maryland 'with several Convicts from this City, Gloucester, etc, was taken about a Week after she sailed which was the 18th past, by a Bayonne Privateer of 8 Carriage Guns and 120 Men about 250 leagues to the westward of Capellear, and sent for St Sebastian's'. The privateer also took two other vessels.

In late June a Bristol newspaper carried a London report on the fate of some convicts:

> The English Convicts lately taken by a French Privateer, and carried into Vigo, Spain, had Liberty to disperse and seek Employment among the Galicians, but being totally ignorant of the Spanish Language, they repaired in a Body to Portugal and committed such Outrages there that Mr Whitehead our Consul at Oporto, found it necessary to take them up, and send them on board the Fleet lately arrived.

Some were subsequently shipped to the Chesapeake from London on the *Neptune* in April 1763.[122] In 1769 a group of northeastern felons on board the *Caesar* were shipwrecked in the English Channel off the coast of Kent on the more familiar southern route. One of them, Robert Bilton from Northumberland, was found at York where, it was reported by the Secretary of State, he had 'behaved himself very well, as hath been humbly certified' by the local authorities. Others such as Durham man

William Smith were pardoned on condition of entering the armed services. The main body of convicts were detained in custody to await another vessel but in the end none of the convicts were transported. The men were enlisted in the army and the navy and the women received a free pardon.[123]

Mutinies tended to occur when conditions on board had already deteriorated due to bad weather or when voyages were unusually long, rations went short and water became undrinkable or exhausted. When sentenced to transportation for the first time James Dalton was shipped aboard the *Honour* for the plantations. Called on to assist the crew of twelve in heavy seas, twenty of the convicts took control of the vessel and directed it to Spain where they disembarked for Vigo. Despite the captain's efforts to retrieve them, Dalton and eight others sailed from Oporto for Amsterdam on board a Dutch man-of-war while eight others left on an English ship for the same destination.[124] In 1764 the *Albion* with a cargo of felons from Bristol only reached the colonies on its third attempt. On the first voyage it was driven back to port 'thro' contrary winds' by which time one convict Mary Jones was dead. On the second voyage, a plot to take over the vessel 'and carry her into Spain' was discovered. 'They had got off their irons with the help of a blacksmith who was one of their number' *Felix Farley's Bristol Journal* reported. One man was shot in the leg, another in the arm. On return to Bristol they were carried to the infirmary and the vessel departed for the third time.

> The Vessel is since sailed again, having got Iron Collars as a farther Security for a Set of such Desperadoes. Tis said there were upwards of 80 sworn to support each other, and to destroy the Crew, which doubtless would have been the Case, had not one of them timely discovered the whole Scene of Villainy.[125]

Another Bristol ship the *Randolph* carrying convicts to the Chesapeake in 1769 was wrecked near Cape Henry and its cargo fled, though many were later recovered.[126]

For the most part transportation proved a largely efficient way of ridding England of those found guilty of felony, whether they were male or female, seasoned criminals, occasional offenders, first-timers, or young thieves. And despite some breast-beating, especially over the perceived crisis over law and order at mid-century, the government of the day failed to take into consideration (although the judge at Poulter's trial had recommended it) the plan that transportee had so artfully proposed in his *Discoveries* 'to prevent any Convict coming back before

their limited Time is out', esssentially by taking a bond from ship's captains not to free any on arrival, and for a register of the names of those
proposing to leave the colonies to be published before sailing and for
the governor to certify that those leaving were not convicts.[127] That no
national system was ever adopted was not because agreement on one
could not be reached but rather because the extent of the problem did
not seem to justify it.

6
Panics and Recriminations: Convergence and Divergence and the Criminal Atlantic

It is clear that convict transportation after 1718 involved a massive effort by the authorities in both England and the colonies. The London government maintained expensive subsidies for shipping felons, and local counties and regions entered into similar, often long-term, arrangements. Equally important were the common interest in criminals which this trade generated, and the exchange of news and cultural representations associated with it. The overall impact on both societies, however, is difficult to gauge. As Bailyn writes, 'how deeply the experience of transportation entered into the consciousness of eighteenth-century Britons and into the fabric of British society and culture can only be surmised, but the evidence of a profound impact abounds'. As we have seen, the visible evidence of 'coffles of manacled prisoners marching through the early-morning streets of London to the Thames or across the English countryside to pens in harbour prisons to await shipment', reports of the transatlantic voyages and accounts of the conditions of work in the 'plantations', indeed the imagery of virtual slavery in the colonies, were all deeply embedded in popular consciousness.[1] In the colonies themselves, the purchase of convicts became a routine part of the acquisition of long-service unfree labour in the eighteenth century, despite the misgivings of the local authorities in the previous century. Convicts were relatively cheap to acquire, and involved only a little additional surveillance to that devoted to slaves and other servants. As the previous chapter has shown, colonial society was in some ways already set up to control unfree labour, to detect and recapture runaways. From the start, however, there were some doubts as to the consequences of such a policy. If some colonies such as Maryland tried to prevent a flood of Catholics by levying five pounds per head for each 'recusant' who would not take the oath of loyalty on landing, then the arrival of so many convicts was likely to provoke even more serious misgivings.[2] For example, between the first and the second edition of his history of Virginia – by 1722 in fact – Robert Beverley had changed his views from welcoming convicts to alleging that Virginia had suffered 'many Murthers and Robberies' since the 1718 Transportation Act, which he claimed were 'the effect of that new Law of England'. He was not alone, as William Bradford commented in the *American Weekly Mercury* in 1721 of the westward spread of the colonies:

> In these Western Parts . . . it is the Desire of our Legislators . . . [that] all possible Care is taken to cultivate and encourage Morality and Industry, that our Sovereign King *George* may find a plentiful Territory and ample Strength and Happiness from our Colonies . . . But by these Ways of transporting villains amongst such a flourishing People, is to less[en] our Improvements and Industry, by filling the Vacancies of honest Men with tricking, thieving and designing rogues, who will hardly be brought to get their Livelihood by such laborious and settled Means; the ill Consequences of which would without doubt be remedied in Great Britain, were they as sensible of 'em as we who are made so by living amongst them.[3]

Yet an unresolved ambivalence towards convicts persisted throughout the colonial period. The economic advantages, their length of service, relative cheapness during it, and above all the way that their price could be negotiated, varying according to their personal qualities and criminality, meant that they were always in demand. As Farley Grubb has demonstrated in his analysis of the 'spot market' for convicts at their landing in the Chesapeake, the advantages for potential purchasers lay in the way that factors of health, gender, age and criminality all combined to allow considerable scope for bargaining a good (low) price for labour. There would always be some who wanted that kind of worker, as Beverley had bitterly commented. Meanwhile, there was also considerable opposition to convicts being imported at all, particularly from those who did not wish to employ them.[4] It is worth noting that even among the enthusiasts for British development of the colonies, such as Malachy Postlethwayt, there were some doubts about convict transportation. He noted that there were 'prodigious numbers of vagabonds' in England, 'who live no one knows how', as well as petty criminals:

> Many people are daily convicted of small crimes, and, from the ignominy of the conviction and punishment, rendered desperate,

and come to the gallows: it would certainly be good policy, as well as charity, to put them in the way of honest labour, before they become superlatively wicked.

However, he was very anxious that they should be sent abroad to America 'not like transports or negroes', but importantly with 'nothing in it of shame, and as little of compulsion as may be', so that they would be willing and productive labourers for the colonists. He was one of the few English commentators in the middle of the eighteenth century to acknowledge the possible damage to colonial society of importing a criminalized class of unfree workers.[5]

In the analysis here, we aim to explore the dynamics of this ambivalence during the colonial period from 1718 to the Revolution. We provide somewhat artificial groupings of attitudes to convicts, varieties of convict narratives and their implicit messages: they are separated into three distinctive periods or phases, which must be conceived as occurring in only a rough historical order. They overlap in time, and included some of the same personnel, but are distinguishable largely by their different emphasis and direction of argument. The first was what can be called the 'foundation myth' of transportation, the myth of both the dominance of serious criminals and of their return. Many in Britain held that most criminals went out to America and returned with ease if they wished. Some of the most famous examples of the narratives supporting this contention have been explored in Chapters 4 and 5. This was accompanied by the parallel and essentially similar American view that the colonies had imported a criminal class (though that is not a word they used) which was having deleterious consequences for colonial society. Such threats to both England and America were, in this period, deemed containable. The second phase, however, consisted of the shared crisis in the middle of the century as crime appeared to be out of hand on both sides of the Atlantic, and the punishment of transportation was evaluated in terms of its consequences for both Britain and America. At this time, there was a kind of mutual panic in the transatlantic world, in which both sides recognized a shared problem of crime. Severe measures were taken in England and in the colonies, and both societies seemed to suffer a kind of common shock at the criminality in their midst. The third period was more complex, involving the use of mutual accusations of criminality by both British and Americans to denigrate each other, firstly at the end of the colonial period and then in the Revolution. Criminality became intertwined in the increasingly hostile construction of the 'other', the British for their part creating an American identity of a people made up of slave-drivers and convicts, and the newly self-identified 'Americans' deploying moral judgements as an essential part of the denunciation of the criminally oppressive policies pursued by the British government. Antipathetic national identities were thus constructed on the basis of the *criminal* other. The British denigration of the Americans which followed the Revolution therefore had a precursor in the late colonial period, one in which criminal transportation played a central part.[6] This final phase consequently marked the end of a time when shared perceptions and the exchange of news constructed common images and discourses about convicts. A common interest in crime was replaced by a mutual exchange of accusations of criminality.

The foundation myth

Whether true or not, the legendary ability of some criminals to escape punishment and return was well established within twenty years of the 1718 Transportation Act, occasioning questions to be raised at the highest levels of government. That the problem of returning transportees should be prominently discussed in London is hardly surprising in the light of the numbers transported from the capital and its role in the transatlantic trade. Given the volume of goods and people packed into the metropolis, the concentration of taverns and alehouses and the market for stolen goods, it 'was undoubtedly easier to sustain a criminal career of any type in London', as Beattie has remarked, 'where victims and receivers were more plentiful and surveillance less obtrusive and intense'.[7] With its many newspapers and large, diverse print industry, stories of criminals and their return would be given wide currency. In 1728, the chairman of the sessions of the peace for Middlesex was informed that:

> His M[ajes]ty being very much concerned at the frequent Robberys of late committed in the streets of London, Westminster, & parts adjacent, & being informed that they are greatly to be imputed to the unlawful return of Felons Convict, who have been transported to his M[ajes]tys Plantations, has been graciously pleased for the better discovering and apprehending of such Felons to give orders to the Lords Commissioners of his M[ajes]tys Treasury to be caused to be paid to any person or persons, who before the first day of March next shall discover any of them so as they may be apprehended and brought to Justice, a reward of forty pounds for each felon convict

returned, or that shall return from Transportation, before the expiration of the term for which he or she was transported, who shall by the means of such discovery be brought to condign Punishment.[8]

Certainly this picture was already part of the literary representation of criminals, particularly in the year of *The Beggar's Opera*, and, as seen in earlier chapters, part of their image in biographies, last dying speeches and news reports. Perhaps convicts learnt that return was a real possibility, and could plausibly use the threat of it in bargaining with the authorities. In 1740, Somerset man Thomas Pope, arrested for burgling the dwelling house of John Bacon and stealing three gold rings and about nineteen shillings in money, threatened Bacon (the prosecutor) with the words 'they can but transport me and if they do, I'll be back in a 12 month'. He tried to persuade his victim to drop the case if the property was returned. This incident unknowingly confirmed Henry Fielding's allegation that many criminals learnt from each other – in his words, that they learnt their 'intrepidity' by hero-worshipping the examples broadcast by the press and made famous by their performances on the gallows.[9]

On the other side of the Atlantic, another myth was taking shape, one that was presaged in the writings of Beverly and Bradford in the 1720s – that of the convict as a 'vile offender', a murderer, robber, rapist or embezzler condemned to the gallows but reprieved on condition of banishment. Yet as Beattie observes, and his judgement is confirmed by the data we have collected from very different regions of England (see Chapter 3), what the Transportation Act accomplished was not the expulsion of the serious malefactor from Britain's shores but that of the non-capital offender, mostly involved in petty crimes. Expelled from England and Wales, Ireland and Scotland, these convicts were to contribute to the increase in population in the colonies – it was hoped that they 'might be the means of *improving* and making the said colonies and plantations *more useful* to *his majesty*'. In theory, they could be sent to any part of the American colonies but in reality they went only to the Chesapeake, to either Virginia or Maryland. Convicts moved one way and tobacco the other (see Chapter 2). And despite the fact that the overwhelming majority of convicts were non-capital offenders, colonial discourse regarded the reprieved felons – the lucky 'gallows birds' – as typical of the whole.[10]

The authorities in Virginia and Maryland were no less disturbed at receiving convicts in bulk than was His Majesty's government in learning of their propensity to return to the capital. Responses varied. At the local level, one Maryland county clerk copied out the core sections of the Transportation Act into the county order book, along with the names of the first convict arrivals. At a higher level, the colony's legislators moved quickly in 1719 to require those purchasing convicts to give security for their good behaviour but the ambivalence of the upper house over the legality of the bill led to its failure.[11] The Virginia response came in an Act passed in 1722 concerning servants and slaves and 'for the better government of convicts' that attached so many liabilities to their entry and sale that it amounted to a virtual prohibition.[12] Already, it was claimed 'of late yeares many persons Convicted of Felonies and other notorious Crimes in Great Britain', who had been transported into Virginia, were responsible for 'many Cruel murders and frequent Thefts and Robberies . . . whereby the Lives and Estates of his Majesties good Subjects are in great danger'.[13] Under the 1722 Act, convicts were not to be allowed ashore until or unless they were sold; their numbers and names were to be registered on entry by those bringing them into the colony, and again, along with the reason for their transportation, at county courts by their purchasers. The latter were required to enter into a recognizance with security for the convict's good behaviour.[14] Provision was also made for a number of eventualities. For a first offence commited in the colony, a justice of the peace was to order a convict 'whipped naked', but thereafter the master, mistress or overseer of such a convict could on the commission of a subsequent crime 'strip and whip such Convict, without any further order and without being liable to any penalty for so doing'. Servants who ran away were expected to serve an extra six months, or even longer, depending on circumstances. Since the problem of convicts was envisioned as colony-wide, the legislators made provision not only for a copy of the Act to by sent to and publicly displayed by all Collectors and Naval Officers but to the courts of each county which were to cause the Act 'to be read publicly at the Court house door of their respective Counties in the months of April and May yearly'. The Act was disallowed by the Privy Council.[15] In the 1730s, Virginians perceived themselves to be under threat from rising levels of crime which they attributed to the number of convicts in their midst. In 1732, Virginia's attorney general, John Clayton, sought an increase in salary in line with the growing volume of criminal business. Matthew Kemp, clerk of the General Court, sought higher renumeration on the same grounds one year later, while in 1737 the Virginia Assembly raised the fees of the Rev. William Dawson, who accompanied condemned prisoners to the gallows, on account of the increased demand for his services.[16] Even if evidence for the extent of this crime wave is thin, these measures taken as a whole reflect a level of heightened anxiety in official circles about the problems posed by the importation of convicts. However, almost every attempt to control their entry, or raise the level of security demanded of the shippers, provoked fierce opposition from the merchants.[17]

The legislatures of Maryland and Virginia continued to reconsider or reform the legal status of convicts throughout the colonial period. Alan Atkinson has argued that although convicts were treated much like indentured servants in both Maryland and Virginia for the first half of the period between the passage of the Transportation Act and the American Revolution, in the second 'there was a tendency to assimilate convicts, in principle, with slaves rather than with ordinary indentured servants', but it is difficult to perceive such a sharp distinction between one period and the next and his explanation that new legal measures were due 'to a new concern with the moral basis of citizenship' is open to question.[18] Attempts to redefine the legal status of the convict in Virginia law are evident well before the last decades of the colonial period and have their origin in local factors in the Northern Neck of Virginia.

Situated between the Rappahannock and Potomac Rivers, the Northern Neck received numerous convicts in the 1720s and 1730s. Governor Gooch described the area in 1732 as:

> remote from the seat of government, where the common people are generally of a more turbulent and unruly disposition than anywhere else, and are not like to become better by being the place of all this Dominion where most of the transported convicts are sold and settled.[19]

The region was also the centre of opposition to the Tobacco Inspection Act adopted in 1730 which saw some public warehouses burnt to the ground in protest.[20] Petitions to the House of Burgesses from the lower counties of the Northern Neck and the south side of the Rappahannock River began at this time. The earliest petitions emanated from Westmoreland and Richmond counties in 1730 and 1732 and were most likely prompted by the spectacular fire that consumed the Mount Pleasant home of Colonel Thomas Lee, Collector of the Potomac, in Westmoreland County, a disaster which was widely attributed to convicts, though this was never proven.[21] News of the outrage appeared in the *Maryland Gazette* – there was no Virginia newspaper at the time – and a public reward was offered for information leading to the apprehension of the culprits.[22] Informing the Board of Trade of the occurrence, Gooch was convinced that it was linked to Lee's dealing with convicts as a justice of the peace and sought compensation from the home government for his losses.[23] Two years before, at an examining court in Richmond County, convict servant John Hesrook, a former horse thief, confessed to the murder of his master and mistress and was committed to Williamsburg for trial. He had robbed the house with a view to securing passage aboard a vessel sailing to England.[24] Nothing short of a miracle could save him from the hangman. The threat of convict violence was therefore not entirely imaginary.

The Richmond-Westmoreland petitions sought to restrict the movement of convicts and to encourage masters to discover their crimes and bring them to justice, but they also sought to give county courts jurisdiction similar to that already enjoyed in the case of slaves charged with capital offences.[25] The bills failed and the only successful measure to get through the Assembly was one in 1738 that denied convicts the right to a jury of the vicinage, substituting in its place a jury of 'bystanders'. The change was advocated on the grounds that it was 'burthensome and expensive to the public, as well as grievous to many of his majesty's good subjects, who live in the remote counties'. The Act also claimed that 'most of the felonies, and other capital offences committed in this colony, are perpetrated and done by persons who have been convicted of felony, or other crimes in Great Britain, or Ireland'.[26]

Although the 1722 Virginia Act sought to constrict the actions of sellers off the boats, and specified the responsibilities of buyers for the behaviour of convict servants as well as rules for their punishment, it did not equate convicts with slaves. A Maryland grand jury meeting one year later did so when, contemplating the impact of convicts on servants and slaves, its members expressed the fears that the example of the former would lead the latter 'into the same Wicked Practices'.[27] Rather than the moral dilemma which Atkinson raises, a more likely explanation for the desire of colonial planters to restrict the legal rights of convicts may lie in their racial sensitivities and fears, real or imaginary, an insight into which is conveyed by Governor Gooch in his correpondence with Alured Popple, legal counsel to the Board of Trade, in 1736. In response to queries relating to the exclusion of 'free Negroes' from the franchise in an Act passed some twelve years earlier, Gooch defended the measure as a matter of necessary social control.[28] Although the Act excluded free negroes, mulattoes and Indians from voting, the exchange between His Majesty's government and the governor revolved around the situation of the free negro. Gooch's problem was that while class exclusion from political rights on the grounds of property qualification was understood by the British authorities, racial exclusion was not: all freemen were regarded alike, whatever their colour. However, Gooch had to argue that the Virginia provision was part of a larger Act forced on the colony in the wake of a conspiracy

> among the Negros to Cutt off the English, wherein the free-Negros & Mulattos were much Suspected to have been Concerned (which will forever be the Case) and tho' there could be no legal Proof, so as to Convict them, yet such was the Insolence of the Free-Negros & Mulattos by excluding them from that great Priviledge of a Freeman, well knowing they always did, and ever will, adhere to and favour the Slaves.

Gooch also complained 'of the Nature of Negros, and the Pride of a manumitted Slave, who looks on himself imediately on his Acquiring his freedom to be as good a Man as the best of his Neighbours'. This was especially true, he thought, if they were descended of a white father or mother, 'lett them be of what mean Condition soeever'. Moreover, he alleged:

> As most of them are the Bastards of some of the worst of our imported Servants and Convicts, it seems no ways Impolitick as well for discouraging that kind of Copulation, as to preserve a decent Distinction between them and their Betters, to leave this mark on them.

In this way, Gooch confirmed 'the present Disposition in the Country to Continue it' in the cause of preserving a proper racial and social hierarchy.[29] Other legal distinctions were also made in terms of the rights of different kinds of servants. In a Virginia Act in 1753 ordinary servants were guaranteed 'freedom dues', that is, a substantial gift at the end of their term of service, recoverable by law if the master or mistress refused. Convicts were excepted, but this exclusion was not mandatory: employers could still choose to treat convict servants in the same way as the others. This law has been interpreted as a measure to deprive convicts of hitherto customary rights, but in fact it seems that their freedom dues were not forbidden, only not compulsory and legally enforcible. Evidence is thin, but it seems that in some areas, certainly in Maryland in the Ridgely ironworks, some convicts were treated as well as ordinary servants when it came to freedom dues.[30] In advocating a complete end to payment of freedom dues to convict servants in 1741, Councillors

Thomas Lee and William Fairfax, both from the Northern Neck, were unsuccessful. They entered their dissent in the Council records, cautioning against the prospect of closer ties between convicts and slaves. 'Freedom wears a Cap', they maintained 'that can without a Tongue call together all those that long to shake off the Fetters of Slavery'. Virginia faced the prospect of 'sure and sudden destruction' from a 'union of slaves and convicts'.[31] This debate about convicts' rights was therefore part of a set of legal measures which did not add up to a wholesale reduction in the status of white convict servants. In general, poor whites, who had shown a tendency towards collective violence in the seventeenth century, were no longer regarded with so much anxiety in the eighteenth. Rather, the measures taken after 1718 reflect a concern to prevent alliances between the races, whether sexual or criminal, and a desire to maintain the social hierarchy emerging after the large-scale importation of convicts complicated the status of servants. There is no evidence that in the period before the 1750s there was a drive to contain convicts through construction of a single, subordinate, collective legal status.[32]

The mid-century panic

The second stage of representation, shared by British and colonial commentators alike, was a conviction that transportation was, at best, a failed punishment or, at worst, a dangerous one. A combination of rising crime and some striking cases in the newspapers provoked a crisis of confidence in the judicial system in the middle of the eighteenth century. In the 1750s, on both sides of the Atlantic, transportation became the object of sceptical penological and political discourse, part of a much wider re-evaluation of policies of punishment. John Beattie notes the paradox. On the one hand, transportation to America had introduced stability and flexibility into the administration of the law in England, providing, through a secondary, non-capital form of punishment, scope for a level of 'discretion that made the increasing capital statutes tolerable'. At mid-century, he says, 'it had been a striking success for thirty years'. On the other hand, while transportation was reaching its peak, there was increasing criticism. Moreover, 'some people had always opposed sending men and women to America'. By the 1740s, the magistrates (in London particularly) were complaining that large numbers of 'old offenders' sent to America were making their way back to England very quickly and used this as an explanation for serious crime in the capital in the late 1740s and 1750s.[33]

This second group of narratives, more serious and fearful, concentrated around the middle of the century, had a double purpose. In England they provided a discourse critical of the efficacy of transportation as a punishment, and in America, they demonstrated the criminal consequences for the colonies. Added to the colonial concern about crime in subsequent years were anxieties about rebellion. Certainly there seems to have been a cluster of reports in the American newspapers during the 1750s of mutinies and rebellions by convicts on the ships transporting them. Murders of incoming captains and seizures of the ships seemed suddenly common. One of the stories of mutiny ended with the rumour that the convicts had turned 'pyrates in the Bay', confirmed by their arrest a few weeks later.[34] Fear of revolt was also a feature of English attitudes at the time. Nicholas Rogers notes Henry Fielding's fear of insubordination and disorder arising from patterns of riots and strikes between 1747 and 1753, resonating among the propertied classes of the capital and elsewhere. The common people whom he described as 'so audacious, insolent and ungovernable' were collectively out of control and in danger of subverting the accepted order.[35] In the colonies, some individuals too, at first favourable to convict transportation, were beginning to have their doubts. William Byrd II initially welcomed them as a means of settling the country but later changed his mind, describing them as 'a vile commodity' better sent to Georgia where they might quickly perish or else live miserably. They had flourished in Virginia where they contributed to the rising level of crime.[36] Servants in England were always a source of anxiety, though concerns focused increasingly on their criminality rather than on any capacity for collective rebellion.[37] In Virginia, as has been stressed earlier, there was the added complication of relations between servants, slaves and convict servants. Maryland too had its problems, especially with the approach of war, aggravated by the number of Irish Catholic convicts in its midst.[38]

There were striking gender differences in these attitudes towards servants. In England, the idea that women could be criminals in the home was a common anxiety, as in large urban settings such as London servants were 'ubiquitous but invisible'. With so many women, particularly young women, before the courts, this problem had an effect on penal theory, since it reinforced the idea of transportation as a useful secondary punishment, placed between the gallows or local punishment. To some it might be ideally suited to women. To many colonists, however, male servants, particularly convicts, were thought to be more of a menace, posing threats of theft and violence. Despite these gender

variations, the fears confirm the notion that stories of crimes and criminals were never purely about crime, but in part about all kinds of other
fears and anxieties – about social order and moral collapse.[39] None of
these arguments were new at this time, but seem to have been brought
together in many stories and reports which reinforced the image of
public danger and helplessness in the face of convict actions on both
sides of the Atlantic. If there was something of an English crisis of confidence in law enforcement in the late 1740s and early 1750s, there was
a parallel development of American certainty that the colonies were
paying the highest price for that failure. The anxieties were either
vented or created and reinforced by stories in the newspapers. Nicholas
Rogers notes the growing figures of reports of serious crimes between
1748 and 1751 in the *Whitehall Evening Post*, within which there was a
steady increase in the proportion devoted specifically to violent crimes.
In England the first serious gang since the days of Jonathan Wild, the
McDaniel gang, attracted national attention, and aroused the kinds
of doubts about the use of informers and 'thieftakers' which had arisen
two decades before. Detailed, allegedly authentic, autobiographies
such as that of John Poulter confirmed the large-scale organization of
gangs able to move easily within England, and apparently traverse
the Atlantic at will.[40] Parallel developments in the American press are
indicated by the statistics for the 1740s and 1750s, suggesting that
reports of crimes and punishments reached a peak in the middle of the
century. It is surely significant that Maryland, the colony with the
highest population of convicts, had a newspaper that devoted more
space than any other to crime, nearly a fifth at the mid-century. Overwhelmingly, the American press concentrated on serious crimes against
property and persons, that is, the exceptionally dangerous rather than
ordinary minor cases. Even the extreme crimes of murder were misrep-
resented, the press concentrating on homicides between strangers, often
as part of robberies, rather than the more ordinary but equally ugly
domestic killings. In this, the American differed little from the British
newspapers in their broadcasting the 'remarkable and the sensational'.[41]
Whether the press merely reflected the actual crime waves, or acted to
stir up a heightened but exaggerated anxiety about crime, is always a
difficult conundrum in the analysis of crime in the press. In the absence
of continuous runs of crime statistics, in England or America, historians have rather tentatively concluded that newspapers did respond to
some real increases in crime in the middle of the century. At the same
time, the press also formed the public consciousness of crime and the
sense of helplessness in the reading public. In this regard, newspapers

were active participants in the growing political debate on crime and the law.[42]

Certainly there were some ugly crimes committed in Virginia and Maryland at this time. The year 1751 alone produced a number of horrifying murders by convicts and further evidence of convict criminality in several thefts, all given prominence in the newspapers. Convict servant Jeremiah Swift attempted to kill the two young sons of his master John Hatherley in the fields at Elk Ridge before returning to the house to murder their sister with an axe. One boy, John Hatherley, had asked Swift 'if he thought he could make a thousand [tobacco] hills before night'. This was probably a mocking challenge or jeer. However it was meant, Swift 'told the boy he would let him know before night, and immediately, without the least provocation, struck [him] on the head with his hoe', and then repeated his blows 'till he killed him on the spot'. After attacking the other boy, he went to the house and killed the daughter Elizabeth. One of the boys in the fields lived to give evidence against Swift who was executed and his body hung in chains at Elk Ridge within three weeks of the crime. He was born in Braintree, Essex, 'of credible parents', was 'well educated' and about twenty-one at his death. He had been in Maryland less than a year.[43] Daniel Sullivan, an escaped convict, murdered the overseer who had retrieved him after he had run away, despite being treated 'humanely' by him during the journey. The discovery of his victim was particularly shocking, his naked body half-buried in clay and muddy water, gnawed by dogs whose howling alerted a passer-by. Sullivan's body, too, was hung in chains.[44] Another case involved Jacob Windsor,

> who had been convicted at a late Special Court in Queen Anne's County, was there executed pursuant to his Sentence. He was transported from England to America for 14 years, and had been four Times since Whipp'd and Pillory'd, once for stealing a Bible.[45]

John Conner, a convict servant belonging to a gentleman of Elk Ridge, was arrested and confessed to robbing Mr Charles Cole. He was one of the first to take advantage of the law passed in June 1751 allowing a felon's word to be taken as evidence in a criminal case against another convict. Conner accused Thomas Bevan of being his colleague in the robbery, and on this evidence Bevan was convicted and executed in November. Bevan was another 'likely young man who had had a pretty good education'. It was his crime which provoked the *Maryland Gazette* into claiming that 'we have been infested in this town and neighbour-hood for some time past with a parcel of thieves and robbers, but from whence they come, or who they are, cannot be found out, although we have strong suspicions'.[46] That summer Maryland counties tried one by one to impose a £50 security for every convict imported. It was hoped that this, together with the new rule on felons' testimony would 'prevent the sale of those sort of people sent hither for the *better peo-pling of the colonies*'.[47] It is scarcely surprising that the *Virginia Gazette* took up two full columns on its front page in June 1751 with the London story of William Parsons, son of Sir William Parsons, Baronet, graduate of both Eton College and the Kent Assize courts, executed in February that year for being a returned transportee from Virginia (where he had worked for Lord Fairfax). Well-educated British criminals were in the news that year.[48]

It is a truism of studies of the modern media that a few exceptional cases, given an exaggerated and sensational treatment, are sufficient to create a popular belief. Such impressions often become self-perpetuating.[49] As William Smith wrote in a long piece in the *Indepen-dent Reflector* in 1753:

> It is remarked at Philadelphia, that of the great Number of Criminals, for several years past executed there, scarce any of them were Chil-dren of *America*, or honestly came over for a settlement in the country . . . while almost every News-Paper we receive from thence, advertises the Tryal or Execution of an *English* or *Irishman*.

He drew the obvious lesson: 'we want people, 'tis true, but not villains, ready, at any time, encouraged by impunity, and habituated, upon the slightest occasion, to cut a man's throat, for a small part of his prop-erty'. He cited the many thousands of indigent but virtuous Germans as examples of a very different sort of immigrant. This view represents an interesting shift in prejudice, a departure from the contempt for the criminal tendencies of the non-English expressed in some earlier reports of crime in the American press reproducing the reports in the London papers of the spectacular crimes in Germany and elsewhere on the Euro-pean Continent. The terrible actions of the Jew 'Suss' attracted atten-tion on both sides of the Atlantic.[50] It was colonial crime reports like those of 1751 involving British convicts, and the crisis they seemed to reflect, that provoked two notable responses in the middle of the eigh-teenth century. The first was Benjamin Franklin's famous denunciation of convict transportation.[51] The second was the widespread interest of both sides of the Atlantic in the English debate about hard labour (centring on the unsuccessful Hard Labour Bill of January 1752), which, in proposing hard labour in the dockyards as a secondary punishment, explicitly regarded transportation as a failure.

The most famous and impassioned outburst denouncing British convicts in the colonies and the government policy of sending them there appeared in the *Pennsylvania Gazette* in April 1751. Describing the convicts as 'human serpents', the writer asked:

> What good Mother ever sent Thieves and Villains to accompany her children: to corrupt some and murder the rest? What Father ever endeavour'd to spread the Plague in his Family? . . . In what can Britain show a more Sovereign contempt for us than by emptying their jails into our settlements?

A few issues later, in May, there appeared a solution. In a tone heavy with irony, the author suggested that the colonists should transport rattlesnakes to Britain where he proposed they should be

> carefully distributed in St. James's Park, in the Spring-Gardens and other Places of Pleasure about London; in the Gardens of all the Nobility and Gentry throughout the Nation; but particularly in the Gardens of the *Prime Ministers*, the *Lords of Trade* and *Members of Parliament*; for to them we are most particularly obliged. Our *Mother* knows best for us. What is a little Housebreaking, Shoplifting, or Highway Robbing; what is a *Son* now and then *corrupted* and *hang'd*, a Daughter *debauch'd* and *pox'd*, a Wife *stabb'd*, a Husband's *Throat cut*, or a Child's Brains beat out with an Axe, compar'd with this IMPROVEMENT AND WELL PEOPLING of the Colonies![52]

Franklin signed it 'Americanus', significantly. His lengthy outburst was more than likely triggered by the brutal murders committed by Jeremiah Swift and the several other Chesapeake cases which appeared in the 11 April 1751 issue of the *Pennsylvania Gazette*. These also included the account of the shipboard mutiny by Liverpool convicts, as well as that of a convict servant who, intent on killing his mistress only to change his mind, chopped off his hand and, throwing it at her, challenged her to repeat her orders. Franklin's sentiments were widely reproduced in the northern and mid-Atlantic colonies, appearing in the *New York Evening Post*, *Maryland Gazette*, *Boston Gazette*, *Boston Evening Post* and

Virginia Gazette.[53] When reporting local crimes, the influence of convicts was often asserted as a likely source of moral corruption. In the same edition of the *Virginia Gazette* that printed Franklin's 'rattlesnake' letter, there was a further pronouncement, following the news of several incidents:

> *Extract from a Letter from Maryland, dated April 26.*
> I believe we have every Year three or four Hundred felons imported here from London; and if, when their Times are out, or before, they were not many of them to move away to the Northward, and elsewhere, we should be over-run with them. Some few may possibly have been transported for small Matters, or thro' false Accusations; but the most well deserve Hanging at home; And we have now no occasion for imported Thieves in America, as the Breed seems to thrive among us, and we are like to have enough of our own Growth. Not only our other Servants and Negroes are corrupted and spoilt, but even our Children begin to be vititated by them.

This was not an unusual idea. Also in the same edition, a case of forgery committed by a young man of a 'respectable family' in Maryland was attributed to the fact that he may have had 'the advantage of being improved by the conversation of some of those Gentry, who are sent over *"for the improvement and well peopling of the colonies"*'. Franklin's language rapidly became common currency.[54]

The denunciation of transportation and the individual cases of convict wrongdoing were carried back across the Atlantic in colonial newspapers arriving probably in West Country ports and appearing in west-country papers. The *Sherborne Mercury* carried all three convict stories (Jeremiah Swift, the mutiny by Liverpool convicts, and the story of the severed hand) in its 17 June edition. Franklin's essay on transportation appeared a month later when it was described as a 'letter lately published in Virginia'. The *Gloucester Journal* also carried all three stories, with a New York dateline of 22 March for the tale of Jeremiah Swift, and an 11 April dateline for the other two accounts.[55] The convict stories and Franklin's sentiments became front page news in the Historical Register of the *Gentleman's Magazine* in June 1751 and appeared in the *London Magazine* in July.[56] Exchange of information of this nature may have led to the assumption in another entry in the *Gloucester Journal* later in 1751, that the British government was willing to heed colonial complaints over transportation policy when it reported:

There is said to be a Scheme on Foot for redressing the *Grievances complained of from the sending Felons over into the Plantations*, and, at the same Time, for rendering them more *servicable* to the *Community*; but *in what Manner* is not yet publically known.[57]

By this time the House of Commons Committee on the Criminal Laws had already been sitting for a number of months, a response to the crime wave rocking the capital. An innovation in policy making, the committee had a remit to investigate the defects of the laws and advise how they might be made more effective.[58] American newspapers observed the British debate on the efficacy of punishment with some cynicism:

It has occurred to some persons, who are sincerely sollicitous for the Public Welfare, that if, instead of being transported for small crimes, able-bodied fellows were condemn'd for seven or fourteen years to work in quarries, or in mines, and care taken to see that sentence duly executed; it would have very good effects.

Two weeks later, as reports suggested northern colonies would ban convicts from entering, the *Virginia Gazette*, referring to the British Parliament, asserted that 'it is apprehended the Legislature will be at last obliged to contrive some way to keep and employ those Wretches at Home'.[59] In fact, the legislation failed, and the response was in part one of increased severity. The Murder Act of 1752 allowed English judges to sentence killers to execution within two days, and their bodies to lie unburied after dissection by the surgeons. The time limit meant that those condemned at any distance from London would not have time for an appeal. Far from signalling the age of reform, it is true to say, as Beattie has, that the crisis of mid-century provided justification for selective severity. Indeed, the response on both sides of the Atlantic was to insist on the most unpleasant and horrifying executions.[60] In the 1750s, execution rates in London rose steeply to levels not seen since the 1720s, as the proportion reprieved from execution fell: more than half of those convicted of capital offences were hanged. This seems to have been one demonstrative response to the crisis.[61] To some in the English establishment, perhaps, transportation had 'almost ceased to be a punishment' as a judge said in 1766, and this remark was not widely criticized or even commented on.[62] However, the problem of making transportation an effective punishment, or of finding an adequate substitute, remained unresolved. The convict trade was a matter of convenience for the British government, as even more people were shipped out in the 1750s and 1760s than before, but it also provided grounds for continuing anxiety in the minds of some of the colonists.

The endgame: Mutual recriminations

The third group of accounts and allegations came towards the end of the colonial period and during the Revolution, although hints of colonial resentment over British assumptions about American inferiority and justifiable subordination to central control can be found earlier. As tension on the Virginia frontier mounted, *Felix Farley's Bristol Journal* carried an 'Extract of a letter from Virginia' dated Williamsburg, 4 June 1754, in which the author lamented English indifference to French ambitions and activities in North America when compared 'upon every paltry Alarm' with the generosity lavished on 'some *German Princes . . .* merely for the Sake of preserving, as the Ministers call it, the *Balance of Power*':

> In short, and to tell the plain Truth in few Words, we are looked upon, by your *Great Men* – as a Subject too low for their sublime Politics; by your *Country Squires* and *Coxcombs*, as a Set of Transports and Vagabonds: – And by your *Boards*, as unruly Children, that want more to be corrected than encouraged. Thanks to their Wisdoms in taking too little Care of our *Breeding*.[63]

Already, it would seem, some colonists were beginning to entertain the notion that people in Britain perceived them as 'transports and vagabonds'. The *Virginia Gazette* also copied letters and comments critical of the Euro-centric policies of the British government, one letter from Amsterdam in 1767 calling the balance of power 'a phantom which we have been pursuing for upwards of a century', at great cost to the national debt.[64] The language of British irresponsibility – the careless parent neglecting the American child, seemed to grow more common from the 1750s. New forms of mutual definitions and distinctive identities were emerging.

As the British government's disdain for colonial rights became increasingly transparent and American alienation grew, questions of identity assumed a new and radical significance. Drawing upon new approaches to nationality and empire, T. H. Breen has argued that recent work in transforming the political landscape of eighteenth-century Britain and reconceptualizing the British empire requires historians to rethink aspects of the American Revolution relating to nationalism and ideology. He observes how during the 1740s, for reasons that are not altogether clear, 'English men and women of all social classes began to express a sentiment that might be described variously as a dramatic surge of national consciousness, a rise of aggressive patriotism, or a greatly heightened articulation of national identity'.[65] And even if eighteenth-century developments were not entirely new but only 'an intensification of an imaginative project with ancient roots, it nevertheless involved a much broader percentage of the population. It was now sustained by a new commercial press that brought stories about the empire to urban coffeehouses and country taverns'.[66] This form of nationalism was exclusive, not inclusive; it 'was actually English nationalism writ large'. It defined the colonial Americans 'as "other," as not fully English, or as persons beyond the effective boundaries of the new national imagination', that is marginalized and on the periphery. Viewed from this perspective, the Stamp Act delivered a body blow. It caused colonial newspapers to ask 'Are not the People of America, BRITISH subjects? Are they not Englishmen?'[67] It was the abrupt discovery of inequality, argues Breen, and the accompanying sense of rejection and humiliation, as much as the radical whig political tradition, that accounts for 'the shrill, even paranoid, tone' of colonial political rhetoric seemingly so much at odds with injuries actually sustained.[68] This view places growing British nationalist sentiment, and the centralizing tendency of government, at the root of the crisis in *American* identity. There are other attempts to identify the points of transformation in British-American relations. Stephen Conway pinpoints the Seven Years' War as a crucial turning point in British perceptions of the Americans, arguing that in the earlier Austrian war of 1739–48, British people viewed American colonists 'not simply as fellow-subjects of King George but as fellow-Britons'. However, the inability of the colonists to pay for, or achieve successful, self-defence against the French in the late 1750s and early 1760s, forced British government circles to the realization that they would have to take a more direct role in the details as well as the broad structures of colonial affairs. This sense of increasing global responsibility was reinforced by the successful campaigns in India and new possessions in West Africa. The Americans could not cope with their own situation, economically or militarily.[69]

Breen, however, also points to changes in the direction of colonial culture, particularly in the writings of some of the leading colonial protagonists at this time, which increasingly differentiated the colonial from British attitudes. In the works of John Adams, James Otis Jr and Daniel Dulany, Breen identifies a neglected strain of racism which he also attributes to the shock of dislocation. 'We won't be their Negroes', wrote John Adams in the *Boston Gazette*, using the name Humphrey Ploughjogger, 'I say we are as handsome as old English folks, and so should be as free'. James Otis Jr, taking the name John Hampton, wrote accusingly in the same newspaper 'You think most if not all the Colonists are Negroes and Mulattoes – You are wretchedly mistaken – Ninety-nine in a hundred in the more northern Colonies are white, and there is as good blood flowing in their veins, save the royal blood, as any in the three kingdoms'. It was a necessary correction, because, as one American found in talking to people on a visit to Britain, 'more than two thirds of the people of this island thought the Americans were all negroes'.[70] In another defensive piece, Daniel Dulany of Maryland rejected the characterizations of British officials in his famous pamphlet, *Considerations on the Propriety of Imposing Taxes in the British Colonies*, printed in Annapolis and widely circulated.

> What a strange animal must a North American appear to be from these representations to the generality of English readers, who have never had an opportunity to admire that he may be neither black nor tawny, may speak the English language, and in other respects seem, for all the world, like one of them![71]

The British, as Governor Gooch had found out, had in some ways failed to understand colonial sensibilities about racialized systems of inequality. Now the Americans were becoming anxious that they were viewed increasingly as inferior, racially as much as morally and politically. The presence of convicts as well as Africans was becoming an awkward factor, almost embarrassing.

Individual Americans such as Franklin and Arthur Lee sought to counter the allegations of specific individuals. Adam Smith's depiction of the founders of the American colonies in the *Theory of Moral Sentiments* (1759) as 'the refuse of the jails of Europe' caused a shock. The phrase occurred at the end of a paean of praise to the moral nobility of savages in America and Africa, particularly in their cultural attitudes to death:

> There is not a negro from the coast of Africa who does not . . . possess a degree of magnanimity which the soul of his sordid master is too often scarce capable of perceiving. Fortune never exerted more

cruelly her empire over mankind, than when she subjected those nations of heroes to the refuse of the jails of Europe.[72]

The remark provoked a response from Arthur Lee, one of the younger sons of Councillor Thomas Lee of Virginia, whose *An Essay in Vindication of the Continental Colonies of America* (1764) denounced British policies and declared that American slaves were not nearly so heavily shackled as their owners, 'their manufacturing hands tied up; their commerce confined'; their tobacco 'oppressed with such intolerable exactions, that it yields to the labouring planter scarce one tenth of its original value'.[73] Dr Samuel Johnson's depiction of the colonists in the same decade as 'a race of convicts' who 'ought to be thankful for anything we allow them short of hanging' may be better known to historians than contemporaries.[74] Like the slave, the convict also constituted a real presence in the colonies and was invoked in James Otis Jr's equally famous 1765 pamphlet, *A Vindication of the British Colonies*. Quoted by Breen though not pursued is Otis's rhetorical question, 'Are the inhabitants of British America all a parcel of transported theives, robbers, and rebels, or descended from such? Are the colonists blasted lepers, whose company would infect the whole House of Commons?' In the midst of trade and Stamp Act disputes, Scotland acquired the legal framework to begin transportation of convicts. As one long pro-American article in the London press put it, 'the Americans remembered the act authorizing the most cruel insult, that of emptying our goals [sic] into their settlements'.[75] By November 1775, at least one member of the House of Commons, William Innes, would have answered Otis's question in the affirmative. 'It has been asserted,' he remarked,

> that the colonists are the offspring of Englishmen, and as such, entitled to the privileges of Britons. [But] I am bold to deny it, for it is well known that they not only consist of English, Scots, and Irish, but also of French, Dutch, Germans innumerable, Indians, Africans, and a multitude of felons from this country, Is it possible to tell which are the most turbulent amongst such a mixture of people?[76]

An indication of how alien the colonies appeared to British commentators is a letter on behalf of two Bristol women reprieved for transportation in 1774. The younger evoked more sympathy – 'banished from all her friends, an affectionate Mother, and other ties more tender, to a foreign country'.[77] Part of that strangeness was the use of unfree workers in such numbers. Visitors to the colonies like the 'French

Traveller' (probably a spy) in 1765 found 'the number of Convicts and Indented servants to Virginia amazing, besides the numbers of Dutch and Germans, which is also Considerable'. He wrote of North Carolina as:

> the azilum of the Convicts that have served their time in Virginia and Maryland. when at liberty they all (or a gret part) Come to this part where they are not Known and setle here. It is a fine Country for poor people, but not for the rich.[78]

The notion that colonists *were* convicts, vagabonds and slaves took a stronger hold on the imagination of some people on both sides of the Atlantic in the last quarter of the colonial period. In fact, in 1766 Franklin found himself fighting off the extension of the Transportation Act of 1718 to Scotland, and failing.[79] Indeed, if anything, the British government seemed prepared to expand the practice to different categories of offenders and different parts of the Americas.[80] Franklin's identification of the passage of convicts to the colonies with the euphemism 'for the well peopling of his Majesty's colonies' in 1751 had become for 'the better peopling of Your Majesty's Colonies' in 1774. Characteristically, Samuel Johnson deployed reptilian wit when he turned Franklin's demographic rule that the American population was doubling every twenty-five years into a sardonic comment: 'they multiply with the fecundity of their own rattlesnakes, so that every quarter of a century doubles their numbers'.[81]

If the 1750s were the period of maximum convergence of convict representation and criminal concern between the two sides of the Atlantic, the conflicts at the end provided each side with a new usage of the convict narrative. If the stories confirmed to British patriots that the Americans were a nation of convicts, they also indicated to Americans that they had been oppressed by little more than criminals. A curious 'Letter from a gentleman at Boston to his friend in London' appeared in the *Virginia Gazette* in June 1769. Its contents were provocative. Convict ancestry, now made explicit, furnished the grounds for denying that the colonists were, in fact, 'the children of Great-Britain':

> After a tour to the southward, I arrived here about three weeks ago. Things are much quieter than I expected. The troops have awed the licentious into silence; but through all the provinces the common cry is LIBERTY and INDEPENDENCE. Virginia and Maryland, with some reason form a pretension to independency. The bulk of the

inhabitants, or their progenitors, forfeited their rights as subjects in England, and were banished to America to expiate the crimes they had committed in Europe. They suffered, after their emigration, the punishment of the lash for seven, fourteen years, or their Life; which if anything can, is certainly a reason to say, that they are not the children of Great-Britain. But they should not forget that they came over as slaves; that there are many daily arriving in that capacity; and that two thirds of the inhabitants, white or black, are now actually slaves.[82]

There were a series of such denigratory comments in the 1760s and 1770s by the 'British' about the 'Americans' as the two identities became more clearly defined. The convict reputation – in effect, being smeared as criminals, produced some resentful responses among the Americans before the Revolution. One reaction was close to embarrassment for being associated with convict states. Another was more directly economic. At the time of the Association in 1774 eight Virginia counties added the importation of slaves to the list of prohibited goods, three Virginia counties – Culpepper, Princess Anne and Surry counties – also resolved to prohibit the importation of convict servants. According to the Surry resolves, 'the population of this colony with freemen and manufactures is greatly obstructed by the importation of slaves and convict servants'.[83]

As the formal relationship between Britain and the continental American colonies dissolved after Lexington and Concord, loyalists took flight, some heading for England, others for Canada or the West Indies. The *Virginia Gazette* carried a report from Maryland

> Every ship has at least six or seven passengers. The one I was yester-day on board of carries out parsons Addison and Boucher, with their families. Annapolis is thinned; Lloyd, Dulany, and many others, with their families, are embarked. Old Mr Dulany takes his daughter to Nova Scotia, for the recovery of her health; which it is said, she was not known to want.

The writer rejoiced at the departure of 'all those filthy, grovelling vermin' and envisaged a situation in which instead of the cordial reception which they anticipated, they would be met by a mob of 'honest Englishmen' and that the King, 'to stop their murmers of disappoint-ment, transport them back again to America, in the capacity of con-victs, that they may enjoy slavery and infamy in a land where they could not brook freedom and glory'.[84] When John Adams passed through Maryland some eighteen months later he was hardly less disparaging of Maryland society and its aspirations than its most strident critics. 'The lands are cultivated', he wrote,

> and all sort of trades are exercised by Negroes, or by transported convicts, which has occasioned the planters and farmers to assume the title of gentlemen, and they hold their negroes and convicts, that is all labouring people and tradesmen, in such contempt that they think themselves a distinct order of beings. Hence they never will suffer their sons to labour or learn any trade, but they bring them up in idleness or what is worse in horse racing, cock fighting, and card playing.[85]

As fighting continued, American reports of an English convict's execution confirmed the criminal character of those who had resisted the revolution. In May 1778 the *Pennsylvania Gazette* noted the execution in London of Frances Mercier, for murdering a jeweller. This 'atrocious criminal', as the *Gentleman's Magazine* called him, tried to avoid trial by pretending madness, remaining silent in court when asked to plead to the charge. A special jury had to be empanelled to see if he was standing mute 'through obstinacy, or by the visitation of God'.[86] They decided the former, and he was accordingly convicted of murder, and sentenced to be hanged and dissected by the surgeons. The American press was interested in him for other reasons. He had been transported from Middlesex in 1773 after being reprieved from execution for horse stealing.[87] After the voyage over, he was accused but cleared of poisoning the ship's captain, and was a little time later condemned for stealing from a druggist's in Baltimore, but pardoned. He subsequently went north where it was believed he was hanged at New York. However, this was a false rumour, for he next turned up serving briefly in the revolutionary army before being imprisoned in New York for desertion. He escaped and joined the British when New York was seized by Howe. He was then given the care of American prisoners, including his former gaoler there, but crucial to his behaviour was a beneficial rule that 'the effects of all persons who died under Mercier's care became his property'. Allegedly he gave infected clothing to his charges, and this created a 'pestilential disorder' which killed 573 people. As prisoners began to perish, he is reported to have told General Howe, 'the rebels died like fun'. Not surprisingly, the story was told in the American press (on the front page) in order to rebuff those criticizing stories of 'British cruelty' who called the American accusations exaggerated. This kind of tale reinforced the impression of the deviousness of a British leadership who would hire criminals as easily as they would slaves or Indians to oppose the Revolution. It was entirely believable when newspapers reported in 1775 that regiments of loyal Americans were being recruited by the British from among 'head Tories, a few Negroes, and some Scotch rebels and convicts'. After all, Dunmore had tried something similar with slaves in Virginia.[88] Nicholas Cresswell, an Englishman on the Virginian frontier, wrote in his Journal for 3 March 1777 how he had been at Leesburg where he 'saw a review of Capt William Johnston's company', and commented derisively, 'a set of rascally servants and convicts most of them just purchased from their masters. A ragged crew indeed'.[89]

If the Americans accused the British of trying to turn convicts into patriotic soldiers, there were also images favoured by the British suggesting they could become true Americans. That convicts might prosper in America led some commentators to regard America as a land of dubious social origins and personal success. As Dublin's *Freeman's Journal* commented in 1787, hearing of the transportation of Irish felons to America, rather than Botany Bay:

> They ought to receive a welcome, from the infinite use which many of our former transported convicts were of to the American cause, in fighting its battles, and assisting in acquiring its present independency. It is not improbable, therefore, from the present state of the Western empire, that the children of some of our late transported gentlemen and ladies will sit in Congress in less than half a century, as it is an indisputable fact that some former convicts have already obtained that honour.[90]

Even after independence, the stigma of being a convict colony could still hurt. When representing his country in France Thomas Jefferson was consulted over an entry on America prepared for the *Encyclopédie*, and he was appalled to find that it had drawn on the work of the Abbé Raynal according to whom America was made up of three classes of people: servants, slaves and convicts. He replied:

> The Malefactors sent to America were not in sufficient number to permit enumeration as one class out of three which peopled America. It was at a late period of their history that this practice began. I have no book by me which enables me to point out the date of it's

commencement. But I do not think the whole number sent would amount to 2000, and being principally men, eaten up with disease, they married seldom and propagated little. I do not suppose that themselves and their descendants are at present 4000, which is little more than one thousandth part of the whole inhabitants.[91]

What was implicit in Jefferson's comments was made explicit in Edmund Randolph's *History of Virginia*. A contemporary of Jefferson, governor of Virginia and the first Chief Justice of the Supreme Court, Randoph wrote that there was 'no risk of contamination from a matrimonial alliance of convicts with decent families'. Randolph believed that Adam Smith had been misled into thinking that 'the population of a very large district of America' was descended from those 'who were convicted of criminal offences', citing William Stith's history of early Virginia as a possible source of the error. Stith had protested that a policy originally designed 'for the advancement and increase of the colony' had proved a hindrance to its growth. 'For it has laid one of the finest countries in British America under the unjust scandal of being a mere Hell upon earth, another Siberia, and only fit for the reception of malefactors and the vilest of the people'. As a consequence, 'our younger sisters, the northern colonies . . . have outstripped us so much more in the number of their inhabitants and in the goodness and frequency of their cities and towns'.[92] In effect, the presence of convicts in the colonies ceased to be a matter of any consequence except for Virginians and their historians. Although Timothy Pitkin discussed criminal transportation in some detail in his two-volume history published in 1828, the subject received little attention until Bancroft and Butler took it up at the end of the nineteenth century. Butler's work in particular met with a cool reception in Virginia and its ramifications were still being discussed in the pages of the *Virginia Magazine of History and Biography* at the end of the Second World War. The convict reputation produced a long history of commentators either reducing their number, transforming their character, or recruiting them into the army. In sum, Virginians purged them from their past.[93]

Conclusion

Much of this study has concentrated on reconstructing the published representations of convicts in an Atlantic world where a growing market for information and print culture created a public sphere embracing both sides of the Atlantic. But within this world of trade in goods, information, convicts and slaves, new identities were emerging, some of which would lead to new nations. A reading – and listening – public was increasingly well informed about events and policies, and with this information came recognition of similarities and differences between the societies either side of the Atlantic. The purpose of this chapter has been to see what the two shared in the exchange of criminal representations, and where (and when) they differed. It seems that what had begun as anxious dialogue ended in acrimonious mutual insult. There were shifts in emphasis, and developments or reproductions of older images, but they do not add up to a sequence of utterly distinct representations. All three of the modes of representation outlined here could coexist at any one time. As Rawlings put it,

> understanding changes in the literature is not simply a matter of identifying a time and an event as denoting a clean break with the past . . . Change is rarely instant and total, but more often it involves a dynamic discourse between present and past, in which the new is never entirely new, and the old never entirely forgotten.[94]

There were patterns of broad agreement at the beginning, when in the aftermath of the 1718 Act the first large-scale shipments of convicts were made, and British and colonial authorities debated how to contain what were seen as essentially manageable dangers. At mid-century there was a period of convergence and shared anxiety as serious disadvantages of the convict trade were identified, and its failure to reform criminals was the subject of confident assertion. Finally, as relations between Britain and her North American colonies worsened, there was a collapse into mutual recrimination. The convicts became a source of bad blood between the 'mother country' and her colonies. To the British they furnished proof of the polluted – hence illegitimate – society demanding independence. This dismissive image had racial overtones, in the sense that a criminal class could be conceived as a kind of hereditary difference, an 'other' whose stigma could not be removed. The picture has parallels in later developments of racial theories of criminality in the more biologically minded nineteenth century. In the middle of the eighteenth century, however, it may be that Malachy Postlethwayt's warning of the consequences of inflicting 'shame' on the transported convicts was actually a reflection of that tendency, already half-developed in British society by the 1750s, to see the convict colonies as marked for ever by inferiority. This damning image of a criminal colony involved an extension of some old associations rather than an entirely newly invented narrative. Colonial society had long figured in tales of the exotic and the picaresque – a place of wild people and animals, strange creatures and repressive social relations. The slave colonies in particular had acquired a bad reputation in many British prints in the first half of the eighteenth century in narratives of capture and exploitation. Their moral inferiority was therefore already presaged by tales in print before 1750, and confirmed by insults after that. By way of reply, the country receiving the criminals became increasingly resentful of those producing both the convicts and the stereotypes. As long as the Americans saw themselves as 'British', the debate could take the form of relatively limited criticisms of transportation as a policy, proposals to reduce its detrimental consequences for the colonies, or ideas to make it more effective. Once the Americans recognized how the British derogated their status, in effect, once they realized that their Britishness was second class, then criminality became a key characteristic of the over-mighty 'other'. Colonial rule itself became seen as criminal. In this period of intense political and military conflict, both sides deployed the criminal stereotype to diminish the moral authority of the other. The 'criminal Atlantic' was irrevocably split in two.

7
Conclusion

The American Revolution did not end the story of transatlantic convict transportation. As the last ship to arrive before hostitilies fully developed, the *Jenny* from Newcastle, came in to the Chesapeake to land its cargo in April 1776, no one in Britain imagined that this was the demise of the convict trade to America.[1] In 1769, the *Virginia Gazette* noted that the Conversation Club in London had debated the question, 'is transportation a proper method of punishing criminals?', but without noting the outcome.[2] For the British government the answer was always affirmative, though this proved difficult to implement after 1776. Before the Revolution, however, alternatives to the mid-Atlantic colonies had already been mooted, notably in 1767 when it was reported that William Pitt, Lord Chatham, exercised his 'utmost endeavours to obtain pardons for all the rioters' condemned to death, on condition that they be transported to Florida. These probably included those West Country men sentenced to hang in Wiltshire and Gloucestershire in the year of hunger riots, 1766. Significantly, though, this 'act of clemency' was not to be extended to any who were guilty of 'thefts and robberies'. Yet later the same year this idea seems to have taken root, when it was reported as a firm proposal for 'felons of either sex convicted for transportation, white servants being much wanted in that settlement'. The demand for them had been evinced by petitions from planters desiring convicts to perform the domestic tasks which they had been forced to allocate to negroes. Even in 1775, as 'the Americans' threatened to close their ports to convict shippers, there had been rumours in the colonies that the British were contemplating shipping convicts to Florida, which might be dangerous since they would be vulnerable to the subversive influence of French agents.[3] Other locations had been mooted: in 1773 judge Lord Mansfield, reportedly as the result of a 'remonstrance from the

Provinces of Virginia, Maryland and Connecticut', had proposed sending convicts to the East Indies, or imprisoning them for life in 'strong houses'. The colonies had apparently complained of the 'inundations of vagabonds from Great Britain and Ireland'.[4]

The outbreak of war did not at first force the British authorities to renew these plans. However, a few years later, as the gaols had filled up by the end of the American war, there was a continual search for alternative destinations for felons. Local authorities hatched schemes for the West Indies, Newfoundland, and Nova Scotia. Some shiploads were even sent, with various results. This was followed with great interest in the newly independent United States – the press in Maryland noting the report of about 90 London convicts sent on their way to Nova Scotia, 'the land of frost and freedom'.[5] There were even attempts to send convicts to the Chesapeake, as though nothing had happened to make the colonies an independent country. As Ekirch comments, it must have been 'an act of desperation' by the authorities to try to resume the traditional policy. Nevertheless, 143 convicts were sent from London in 1783, on a voyage of variable fortunes. The ship, newly named *The Swift* to disguise its identity, was almost wrecked on the southern English coast, and even when it arrived in America, the convicts found themselves left almost starving by the reluctance of any masters to buy their services. It does seem correct to say that 'when peace was negotiated with the Americans in 1782, both Dublin and London hoped that the system could be re-established and subsequently attempted to do so'.[6]

The interruption to transportation was therefore at first scarcely acknowledged, particularly by the Irish authorities, who tried repeatedly to transport their convicts in the 1780s to various parts of North America. This was partly because the emergency legislation passed in Britain to employ convicts in dredging the Thames was not extended to Ireland, and even the first Act authorizing transportation to Australia excluded the Irish. The Irish government was therefore left with a serious problem. Their strategies in the 1780s have been the object of a recent study by Reece, which establishes that the renewal of Irish transportation was frequently disastrous. Although 'entrepreneurs, politicians and officials responded quickly to the opportunity to renew commercial relations with America', their choice of destination and methods of landing and disposal were often fatal. One shipload in 1784 was aiming for Barbados, but when they were landed in the Canaries thirty-six convicts were massacred by the Spanish garrison. The remainder were sold in the Leewards, but some caused trouble in St Kitts and were arrested for thefts, and the island's legislature voted to pay £30 to a ship's captain to take them to one of the American ports. Other attempts were rather more successful, but aroused critical opposition in the American press. A large batch of Irish convicts left in 1787 for Alexandria, Virginia, and were reportedly sold to John Fitzgerald 'in one lump' for the Potowmack Canal Company, whose president was George Washington. This venture was hardly an attractive form of employment, as the work cutting a canal to the Ohio was extremely dangerous, and injury and mutiny were frequent. Other ships tried to sell their cargoes in Connecticut, or were forced to abandon them in New Brunswick because Nova Scotia refused to take them.[7] The London authorities, meanwhile, despite the dispatch of the first fleet to Australia, explored the possibility of sending some of the inmates of their crowded gaols to Newfoundland while awaiting reports of the success of the Botany Bay colony. This was in 1789, and in fact the idea was taken up by the Irish government, and the ship, the *Duke of Leinster*, was probably the last to take convicts across the Atlantic. Among them was one whom the Dublin press called the 'best shoplifter in Ireland'. The enterprise was not a success. Abandoned on shorelines a few miles from St John's, the convicts began to 'straggle' into town, and caused widespread dismay and anxiety. The men were imprisoned, and eventually the bulk of convicts were shipped back to England, though about thirty of the original 114 seem to have disappeared. At least twelve were subsequently shipped from Cork to Australia. There were no further ventures of this kind: whatever the potential popularity of the idea in England, Canadian opposition, by local officials as much as their public, drove the British to seek alternative destinations. Despite discussion of extending the Botany Bay scheme to the Canadian North West, nothing came of the idea. As one historian has pointed out, the Canadian authorities, even in under-populated places such as Newfoundland, were not without organization or influence.[8]

The problems for the British government were compounded by the pressure from the local authorities in the counties of England and Wales, whose gaols were increasingly full and dangerously unhealthy. Petitions poured into the Home Office requesting the resumption of transportation. To take one example, the chairman of the Lancashire bench, on instruction of his grand jury, pleaded in 1784 that:

> The gaols are crowded beyond example and a pestilential fever peculiar to these mansions of misery prevails in very many of them which threatens danger to the whole nation. Convicts sentenced to transportation in accumulated numbers are there kept from year to year,

because there are no methods of carrying their sentence into execution. Whilst another description of them who are confined for terms in our houses of correction, continually add to the number of prisoners and will soon occupy the whole of our small ill contrived gaols.

The following year there were more than fifty people held in Lancaster gaol, under sentence of transportation or awaiting trial.[9] Other counties were also in desperate difficulties, they reported to London, as their gaols became crowded. It is not surprising that a parliamentary committee in 1785 searched for a suitable destination for these felons. They conceded that gaols so full of convicts led to conditions which made 'a separation of offenders impracticable, and that by constant intercourse they corrupt and confirm each other in the practice of villainy'. They also had to admit that transportation, 'though the next punishment in point of severity to a capital sentence, . . . answers very imperfectly the purpose of example', and rather reluctantly suggested West Africa as a possible destination. Many people wrote to the Home Office proffering cultural and practical assistance. This included the keeper of the New Gaol in Surrey, who, hearing that the East Indies was to be the destination, volunteered knowledge of the 'manners and customs of the nations of Indestan', and the commander of naval forces in Africa, now based in Bedfordshire, with a plan for managing the shipping to Africa where a punishment could be arranged which would be less than hanging and therefore 'highly acceptable to the state and the nation'. Eventually, after a protracted process, the government was persuaded to adopt Australia as its first penal colony.[10] The progress of the Botany Bay decision was followed with interest in America and more carefully in Britain. Provincial newspapers published detailed accounts of the first fleet's arrival and settlement in Australia.[11]

For Americans, however, the period of transportation was conveniently forgotten, with the contribution made by convicts in effect wiped from the collective national memory for 100 years. Only occasional references by historians countered the convenient amnesia: Pitkin, for example, turned the willingness of the British government to let loose in America 'those villains, who, by their enormous crimes, had become unfit for society in England' into an indictment of colonial policy and a justification of American indignation.[12] For most writers, however, perhaps for reasons of national pride, because of the need to assert moral superiority, or simply because of anxiety about racial purity, the criminal ancestry of many white Americans was deleted. Yet some heritage remained. Transportation had always been one part of the

British criminal laws not fully adopted by the American colonies, though they were not above trying, convicting and deporting troublesome Native Americans under legislation drawn up for specific cases.[13] After independence, however, some states, Virginia among them, formally adopted a general punishment of 'deportation' for rebellious black slaves. One estimate suggests that more than 900 were transported out of the state in nearly sixty years. Initially sold out of the United States entirely, usually to parts of the West Indies, these slaves, many of them convicted and condemned for violent offences against whites, were later deported to other slave states in the South, which produced predictable protests that Virginia was dumping its criminals.[14] For whites, though, the Revolution brought an ending, not only to transportation, but eventually to most forms of servitude. Historians have explored the complexities of this fundamental shift in both the immigrant and native American experience. Fogleman regards independence as a watershed leading to the end of formal servant servitude. 'For nearly two centuries most immigrants arrived in British North America in some condition of unfreedom, and the colonists regarded this as normal. Yet in the late eighteenth and early nineteenth centuries, the trend suddenly reversed' – 'the character of American immigration had permanently changed'. Part of that change was the ending of British convict transportation, though, as we have seen, this was more drawn out than was once thought. Both slave and convict trades declined in the American Revolution, as trade of all kinds was thrown into chaos. More importantly, Fogleman argues, the Revolution also led 'to the demise of indentured servitude'. What had once been essential was now discarded.[15]

The period of white servitude had been a crucial part of the development of the Chesapeake colonies and Pennsylvania, and convicts had been the longest-serving group among them:

> White servitude was one of the major institutions in the economy and society of colonial British America. Indentured English men and women constituted the principal labour supply for many of the early British settlements in the New World, and their successors continued to make up an important part of white British colonies in America throughout the seventeenth and eighteenth centuries.

In many ways, the indenture system had been the outcome of the efforts of early British colonizers of America to transplant the English system of service in husbandry to the New World.[16] As we have seen, convicts were a major source of this labour between 1718 and 1776. Yet

Fogleman argues that a fundamental shift in labour relations occurred after the Revolution, though it took perhaps forty years or more to come to fulfilment. There was continuity, but socially and culturally America, or rather the new United States, was a different place with changing values, and white unfree labour was not given a future. Immigration, once characterized by 'degrees of servitude', was transformed into 'one characterized by freedom'.[17] Others have been more sceptical, or less emphatic about the transformation.

The absolute distinction between free and unfree can be overdone. As is clear from the first ninety years of the history of the United States, freedom for some may have been accompanied by slavery for others. Moreover, some scholars have warned that the idea of radical progress ignores some of the continuities in the coercion of labour. As has been pointed out by Christopher Tomlins, the ending of formal indentured servitude (under the Thirteenth Amendment) did not in fact stop the legal arrest and imprisonment of workers for leaving their employment.[18] This argument concentrates not on the label of servitude and ownership but on the degree of coercion enshrined in legal *practices* at different times, a perspective that leads to much overlap of the unfree and free phases of American labour. Similarly, the widening of restrictions on British labour, which made it an imprisonable offence to leave your employment, even if hired for only a year without indentures, indicates, as Steinfeld has suggested, that apparently free markets in labour could go hand in hand with the extension of coercion. The laws of mid-eighteenth-century England remained in force until the 1870s.[19] There are other reasons for doubting the dramatic character of changes after 1776. Some significant developments had already occurred before American independence. Indentured labour may have ceased as a means of attracting people to America, but that may be because, even before 1776, families had begun to dominate migration, particularly from northern England and Scotland. These families flooded into the backcountry of the colonies, and this trend continued after the Revolution. The old-established pattern of single, mostly male, migration, from the southern regions of England, was slowly declining, and in many ways surpassed by this family movement. It is therefore possible that the supply of individual servants was already falling, before demand for them declined.[20] Elsewhere, unfree labour persisted, like convict transportation, with legal and extra-legal forces of coercion applied to the subordinated. In the British Empire the state-managed movement of labour that replaced the slave trade involved the indenturing of millions of Indian workers shipped to places as far apart as Trinidad and

Fiji. This trade far exceeded that of slaves across the Atlantic, and was part of an early globalization of labour migration. It has been said that, in the formation of the modern world,

> coercion was essential to labour regimes throughout the emerging world order, whether it was to control impressed gangs of seamen for the British navy, Irish indentured servants in the West Indies, . . . or enslaved Muslims from the Sokoto Caliphate in Brazil.[21]

While there is still a tendency to assume that the progress of capitalism will inevitably lead to personal freedom and the emancipation of labour, there is still much concern about forms of unfree labour in developing countries, a live issue to this day.[22]

To the last, the image of the dangerous British criminal dominated, particularly in the minds of Americans. In the controversy over the resumption of transportation to Virginia when the convicts from Ireland were landed, for example, the *Virginia Journal* commented that 'you will have to dread robbers, murders etc. if they are permitted to land. *Query*: would not the Captain do an equal favour to the States by introducing a load of serpents?'[23] This could have been said at any time in the previous 100 years, and as so often before, the images of convicts and poisonous snakes had become associated with each other. As Kenneth Morgan points out, the colonial attitude to convicts had been a mixture of anxiety and acquiescence. Ambivalence was the core, but the convict trade was 'maintained until 1775 because it suited the social needs of the home government and the economic needs of buyers in Maryland and Virginia'.[24] What perhaps is worth reiterating is that the metropolitan, specifically London, criminal dominated the representations of the convicts, entirely in the face of the evidence. In effect, London not only shaped the direction of transportation as a national policy, as John Beattie has established: the city's criminal life and the reputations of its convicts also dominated the print image of convicts to America. The organized violent criminal gang was indeed something to fear, whenever it was found. Members committed crimes on both sides of the Atlantic, and apparently passed easily through transportation, memorably described as being to them but a 'country journey, they returning when they please'.[25] But, despite the many narratives, few convicts sent to colonies presented that level of menace. The reality for both the convicts and their new colonial employers was very different. The provincial convicts, many produced by quarter sessions for minor crimes, were most likely to have passed blamelessly through their servitude, neither running away nor committing further crimes. They served a little longer, and were perhaps subject to greater suspicion and surveillance, than ordinary servants, but it was a marginal difference. There is little evidence that they acquired a permanent stigma as convicts, or 'prisoners' as they were called years later in Australia. The legal tendency in Virginia and Maryland to 'assimilate convicts, in principle, with slaves rather than ordinary indentured servants' can be exaggerated, as it seems that they, like many servants, joined the poor whites of the Chesapeake on completion of their service, or left to find other opportunities. They were perhaps among those former servants seen by Father Mosley on the Eastern Shore of Maryland, 'strolling about the country without bread'.[26]

For the British, as long as American transportation lasted, it was seen as an efficient if not entirely successful punishment. America was not a penal colony but an established society, if rather different from that in England, into which convicts were being fitted. Debate concentrated on whether the punishment worked, whether felons were rehabilitated, or whether they returned to their criminal ways, either in the colonies or, even, in England. The American experience shaped British narratives of Australian transportation, with the exception that, gradually, the penal colonies of the early 1800s acquired a fearful reputation and political opposition both at home and in Australia itself. This was also part of a common reaction in Britain and America to old forms of punishment, though most initial opposition was to ancient forms of corporal punishment and more extreme forms of cruelty.[27] What made Australia distinctive is that it was from the outset a penal colony in which labour was regulated by government. By contrast, the American colonies had their own 'customs of the country', labour relations and legislatures. The British could send convicts, and they might be granted a qualified welcome, but the society in which they were received could not be controlled. The Atlantic world was in many ways a voluntary one, driven by trade and connected by mutual interests. There was no single managing force, nor any realistic attempt at legal uniformity. The result was that the convict world on the two sides of the Atlantic differed in terms of law, culture and society. What bound them together, for a while at least, was the movement of convicts and their stories.

Notes

Chapter 1 Introduction – the formation of the criminal Atlantic

1. *Maryland Gazette*, 27 Aug. 1752; see theatre notice for Williamsburg, *Virginia Gazette* (Purdie and Dixon, and Rind), 26 May 1768; Henry T. Tuckerman, *America and her Commentators, with a critical sketch of Travel in the United States* (New York: originally 1864, reprinted August M. Kelley, 1970), p. 173, referring to the visit of Rev. Andrew Burnaby; for the history of colonial American theatre, see Walter J. Meserve, *An Emerging Entertainment – the Drama of the American People to 1828* (Bloomington: Indiana University Press, 1977); on population and convicts in Virginia and Maryland, see A. Roger Ekirch, *Bound for America: the Transportation of British Convicts to the Colonies, 1718–75* (Oxford: Clarendon Press, 1987), pp. 116–18.

2. David Nokes, *John Gay: a Profession of Friendship. A Critical Biography* (Oxford: Oxford University Press, 1995), p. 443; for the impact of *The Beggar's Opera* in America, see Julian Mates, 'Some Early American Musical Stage Forms', *Popular Music and Society* 13 (2) (1989), 67–75, p. 68.

3. Andrea Mackenzie, 'Making Crime Pay: Motives, Marketing Strategies, and the Printed Literature of Crime in England, 1670–1770', in Greg T. Smith, Allyson N. May and Simon Devereaux (eds), *Criminal Justice in the Old World and the New: Essays in Honour of J. M. Beattie* (Toronto: Centre for Criminology, 1998), p. 243.

4. Her account, as Mary Young, is in Philip Rawlings, *Drunks, Whores and Idle Apprentices: Criminal Biographies of the Eighteenth Century* (London: Routledge, 1992); *The Complete Newgate Calendar*, 6 vols (London: Navarre Society, 1926), vol. 3, pp. 102–8, 'Mary Young *alias* Jenny Diver', *Old Bailey Sessions Papers*, 16 Jan. 1741; *Newcastle Courant*, 26 May 1738, as an example of a provincial newspaper taking an interest; John Gay, *The Beggar's Opera*, ed. Edgar V. Roberts (London: Edward Arnold, 1968; originally University of Nebraska Press, 1968), p. 39

5. Gay, *Beggar's Opera*, p. 27.

6. *Maryland Gazette*, 10 June 1756 – Poney had earlier been branded for burglary, *Maryland Gazette*, 12 June 1751; for two alternative stories on Ketch, see Walter Thornbury and Edward Walford, *Old and New London: a Narrative of its History, Its People and its Places* (London, 1897), vol. 5, p. 196 (cited in Roberts' edition of *The Beggar's Opera*, p. 27) and V. A. C. Gatrell, *The Hanging Tree: Execution and the English People, 1770–1868* (Oxford: Oxford University Press, 1994), p. 116. There are parallels in the late nineteenth-century creation of the 'hooligan' in England, which was based on a mythical London gang led by someone called Hooley: see Geoff Pearson, *Hooligan: a History of Respectable Fears* (London: Macmillan, 1983).

7. From the film *The Man Who Shot Liberty Valance*, John Ford, 1962.

8. John Brewer, *The Pleasures of the Imagination: English Culture in the Eighteenth Century* (New York: Farrar, Straus and Giroux, 1997), pp. 436–7.
9. Ebenezer Cook, 1667–1733, *The Sot-Weed Factor; or a Voyage to Maryland etc.* (London, 1708), reprinted in Paul Lauter (ed.) *The Heath Anthology of American Literature*, 2 vols, 2nd edn (Boston MA: Houghton Mifflin, 1994), pp. 631–49; Daniel Defoe, *The Fortunes and Misfortunes of the Famous Moll Flanders*, ed. David Blewett (London: Penguin, 1989); on non-criminal migration, see David Souden, ' "Rogues, Whores and Vagabonds?": Indentured Servant Emigrants to North America and the Case of Mid-Seventeenth Century Bristol', *Social History* 3 (1978), 23–41; for a positive assessment of the opportunities for convicts in the colonies, see Michael J. Rozbicki, *The Complete Colonial Gentleman: Cultural Legitimacy in Plantation America* (Charlottesville, VA and London: University Press of Virginia, 1998), pp. 92–6.
10. P. Spierenburg, *The Prison Experience: Disciplinary Institutions and Their Inmates in Early Modern Europe* (New Brunswick and London: Rutgers University Press, 1991), p. 264, argues that in Britain, uniquely in Europe, the importance of imprisonment declined during the period 1720–80 as transportation to the colonies was adopted; J. M. Beattie, *Crime and the Courts in England, 1660–1800* (Princeton, NJ: Princeton University Press, 1986), pp. 498–9 and 548–9, documents the decline of imprisonment after 1718 in Surrey and Sussex.
11. Stuart B. Schwartz, 'The Formation of a Colonial Identity in Brazil', in Nicholas Canny and Anthony Pagden (eds), *Colonial Identity in the Atlantic World, 1500–1800* (Princeton, NJ: Princeton University Press, 1987), 15–50, p. 21; Timothy J. Coates, 'Crime and Punishment in the Fifteenth-Century Portuguese World: the Transition from Internal to Imperial Exile', in Donald J. Kagay and L. J. Andrew Villalon (eds), *The Final Argument: the Imprint of Violence on Society in Medieval and Early Modern Europe* (Woodbridge: Boydell Press, 1998), 119–39, noting a 1903 statement by a Portuguese author, p. 139; for France see James D. Hardy, 'The Transportation of Convicts to Colonial Louisiana', *Louisiana History* 7 (1966), 207–20, p. 220; for the later French practice, see Richard Price, *The Convict and the Colonel* (Boston, MA: Beacon Press, 1998); Stephen P. Frank, *Crime, Cultural Conflict and Justice in Rural Russia, 1856–1914* (Berkeley, CA: University of California Press, 1999).
12. Simon Devereaux, 'In Place of Death: Transportation, Penal Practices and the English State, 1770–1830', in Carolyn Strange (ed.), *Qualities of Mercy: Justice, Punishment and Discretion* (Vancouver: University of British Columbia Press, 1996), 52–76, pp. 58–9; Morgan and Rushton, *Rogues, Thieves*, Chapters 7 and 8; Joanna Innes, 'The Role of Transportation in Seventeenth and Eighteenth-Century English Penal Practice', in Carl Bridge (ed.), *New Perspectives in Australian History* (London: Institute for Commonwealth Studies, Occasional Papers no. 5, 1990), 1–24.
13. Lois Green Carr, 'Emigration and the Standard of Living: the Eighteenth-Century Chesapeake', in John J. McCusker and Kenneth Morgan (eds), *The Early Modern Atlantic Economy* (Cambridge: Cambridge University Press, 2000), 319–43, p. 320; see also Marilyn C. Baseler, *'Asylum for Mankind': America 1607–1800* (Ithaca, NY: Cornell University Press, 1988), p. 104; servitude in the colonies was very different from its equivalent institution in Britain.

14. David Armitage, 'Three Concepts of Atlantic History', in David Armitage and Michael J. Braddick (eds), *The British Atlantic World* (London: Palgrave Macmillan, 2002), 11–27, p. 26.
15. See Ian K. Steele, *The English Atlantic, 1675–1740: an Exploration of Communication and Community* (New York and Oxford: Oxford University Press, 1986); Part 1 is organized around products and routes.
16. Alison Games, 'Migration', in Armitage and Braddick (eds), *The British Atlantic World*, 31–50, p. 41 and Table 2.1 on that page.
17. Kenneth Morgan, *Bristol and the Atlantic Trade in the Eighteenth Century* (Cambridge: Cambridge University Press, 1993), p. 126; also see his 'Business Networks in the British Export Trade to North America, 1750–1800', in McCusker and Morgan, *Early Modern Atlantic Economy*, 16–62.
18. Keach Johnson, 'The Baltimore Company Seeks English Markets: a Study of the Anglo-American Iron Trade, 1731–55', *William and Mary Quarterly*, 3rd ser. 16 (1) (1959), 37–60, pp. 49, 54; Morgan, *Bristol and the Atlantic Trade*, pp. 126–7.
19. Johnson, 'Baltimore Company', pp. 46–8; Crowley had previously imported iron in the 1730s from the Principio Company, operating in Virginia and Maryland.
20. Morgan, 'Business Networks', p. 36; T. H. Breen, 'An Empire of Goods: the Anglicization of Colonial America, 1690–1776', *Journal of British Studies* 25 (1986), 467–99; see *Joshua Johnson's Letterbook, 1771–4: Letters from a Merchant in London to his Partners in Maryland*, ed. Jacob M. Price (London: London Record Society, 1979), p. 33.
21. Colin Kidd, *British Identities Before Nationalism: Ethnicity and Nationhood in the Atlantic World, 1600–1800* (Cambridge: Cambridge University Press, 1999), p. 263.
22. Armitage, 'Three Concepts', p. 21.
23. *Quarter Sessions Records for the County of Somerset*, 4 vols, ed. Rev. H. E. Bates (later H. E. Bates Harbin), from vol. 2 (Somerset Record Society, 1907–19), vol. 3, pp. 46, 358–9.
24. Armitage, 'Three Concepts', p. 25.
25. See L. Radzinowicz, *A History of English Criminal Law and its Administration from 1750*, 4 vols, vol. 1 *The Movement for Reform* (London: Stevens and Sons, 1948), where the implications for American or even British society are widely neglected; Ekirch, *Bound for America*; B. Bailyn, *Voyagers to the West: a Passage in the Peopling of America on the Eve of the Revolution* (New York: Knopf, 1986); Aaron S. Fogleman, 'From Slaves, Convicts, and Servants to Free Passengers: the Transformation of Immigration in the Era of the American Revolution', *Journal of American History* 85 (1) (1998), 43–75.
26. P. Gilroy, *The Black Atlantic: Modernity and Double Consciousness* (London: Verso, 1993); Peter Linebaugh and Marcus Rediker, *The Many-Headed Hydra: the Hidden History of the Revolutionary Atlantic* (London: Verso, 2000); called the 'red Atlantic' by Armitage, 'Three Concepts', pp. 14–15.
27. Northumberland, Newcastle-upon-Tyne, County Durham, Cumberland, Westmorland, Lancashire, Devon and Bristol (assizes and quarter sessions); Hampshire, Wiltshire, Dorset, Somerset and Cornwall (assizes only).

28. Gwenda Morgan, ' "One of the First Fruits of Liberty": Penal Reform in the Young Republic' in R. A. Burchell (ed.), *The End of Anglo-America: Historical Essays in the Study of Cultural Divergence* (Manchester: Manchester University Press, 1991), 87–112; Cindy C. Burgoyne, 'Imprisonment the Best Punishment: the Transatlantic Exchange and Communication of Ideas in the Field of Penology, 1750–1800' (unpublished PhD dissertation, University of Sunderland, 1997).

29. Linda Colley, *Britons: Forging the Nation, 1707–1837* (London: Random House, 1994).

30. Charles Coleman Sellers, *The Artist of the Revolution: the Early Life of Charles Willson Peale* (Hebron, CT: Feather and Good, 1939), on Charles Peale, his father, p. 29; see Chapter 4.

Chapter 2 Pedlars in the outports: Transportation, the locality and the Atlantic

1. P. Slack, *Poverty and Policy in Tudor and Stuart England* (London: Longman, 1988), pp. 122–7; A. Fraser, *The Gypsies*, 2nd edn (Oxford: Blackwell, 1995), pp. 132–6 and p. 171, makes the point that 'gypsy' replaced the earlier 'Egyptian' only in the 1713 law; A. L. Beier, *Masterless Men: the Vagrancy Problem in England, 1560–1640* (London: Methuen, 1985). See some prosecutions of gypsies in Yorkshire in 1655, PRO ASSI 47/20/6 NE Circuit Gaol Book, 17 March 1655: four gypsies called Holland acquitted; note the use of transportation as a response to political rebellion in the seventeenth century.

2. A. E. Smith, *Colonists in Bondage. White Servitude and Convict Labor in America, 1607–1776* (New York: Norton, 1971, originally University of North Carolina Press, 1947), p. 92; Slack, *Poverty and Policy*, p. 127; Beier, *Masterless Men*, p. 162, points out that in fact most were sent to the American colonies.

3. Joanna Innes, 'The Role of Transportation in Seventeenth and Eighteenth-Century English Penal Practice', in Carl Bridge (ed.), *New Perspectives in Australian History* (London: Institute for Commonwealth Studies, Occasional Papers no. 5, 1990) pp. 8–9; see below for Devon's policies towards vagrants at quarter sessions after 1718; Paul Griffiths, 'Masterless Young People in Norwich, 1560–1645', in P. Griffiths, A. Fox and S. Hindle (eds), *The Experience of Authority in Early Modern England* (Basingstoke: Macmillan Press [now Palgrave Macmillan], 1996), 146–86.

4. Michael J. Rozbicki, 'To Save Them from Themselves: Proposals to Enslave the British Poor, 1698–1755', *Slavery and Abolition* 22 (2) (2001), 29–50, p. 43.

5. P. W. Coldham, *The Complete Book of Emigrants in Bondage, 1614–1775* (Baltimore: Genealogical Publishing Co., 1988); Coldham, *King's Passengers*.

6. J. M. Beattie, *Crime and the Courts in England, 1660–1800* (Princeton NJ: Princeton University Press, 1986), pp. 472 and 475–6.

7. A. G. L. Shaw, *Convicts and the Colonies: a Study of Penal Transportation from Great Britain and Ireland to Australia and other parts of the British Empire* (London: Faber and Faber, 1966; 2nd edn, Irish Historical Press: 1998), p. 31.

8. See *Calendar of State Papers Colonial, 1574–1660* (London: 1860), p. 457 and *Calendar of State Papers Colonial, America and West Indies, 1661–68* (London, 1880), pp. xxvii–xxx, 35, 98, 220 and 221; *Acts of the Privy Council (Colonial)* (Hereford, 1910), vol. 2, pp. 41–5; W. F. Craies, 'The Compulsion of Subjects to Leave the Realm', *Law Quarterly Review* 6 (1890), 388–409; for the general situation of servant-recruiting in the seventeenth century, see Kenneth Morgan, *Slavery and Servitude in North America, 1607–1800* (Edinburgh: Edinburgh University Press, 2000), Chapter 1.

9. John Wareing, ' "Violently Taken Away or Cheatingly Duckoyed": the Illicit Recruitment in London of Indentured Servants for the American Colonies, 1645–1718', *London Journal* 26 (1), (2001), 1–22, and 'Preventive and Punitive Regulation in Seventeenth-Century Social Policy: Conflicts of Interest and the Failure to Make "Stealing and Transporting Children and Other Persons" a Felony, 1645–73', *Social History* 27 (3) (2002), 288–308; *Calendar of State Papers Colonial, America and West Indies, 1661–68*, p. 221; Marilyn C. Baseler, *'Asylum for Mankind': America 1607–1800* (Ithaca, NY: Cornell University Press, 1988), p. 89; D. H. Sacks, *The Widening Gate: Bristol and the Atlantic Economy, 1450–1700* (Berkeley, CA: University of California Press, 1991), Chapter 9 'Registering the Pilgrimage'.

10. *Quarter Sessions Records for the County of Somerset*, 4 vols, ed. E. H. Bates (Somerset: Somerset Record Society, 1907–19), vol. 1, p. 242; Claire Tomalin, *Samuel Pepys: the Unequalled Self* (London: Viking/Penguin, 2002), pp. 245–6.

11. See *An Essay against the Transportation and Selling of Men to the Plantations of Foreigners, with special regard to the manufactories and other domestic improvements of the kingdom of Scotland . . . by 'a sincere well-wisher to the honour and interest of his Country'*, Edinburgh, 1699 (University of London, Goldsmiths Collection); Baseler, *'Asylum for Mankind'*, pp. 38–9, points out that the Scottish Privy Council had declared against forced recruitment of Scots to servitude the year before.

12. See Chapter 4. For a useful summary of many stories of servitude, see John Van der Zee, *Bound Over: Indentured Servitude and American Conscience* (New York: Simon and Schuster, 1985) who deals with the first two of these; Edward Kimber, *The History of the Life and Adventures of Mr Anderson, containing his strange varieties of Fortune in Europe and America* (London: W. Owen, 1754); this derived from a real case of a man whom he interviewed some years earlier, in his *Itinerant Observations in America* – originally 1745–46 in the *London Magazine* and printed repeatedly since – see Savannah edition, J. H. Estill (1878), and a modern edition edited by Kevin J. Hayes (Newark, DE: University of Delaware Press, 1998).

13. See the differences between the two editions of Carew's story, *The Life and Adventures of Bampfylde Moore Carew, the noted Devonshire Stroler and Dog-Stealer* (Exeter: the Farleys, 1745), and *An Apology for the Life of Bampfylde-Moore Carew* (London: R. Goadby, 1749), discussed in Chapter 4; note that the latter was sold by the W. Owen who printed Kimber's novel; Goadby also printed and advertised in his *Sherborne Mercury or Western Flying Post* (see 13 May 1751) *The Unhappy Voyage and Long Captivity in Barbary of Thomas Pellow of the Borough of Penrynn in the County of Cornwall* – a long description of his 23 years in captivity; Morgan and Rushton, *Rogues, Thieves*, p. 166.

14. J. M. Beattie, *Policing and Punishment in London, 1660–1750: Urban Crime and the Limits of Terror* (Oxford: Oxford University Press, 2001), pp. 288 and 290–1; Innes, 'The Role of Transportation', p. 8; for the best study of the processes of decision-making, see Peter King, *Crime, Justice and Discretion in England, 1740–1820* (Oxford: Oxford University Press, 2000).

15. See the experience in Essex in the 1660s and 1670s: J. A. Sharpe, *Crime in Seventeenth-Century England: a County Study* (Cambridge: Cambridge University Press, 1983), p. 148; and for estimated total 1655–99, see Shaw, *Convicts and the Colonies*, p. 24.

16. Beattie, *Policing and Punishment*, p. 295; Shaw, *Convicts and the Colonies*, p. 32.

17. PRO SP 36/38, pt.2/162–3, concerning George Vaughan, 2 March 1735/36.

18. PRO ASSI 42/1, p. 37, and see also p. 2 for 1665, and p. 32 for 1668; K. Emsley, 'A Circuit Judge in Northumberland', *Tyne and Tweed* 31 (1978), p. 18.

19. Notebook of Isaac Basire, Dean and Chapter Library, Durham, Hunter MSS 137, unpaginated.

20. Coldham, *Complete Book*; seventeen between 1679 and 1685, then two in 1688 and one in 1694, eleven in 1699; PRO PL 28/1, which is foliated on lefthand-sided pages and partially paginated, ff.7 (p. 14), 33v (p. 39), 59v (p. 78), 70v (p. 104); for branding, see 64v (p. 128), 84v (p. 132), f.94v (p. 145); armed services, 100v (p. 158); imprisonment, f.166 (p. 191) and f.188v (p. 194); Devon in Coldham, *Bonded Passengers to America*, vol.5.

21. DRO Q/S/OB 1, p. 193, early 1620s, Q/S/OB 5, p. 269, 25 April 1666; *Guide to the Hertfordshire Record Office, Part 1: Quarter Sessions and Other Records in the Custody of the Officials of the County* (Hertford: Hertfordshire County Council, 1961), p. 28.

22. NRO, QSO, 5, pp. 60 (Michaelmas 1711), 64 and 74.

23. NRO, QSO 5, pp. 86, 110, 120, 124, 340 (long quotation), 341 and 354; and in unpaginated appendix, Jan. 1712, and 26 March 1717, £27 8s 4d costs of apprehending the faws and putting them on 'shipboard'; QSB 51, Michaelmas 1719, f.29, and QSB 55, Midsummer 1721, f.11, for additional payments.

24. NRO, QSB 65, Midsummer 1725, f.9; and *Newcastle Courant*, 7 Nov. 1730; Angus Fraser, *The Gypsies*, 2nd edn (Oxford: Blackwell, 1995), p. 171.

25. Morgan and Rushton, *Rogues, Thieves*, pp. 22–5.

26. Devon RO, QS 1/15 Order Book 1704–18, f.332, Easter 1717; LRO, QSO/2/87, Epiphany 1718, p. 30 (referring to sentence in previous sessions), and Michaelmas 1718, p. 27.

27. Note that Devon for many years distinguished these different types of sentences in its records of convicts – those liable to whipping and those to branding.

28. See A. Roger Ekirch, *Bound for America: the Transportation of British Convicts to the Colonies, 1718–1775* (Oxford: Clarendon Press, 1987), pp. 18, 22n. 2, and map, p. 51.

29. Devon RO, QS 1/15 Order Book 1704–18, f.356v, Easter, f.364, Midsummer 1718, and f.367v, Michaelmas 1718.

30. Devon RO, QS 1/17 Order Book 1725–34, pp. 55 and 60.

31. As Innes has noted, 'The Role of Transportation', p. 4. Devon records suggest that a large proportion of 'larcenies' tried were grand, since petty

larceny is usually carefully recorded where relevant. However, this vagueness allows little precise calculation.

32. Three in both the 1750s and 1760s, and two in the 1770s. Devon RO; for 1739, see QS 129/21, and QS 1/18, ff.105, 106 and 106v, 107, vagrants Abraham Hart, Edward Browne, John Smith, plus Carew, and probably William King on the same ship, owned by Ethelred Davy.

33. Maryland State Archives, Annapolis, Kent County Court Bonds and Indentures 1735–40, p. 108 (Jane wife of Richard Mullins, 1733), p. 155 (Agnes Seller, 1734, Tiverton) and p. 192 (Ann Croscombe, 1739 from Barnstaple); Devon RO, R4/1/C/338, Tiverton Sessions Book, 1740 onwards, 9 Jan. 1749.

34. Eighty convicts are known to have been sentenced before 1776; for the early cases, see Devon RO, ECA 69 and Gaol Delivery.

35. NRO, QS0 6, p. 295 (Morgan); an 'anchor' or anker (*OED*) was a barrel containing 10 old gallons, or 8.5 imperial gallons.

36. Richard Welford, *Men of Mark 'Twixt Tyne and Tweed* (London and Newcastle-upon-Tyne: 1895), vol. 3, pp. 687–9; W. A. Speck, 'Northumberland Elections in the Eighteenth Century', *Northern History* 28 (1992), 164–77, p. 170; NRO, QSO 6, pp. 248, 266 and 321, and QSB 59 (Midsummer 1723), ff.91, 93 and 97; QSB 64 (Easter 1725), f.15.

37. Morgan and Rushton, *Rogues, Thieves*, pp. 73–4.

38. Cumbria RO, Carlisle, CQ 3/1, pp. 53 and 58.

39. Cumbria RO, Carlisle, CQ 3/1, p. 151.

40. Cumbria RO, Kendal, WQ/O/6 1738–50, Appleby sessions, Easter 1737, Stephen Nicholson; WQ/M/1 Rough Minute Book 1733–7, Appleby sessions, Easter 1737.

41. Newcastle: 123 compared with eighty-six sentenced or reprieved at the assizes; Lancashire: 430 from the quarter sessions compared with 206 from the assizes; see Chapter 3.

42. K. Morgan, *Bristol and the Atlantic Trade in the Eighteenth Century* (Cambridge: Cambridge University Press, 1993).

43. N. Tattersfield, *The Forgotten Trade, comprising the Log of the Daniel and Henry of 1700 and Accounts of the Slave trade from the Minor Ports of England, 1698–1725* (London: Pimlico, 1998), pp. 14–5: the 10 per cent tax due to the Royal African Company lasted from 1698 to 1712.

44. Ekirch, *Bound for America*, p. 70.

45. PRO ASSI 42/4, ff.3v-4 and 8.

46. Tattersfield, *The Forgotten Trade*, pp. 305–6; Alison Grant, 'Emigration from Devon in the Seventeenth Century', in Michael Duffy, Stephen Fisher, Basil Greenhill, David J. Starkey and Joyce Youings (eds), *The New Maritime History of Devon, Vol. I: From Early Times to the Late Eighteenth Century* (London: Conway Maritime Press and University of Exeter, 1992), 147–52, and K. Morgan, 'Convict Transportation from Devon', in Duffy et al., *The New Maritime History*, pp. 153–4; Maryland State Archives (Annapolis), Kent County Court Bonds and Indentures 1715–20, ff.65–6; Devon RO, QS1/16, p. 101 Michaelmas 1720, contract with George Buck Esq QS1/17, p. 67.

47. Survey of the surviving bonds and contracts in Devon RO, QS 129/1–93; Devon RO, Exeter City Archives (ECA) Transportation Orders and Bonds 1719–46, and Miscellaneous Sessions Papers, Box 3 Bundle 19, and

ED/M/1482 2 May 1729. Our thanks to Devon Record Office staff for their efforts in making sense of the Exeter records particularly.

48. The work of the Bucks can be reconstructed from Maryland sources particularly well, see Maryland State Archives, Annapolis, Kent County Court Bonds and Indentures 1715–20, ff.64, 65–6 (Devon and Somerset 1719–20), and Kent County Court Bonds and Indentures 1731–35: pp. 55–6 for Devon and Dorset 1731–32 and p. 151 for Hampshire; Kent County Court (Bonds and Indentures) 1743–46; pp. 68–9 for Worcestershire, John Buck and William Buck, 22 Feb. 1743.

49. Devon RO, QS 129/94 piece 6, William Stevenson to Adam Pierce, Exon 11 Nov. 1768, and piece 19, William Randolph to Adam Pierce, 11 May 1770; for a thorough analysis of the role of this firm, see K. Morgan, 'The Organization of the Convict Trade to Maryland: Stevenson, Randolph and Cheston, 1768–1775', *William and Mary Quarterly* 3rd ser. 42 (2) (1985), 201–27, particularly pp. 205–11.

50. Devon RO, QS 129/94, piece 20, 19 June 1770 to Mr Foulkes and Mr Chancellor Carrington.

51. Devon RO, QS 129/94, piece 30, 30 Aug. 1773; Morgan, 'The Organization of the Convict Trade', p. 211, suggests that the firm drew convicts from the western circuit, the west Midlands and Wales, including Cheshire and Staffordshire.

52. Devon RO, QS 129/94, piece 23, 12 Feb. 1771, Stevenson and Randolph to John Baring Esq; piece 27, 27 April 1773; and piece 28, 29 April 1773.

53. *Felix Farley's Bristol Journal*, 4 May 1771, referring to the *Elizabeth* which carried about ninety-one people to America; see P. W. Coldham, *King's Passengers*, pp. 250, 251–4, 255–8, and 260–1; we are grateful to Dr Lorena Walsh, of Colonial Williamsburg, for access to her shipping data based on Chesapeake port books.

54. D. Richardson and M. M. Schofield, 'Whitehaven and the Eighteenth-Century British Slave Trade', *Transactions C&WAAS* 92 (1992), 183–204, p. 183; J. V. Beckett, *Coal and Tobacco: the Lowthers and the Economic Development of West Cumberland, 1660–1760* (Cambridge: Cambridge University Press, 1981), pp. 119 and 135–9 on problems of failure to develop industries other than coal.

55. D. R. Hainsworth, ed., *The Correspondence of Sir John Lowther of Whitehaven, 1693–1698: a Provincial Community in Wartime* (Oxford: Oxford University Press, 1983), p. 666; most of the correspondence and discussion took place in 1699.

56. Beckett, *Coal and Tobacco*, pp. 121, 164 and 169.

57. See Tattersfield, *The Forgotten Trade*, pp. 332–7; quarter sessions records in 1729, 1733 (Cumberland) and 1737 (Westmorland): Cumbria RO (Carlisle) CQ1/3, Oct. 1733, CQ1/4, Oct. 1729; (Kendal) WQ/O/5 Kendal and Appleby, 1724–37, Easter 1737; Edward Hughes made Lutwidge a case study in Cumberland's business community, see E. Hughes, *North Country Life in the Eighteenth Century, Vol. 2: Cumberland and Westmorland* (London: Oxford University Press, 1965), Chapter 2.

58. Cumbria RO, Whitehaven, YDX 79/1, p. 79, about raising loans, to Alex Mackenzie, 10 Nov. 1746.

59. Cumbria RO, Whitehaven, YDX, 79/1, p. 336, to Isaac Cookson, 8 Sept. 1740; see below for Newcastle's rioters shipped to London in October.

60. Cumbria RO, Whitehaven, YDX 79/1, pp. 131 and 133, 24 Dec. 1739; YDX 79/2, p. 39, Copy of Daniel Lamb's letter dated 30 May 1746, Choptank Maryland; for cargoes to the Potomac, see YDX 79/1, p. 425, Oct. 1740, 'callicoes, seersuckers, linen, ginghams, chintz, china silk, bandanoos, dickmansoys, bombay shifts, taffaties'.

61. Cumbria RO, Whitehaven, YDX 79/1, pp. 224–5, the lists of items for slave expeditions to Angola, voyages made 1733, 1735, 1736 and 1737; see Hughes, *North Country Life in the Eighteenth Century*, vol. 2, pp. 45–7; YDX 79/2, p. 566, to John Hardman at Liverpool, 15 Oct. 1749.

62. Cumbria RO, Carlisle, CQ1/3, October 1733 Penrith; CQ 1/4, Rough Order Book, Oct. 1729 (five felons).

63. Cumbria RO (Carlisle) CQ1/5, p. 398, Jan. 1746/7, transportation for John Johnston for stealing deal boards from William Hicks, before Peter How. Unfortunately, there is no record of who carried out his transportation.

64. Beckett, *Coal and Tobacco*, p. 110, and pp. 108, 113 and 117; A. N. Rigg, *Cumbria, Slavery and the Textile Revolution* (Kirkby Stephen, Cumbria: Hewitson and Harker, 1994), pp. 77–8; Richardson and Schofield, 'White-haven and the Eighteenth-Century British Slave Trade'; Cumbria RO (Carlisle), CQ1/3, Jan. 1736, for his first contract, and CQ1/8, Jan. 1764, for the last.

65. PRO ASSI 45/25/1/94–8, evidence against Anthony Mawson, 1753.

66. Cumbria RO, Carlisle: CQ 1/3, 1/5, p. 44, 78 and 297; CQ 1/6, 1/7, 1/8, and CQ 2/2, pp. 125, 143, and 177; CQ 8/1 pp. 272, 363, for many references to How between 1736 and 1764.

67. Tattersfield, *The Forgotten Trade*, p. 346; there was a Charles Lutwidge on the magistrates' bench in 1764; Cumbria RO (Carlisle) Q1/8, Oct. 1764 sessions.

68. Cumbria RO (Kendal) WQ/SR/153 (Sessions Rolls) 1742 (Michaelmas), Appleby; WQ/SP/T/1-44 Transportation Bonds 1739–85 gives Thomas Seal or Seel of Liverpool from 1739–43, but (piece 2) had to take one free after allowing Joseph Coulthurst to escape.

69. Cumbria RO (Kendal) WQ/M/3, Easter 1753.

70. Cumbria RO (Kendal) WQ/0/9 1770–80, 1 Oct. 1770. The standard fee for taking felons to Whitehaven was a guinea, £1 1s : see many examples from the previous decade, WQ/O/8 1760–69.

71. S. Ville, 'Total Factor Productivity in the English Shipping Industry: the North-East Coal Trade, 1700–1850', *Economic History Review*, 2nd ser. 39 (3) (1986), 355–70, p. 361.

72. P. Linebaugh, *The London Hanged: Crime and Civil Society in the Eighteenth Century* (Harmondsworth: Penguin, 1991), pp. 135–6.

73. R. Davis, *The Rise of the English Shipping Industry in the Seventeenth and Eighteenth Centuries* (Newton Abbot: David and Charles, 1962), pp. 62–8: about a quarter of British ships were built in America by the 1760s; the 120-ton *Lowther and Senhouse*, which, despite its Whitehaven name, was built in New England, transported north-eastern convicts in 1772; Northumberland RO QSB 89/26. See also A. W. Purdue, *Merchants and Gentry in North-East England, 1650–1830: the Carrs and the Ellisons* (Sunderland: University of

Sunderland Press, 1999), pp. 155–63, although Ralph Carr said that north-eastern merchants would be crippled by the Stamp Act, owing nearly £1m to the Treasury if they paid the £2,000 bonds (p. 161).

74. PRO E 190 series, 1717 to 1770s, 221/3 onwards.

75. *Newcastle Courant*, 27 Aug. 1726; 24 Sept. 1726; 4 Nov. 1727, the *Esther* for Maryland, with Capt. Alan Giles; G. A. Blumer, 'The Washington and Colville Families', *Archaeologia Aeliana*, New Series 19 (1897), 115–26.

76. *Newcastle Courant*, 10 Aug. 1728, the *Mally* under Capt. John Hodgson.

77. *Newcastle Courant*, 1 July 1741 .

78. PRO, E 190 245/4, 17 March 1743, 10 April 1745, 18 April 1745.

79. *Newcastle Courant*, 1 June 1745.

80. *Newcastle Courant*, 29 June 1745.

81. PRO ADM 2/489, f.237, 17 July 1745, f.339 23 July 1745; the convicts were John Ostwald, John Windram, Thomas Parsons and Henry Bell.

82. *Newcastle Courant*, 30 Sept. 1758; see Pieter Spierenburg, *Prison Experience*, p. 277, on rituals of transportation.

83. *Newcastle Courant*, 18 Oct. 1740.

84. See Chapter 3; B. Bailyn, *Voyagers to the West: a Passage in the Peopling of America on the Eve of the Revolution* (New York: Knopf, 1986), pp. 338, 373, 408 and 420.

85. *Newcastle Courant*, 5 July 1740, and 29 Nov. 1740 (the number of servants had gone down to seventeen by the latter report of the safe arrival).

86. See Chapter 3. Shipment reports suggest an average of just over twelve, but since this is derived from only eight newspaper and certificate accounts of the numbers of convicts on particular ships from north-east England, it must be regarded as very tentative. Most newspaper reports simply refer to 'convicts' or 'the Transports', unfortunately, and as non-dutyable goods, they are not recorded in port books. *Newcastle Journal*, 25 Jan. 1766, and *Newcastle Courant*, 14 Feb. 1767, for the *Jenny*. In the latter the fourteen convicts were accompanied by either ten or twelve 'young artificers'; the *Adventure* carried twenty-five convicts in 1773 (Coldham, *King's Passengers*, p. 242). In the case of Westmorland's convicts, the extant certificates suggest that prisoners were delivered in ones and twos at the most, reflecting the small numbers from that county: Cumbria RO (Kendal), WQ/SR/153.

87. Cook papers, Northumberland RO ZCK 3, letter from Edward Cook, 10 July 1761; on 11 July reported prices as £12 to £15 pounds sterling for seven years' servitude and 'Negroes' from £40 to £60.

88. Rigg, *Cumbria, Slavery*, pp. 70–1, referring to the 1765 and 1767 voyages of the *William*. A ship of that name took convicts in 1769 for Cumberland, Cumbria RO (Carlisle) Q11/1769, Michaelmas, piece 2.

89. Shipping provisions to Africa out of Liverpool, see PRO HCA 26/68, master of the *Fly*; see also Tony Barrow, *The Whaling Trade of North-East England* (Sunderland: University of Sunderland Press, 2001), p. 11. We are grateful to Dr Tony Barrow for his help on many aspects of Tyneside's shipping records and the PRO reference.

90. Cumbria RO, Whitehaven, YDX 79/2, pp. 55 and 500, 16 Oct. 1746 and 13 April 1749; according to Hughes, *North Country Life in the Eighteenth Century*, vol. 2, p. 36, Mackenzie was an old school friend of Lutwidge's son who he claims was by then Attorney-General in Virginia.

91. *Chronicles of the Scotch-Irish Settlement in Virginia, Extracted from the Original Court Records of Augusta County, 1745–1800*, 3 vols, ed. Lyman Chalkley (Baltimore MD: Genealogical Publishing Co., 1965, 3rd printing 1966), p. 360, March 1770: John Grant mortgaged the slaves to How in 1764, and the suit for the debt was filed in 1767.

92. Maryland State Archives, Kent County Court (Bonds and Indentures) 1715–20, ff. 65–6 Somerset and Devon, George Buck, certificates dated 29 Sept. 1719, and recorded 16 March 1719/20, all on the *Sophia* of Bideford, f. 89.

93. Kent County Court (Bonds and Indentures) 1759–67, p. 204, 3 Sept. 1761; see also debt to George and William, p. 285, 1764, and p. 375 they are 'merchants of Devon', with William Kenney of the same as their attorney.

94. *Maryland Gazette*, 15 Dec. 1768, George and William Buck; Kent County Court (Bonds and Indentures) 1767–72, p. 148, William Buck Jr and William Buck Sr acknowledge debt of £4 18s and 180lbs tobacco leaf, 21 Oct. 1769.

95. Blumer, 'Washington and Colville Families', p. 120.

96. Blumer, 'Washington and Colville Families', pp. 117–18.

97. See Blumer, 'Washington and Colville Families', p. 120, particularly for an account of the legal case which went to Williamsburg; advertisements in *Maryland Gazette*, 6 June and 6 Sept. 1760, 12 Nov. 1761, 20 Sept. 1764 and 15 Sept. 1768.

98. 'Washington Letters', *Archaeologia Aeliana* New Series 2 (1858), p. 120; Blumer, 'Washington and Colville Families', p. 123; Harry Piper Letterbook, microfilm at John D. Rockefeller Library, Colonial Williamsburg.

Chapter 3 Cities, regions and their criminals

1. Parliamentary Papers, *Report from the Select Committee on Criminal Laws etc.* (House of Commons, ordered for printing 8 July 1819); some of the data for the Home Circuit went back to 1688 (Appendix 6), and for London at the Old Bailey, 1698 (Appendix 4).

2. *Journals of the House of Commons*, vol. 36, April 1778, pp. 931–2 ('gaol distemper'), and vol. 37, p. 311, April 1779 ('gaol fever').

3. J. Howard, *An Account of the Principal Lazarettos in Europe* (Warrington: William Eyres, 1789), pp. 246–7; see *Guide to the Hertfordshire Record Office*, Part 1, *Quarter Sessions and Other Records* (Hertford: 1961), p. 29 for a surviving return to the House of Commons. For the North East, for example, Howard has ninety-two transportees, while we can find ninety-three – minor differences may derive, not from the date of trial, but the precise date of confirmed transportation of the reprieved, not all of which can be firmly established today. Howard's data form the basis for the regional analysis of convicts in A. Roger Ekirch, *Bound for America: the Transportation of British Convicts to the Colonies, 1718–75* (Oxford: Clarendon Press, 1987) p. 49.

4. J. Howard, *The State of the Prisons in England and Wales* (London, 1792), p. 425, notes that on his 1779 visit the women he had seen previously in Morpeth gaol (Northumberland) awaiting transportation had been released; these were listed reports to the Treasury in PRO E370/39/8/676–7 and 680.

5. Wilfrid Oldham, *Britain's Convicts to the Colonies*, ed. W. Hugh Oldham, commentary by Dan Byrnes (Sydney: Library of Australian History, 1990), p. 29; from PRO CO 201/2, 29 Jan. 1787; *Journals of the House of Commons*, vol. 37, p. 314.

6. Coldham, *King's Passengers, passim*.

7. Ekirch, *Bound for America*, p. 80; J. Perry, 'North Riding Quarter Sessions Records', *North Yorkshire County Record Office Journal* 8 (1981), 65–117, pp. 84 and 87; some of Derbyshire's convicts were shipped from Liverpool: E. G. Green, *Hanged for a Sheep: Crime in Bygone Derbyshire* (Cromford: Scarthin Books, 1981), p. 57.

8. *London Evening Post*, 30 Aug. and 11 Sept. 1766.

9. William Green, the unhappy sufferer, *The Sufferings of William Green, being a sorrowful account of his seven years transportation, wherein is set forth the various hardships he underwent with his parting and meeting again in that Country with his intimate Friend Anthony Atkinson with their joyful arrival in England, after being absent ten years. Likewise an Account of their manner of Living; the Climate of the Country, and in what it principally abounds* (Whitechapel, London: J. Long, undated, but after the author 'returned on the second of June 1774'), two pence.

10. *Virginia Gazette* (Purdie and Dixon), 21 Nov. 1771.

11. James D. Butler, 'British Convicts Shipped to American Colonies', *American Historical Review* 2 (1896), 12–33, pp. 24–5.

12. J. M. Beattie, *Policing and Punishment in London, 1660–1750: Urban Crime and the Limits of Terror* (Oxford: Oxford University Press, 2001), p. 438, Table 9.2.

13. George Birkbeck Hill, ed., *Boswell's Life of Johnson*, 6 vols, revised by L. F. Powell (Oxford: Clarendon Press, 1934), vol. 2, p. 312, based on Dr Lang, *Penny Cyclopaedia*, xxv, p. 138.

14. George Bancroft, *History of the United States of America*, vol. 1 (New York: D. Appleton and Company, 1888), p. 443.

15. Butler, 'British Convicts', pp. 12–13; Charles A. Beard cites Butler's comments on Bancroft at the beginning of his iconoclastic work *An Economic Interpretation of the Constitution of the United States* (London: Macmillan, 1913), pp. 1–2.

16. Fairfax Harrison, 'When the Convicts Came', *Virginia Magazine of History and Biography* 30 (1920), 250–60; Mary N. Stanard, *Colonial V irginia: its People and Customs* (Philadelphia and London: J. P. Lippencott, 1917).

17. Basil Sollers, 'Transported Convict Laborers in Maryland during the Colonial Period', *Maryland Historical Magazine* 2 (1907), 42–4.

18. *Gentleman's Magazine* 34 (1764), p. 261: convicts comprised 1,507 men, 386 women, and eighty-eight persons under sixteen, amounting to 1,981, compared with 6,970 servants 'hired or indented'.

19. R. B. Morris, *Government and Labor in Early America* (New York: Columbia University Press, 1946), pp. 328–9; Nathan I. Huggins, 'The Deforming Mirror of Truth: Slavery and the Master Narrative of American History', *Radical History Review* 49 (1991), 25–48, particularly pp. 35–7; Edmund S. Morgan, *American Slavery, American Freedom: The Ordeal of Colonial Virginia* (New York: Norton, 1975).

20. A. E. Smith, *Colonists in Bondage: White Servitude and Convict Labor in America, 1607–1776* (Chapel Hill, NC: University of North Carolina Press, 1947), pp. 117–19, nn. 22 and 23, pp. 363–4.

21. Ekirch, *Bound for America*, pp. 26–7.

22. Aaron S. Fogleman, 'From Slaves, Convicts, and Servants to Free Passengers: the Transformation of Immigration in the Era of the American Revolution', *Journal of American History* 85 (1) (1998), 43–75, p. 43 and Tables 1 and 2, p. 44 – the latter suggest 52,200 convicts and prisoners compared with 103,600 indentured servants and 151,600 free migrants, 1700–75, from all European countries, and 32,500 convicts of 73,100 English and Welsh migrants, in Table A3, p. 71; Francis D. Cogliano, *Revolutionary America, 1763–1815* (London and New York: Routledge, 2000), p. 182–99; Morris, *Government and Labor in Early America*.

23. Linda Colley, *Captives: Britain, Empire and the World, 1600–1850* (London: Jonathan Cape, 2002), p. 188, and Ferenc M. Szasz, 'Peter Williamson and the Eighteenth-Century Scottish-American Connection', *Northern Scotland* 19 (1999), 47–61.

24. Bob Reece, *The Origins of Irish Convict Transportation to New South Wales* (Basingstoke: Palgrave, 2001), p. 12; Neal Garnham, *The Courts, Crime and the Criminal Law in Ireland, 1692–1760* (Dublin: Irish Academic Press, 1996).

25. Williamson was in fact captured three times, once by Scots, and twice by Indians and French; James Annesley was the most well known of this group; see Chapter 4.

26. Peter King, *Crime, Justice and Discretion in England 1740–1820* (Oxford: Oxford University Press, 2000), p. 355.

27. Max Weber, *Economy and Society*, vol. 2, trans. G. Roth and C. Wittich (Berkeley, CA: University of California Press, 1978), pp. 976 and 1115–16.

28. See Gwenda Morgan and Peter Rushton, 'The Magistrate, the Community and the Maintenance of an Orderly Society in Eighteenth-Century England', *Historical Research* 76 (2003), 54–77, for a local case study of these processes in eighteenth-century County Durham.

29. Morgan and Rushton, *Rogues, Thieves*, Chapter 3.

30. *Exeter Flying Post*, 13 July 1764; 24 Aug. 1764, reporting 23 Aug. gaol delivery for Exeter; 7 June 1765, the next gaol delivery.

31. Beattie, *Policing and Punishment in London*, pp. 26–9; see below for discussion of gender and cities.

32. Morgan and Rushton, *Rogues, Thieves*, p. 70.

33. See Howard, *Lazarettos*, p. 246–7: there were 122 transportees from the quarter sessions of whom twenty-two came from Liverpool, and forty-four from the assizes.

34. Pieter Spierenburg, *The Spectacle of Suffering. Executions and the Evolution of Repression: from a Preindustrial Metropolis to the European Experience* (Cambridge: Cambridge University Press, 1984), p. 101; on the role of 'mercy' in the criminal law, see Douglas Hay, 'Property, Authority and the Criminal Law' in D. Hay, P. Linebaugh, J. G. Rule, E. P. Thompson and C. Winslow (eds), *Albion's Fatal Tree: Crime and Society in Eighteenth-Century England* (London: Allen Lane, 1975), pp. 17–63; for an alternative view, Peter King, 'Decision-makers and Decision-making in the English Criminal Law', *Historical Journal* 27 (1984), 25–58. Though most appeals against the

death sentence were successful, those made against transportation usually failed. In the case of women, pregnancy might serve to delay passage across the Atlantic but it was not a sufficient cause to prevent it.

35. Henry Fielding; 'An Inquiry into the Late Increase in Robbers' in *The Works of Henry Fielding Esquire*, 10 vols (London: Smith Elder, 1882), vol. 7; J. M. Beattie, 'London Crime and the Making of the "Bloody Code", 1689–1718' and Nicholas Rogers, 'Confronting the Crime Wave: the Debate over Social Reform and Regulation', in L. Davison Tim Hitchcock, Tim Keirn and R. B. Shoemaker (eds), *Stilling the Grumbling Hive: the Response to Social and Economic Problems in England, 1660–1750* (Stroud: Alan Sutton, 1992), 49–76 and 77–98; Thomas Laqueur, 'Crowds, Carnivals and the State in English Executions, 1604–1800' in A. L. Beier, D. Cannadine and J. M. Rosenheim (eds), *The First Modern Society: Essays in honour of Lawrence Stone* (Cambridge: Cambridge University Press, 1989), pp. 305–55; V. A. C. Gatrell, *The Hanging Tree: Execution and the English People* (Oxford: Oxford University Press, 1994); Julius R. Ruff, *Violence in Early Modern Europe* (Cambridge: Cambridge University Press, 2001), pp. 22–3.

36. Alan Atkinson, 'The Free-Born Englishman Transported: Convict Rights as a Measure of Eighteenth-Century Empire', *Past and Present* 144 (1994), 88–115, pp. 92 and 94, though footnote 18 gives Ekirch's 19 per cent from Maryland data.

37. Kenneth Emsley, 'A Circuit Judge in Northumberland', *Tyne and Tweed* 31 (1978), 13–18, p. 18; Peter Rushton, 'Crazes and Quarrels: the Character of Witchcraft in the North East of England, 1649–80', *Durham County Local History Society Bulletin* 31 (1983), 2–40; J. Hodgson, 'Calendars of the Prisoners Confined in the High Castle in Newcastle upon Tyne, at the Assizes for Northumberland in the years 1628 and 1629', *Archaeologia Aeliana* 1 (1822), 149–63.

38. Philip Jenkins, 'From Gallows to Prison? The Execution Rate in Early Modern England', *Criminal Justice History* 7 (1986), 51–71, p. 65.

39. Fifty-three of the 118 men, or 45 per cent.

40. John Rule, 'The Manifold Causes of Rural Crime: Sheep-Stealing in England, c.1740–1840', in John Rule (ed.), *Outside the Law: Studies in Crime and Order, 1650–1850* (Exeter: Exeter University Press, 1982), 102–29; on sheep stealing in the North, however, see Roger Wells, 'Sheep-Rustling in Yorkshire in the Age of the Industrial and Agricultural Revolutions', *Northern History* 20 (1984), 127–45; E. P. Thompson, *Whigs and Hunters: the Origin of the Black Act* (London: Allen Lane, 1975).

41. For a detailed study of these 1732 incidents around turnpikes, see Robert W. Malcolmson, ' "A Set of Ungovernable People": the Kingswood Colliers in the Eighteenth Century', in John Brewer and John Styles (eds), *An Ungovernable People: the English and their Law in the Seventeenth and Eighteenth Centuries* (London: Hutchinson, 1980), 85–127, p. 101.

42. According to Dale E. Williams, there were seven hangings for riot in Wiltshire in 1766 with fifty-seven receiving lesser punishments: Andrew Charlesworth (ed), *An Atlas of Rural Protest in Britain 1548–1900* (London: Croom Helm, 1983), pp. 88–92: this may have been true only for the whole country in that year. See John Stevenson, *Popular Disturbances in England 1700–1832* (London and New York: Longman, 1992), 2nd edn, p. 122; on

social crime, see John Rule, 'Social Crime in the Rural South in the Eighteenth and Early Nineteenth Centuries', in John Rule and Roger Wells, *Crime, Protest and Popular Politics in Southern England, 1740–1850* (London: Hambledon Press, 1997), an expanded version of the article first published in *Southern History* 1 (1979), 135–53; for riots in Newcastle and the North East, see Morgan and Rushton, *Rogues, Thieves*, Chapter 9; John Rule, *Albion's People: English Society, 1714–1815* (London: Longman, 1992), pp. 196–201; J. A. Ellis, 'Urban Conflict and Popular Violence: the Guildhall Riots of 1740 in Newcastle upon Tyne', *International Review of Social History* 25 (1980), 333–49; on Stockton, E. P. Thompson, *Customs in Common* (Harmondsworth: Penguin, 1993), pp. 233 and 310–11; Thompson's seminal article 'The Moral Economy and the English Crowd in the Eighteenth Century', *Past and Present* 50 (1971), 79–94 remains indispensable but see John Stevenson's critique, 'The "Moral Economy" of the English Crowd: Myth and Reality', in A. Fletcher and J. Stevenson (eds), *Order and Disorder in Early Modern England* (Cambridge: Cambridge University Press, 1987), 218–38 and Thompson's restatement in *Customs in Common*, 259–351.

43. Thompson, *Whigs and Hunters*, p. 155.

44. *Felix Farley's Bristol Journal,* 22 March 1755.

45. Information of Catherine Watkins, 2 Nov. 1744, Information of Solomon Phillips, 3 Dec. 1744, Voluntary Examination and Confession of Mary Blite, 3 Dec. 1744, Voluntary Examination and Confession of Peter Anderson, 2 April 1745, BRO JQS/P/8; George Lamoine, ed., *Bristol Gaol Delivery Fiats 1741–1799*, Bristol Record Society, vol. XL (Bristol, 1989) p. 2; see also the cases of John Charriton and Christopher Dyer, Examination of Christopher Dyer aged 18 years and John Charriton aged 15 years, 31 Jan. 1772, JQS/P/36, only Charriton was transported, Transportation Bonds, JQS/P/49.

46. DRO, Q/S/OB 11, p. 233; Treasurer's Accounts, Q/F/1, 5 May and 6 Sept. 1757; PRO DURH 17/8.

47. Percentages were 59 per cent of north-eastern women, 56 per cent of north-western; as a percentage of known first charges, 66 per cent of females before the western circuit.

48. Beattie, *Policing and Punishment in London*, p. 20; Tim Wales, 'Poverty, Poor Relief and the Life-Cycle: Some Evidence from Seventeenth-Century Norfolk' and W. Newman Brown, 'The Receipt of Poor Relief and Family Situation: Aldenham, Hertfordshire, 1630–90', in R. M. Smith (ed.), *Land, Kinship and Life-Cycle* (Cambridge: Cambridge University Press, 1984), 351–404, 405–22.

49. On access to courts, Tim Stretton, *Women Waging Law in Elizabethan England* (Cambridge: Cambridge University Press, 1998) – this could be true of female *victims* as much as of the accused: see Morgan and Rushton, 'The Magistrate, the Community', pp. 68–9.

50. As noted below there are some gaps in Bristol's records for the 1750s, but not perhaps sufficient to explain the same phenomenon 1759–76 when transportation bonds are complete. Both Hampshire and Cornwall's assize figures after 1750 show females at below 10 per cent of transported convicts, while all other western circuit counties experienced an increase. See Richard Burn, *The Justice of the Peace and Parish Officer*, 6th edn, 1758, 3 vols; seven years' transportation for wounding animals 'to avoid judgement

of death, or execution thereupon, he may chuse to be transported', stealing £50 reward, and no benefit (includes all oxen, heifers, lambs etc.), vol.1, pp. 220–1; see D. J. V. Jones, 'Life and Death in Eighteenth-Century Wales: a Note', *Welsh Historical Review* 10 (4) (1981), 536–48, on the chief justice of Chester in 1785, p. 542; Wells, 'Sheep-Rustling in Yorkshire; King, 'Decision-makers and Decision-making': 'Jurors sometimes had their own axes to grind – juries of Welsh farmers for example were notorious for their cavalier treatment of those accused of sheep theft', p. 56; on animal theft in Northumberland and Durham, see Morgan and Rushton, *Rogues, Thieves*, pp. 100–1.

51. Morgan and Rushton, *Rogues, Thieves*, pp. 104–5.
52. John Latimer, *Annals of Bristol in the Eighteenth Century* Vol. 2 (Bristol, 1893), p. 292; Kenneth Morgan, 'The Economic Development of Bristol, 1700–1850' in Madge Dresser and Philip Ollerenshaw (eds), *The Making of Modern Bristol* (Tiverton: Redcliffe Press, 1996), 48–75, p. 49; Joyce Ellis, 'Regional and County Centres 1700–1840' and Gordon Jackson, 'Ports 1700–1840' in Peter Clark (ed.), *The Cambridge Urban History of Britain* (Cambridge: Cambridge University Press, 2000), vol.2, 1540–1840, 673–704, pp. 674–5, and 705–31, p. 708 and p. 711. David Hussey, *Coastal and River Trade in Pre-Industrial England: Bristol and its Region, 1680–1730* (Exeter: Exeter University Press, 2000); D. J. Rowe, 'The North-east', in F. M. L. Thompson (ed.), *The Cambridge Social History of Britain, 1750–1950*, Vol.1, *Regions and Communities* (Cambridge: Cambridge University Press, 1990), p. 437.
53. For the missing years, see Lamoine, ed., *Bristol Gaol Delivery Fiats*.
54. Bristol's docket books are extant for the period up to 1753 but there are none for the remainder of the century. Fortunately, transportation bonds exist for the period from 1759 to 1775 which provide details of those sentenced to transportation by quarter sessions and assize courts as well as on those reprieved on condition of transportation.
55. Of the 750 known transportees from Bristol, 1727–76, 255 or 34 per cent are identifiably female; in the later period, from 1759 to 1776 there were 294 transportees for whom there are transportation bonds, of whom ninety-one were female, 31.08 per cent – see Table 3.6; W. S. Wyatt, 'The Transportation of Criminals from Gloucestershire', *Gloucestershire Historical Studies* 3 (1969), 2–16, p. 11, sixty-six females out of a known 612, or 10.8 per cent. See Beattie, *Policing and Punishment*, pp. 65–70.
56. Lynn Mackay, 'Why They Stole: Women in the Old Bailey, 1779–89', *Journal of Social History* 32 (1999), 623–40, pp. 625–6.
57. Patrick McGrath and Mary E. Williams, *Bristol Inns and Alehouses in the Mid-Eighteenth Century* (Bristol: City of Bristol, 1979), p. vi.
58. *Letters of Spencer Cowper, Dean of Durham, 1756–74*, ed. E. Hughes, Surtees Society, vol. 165 (Durham: Andrews, 1950), 1 Sept. 1748, p. 102.
59. *Felix Farley's Bristol Journal*, 7 Sept. 1754.
60. Lamoine, ed., *Bristol Gaol Delivery Fiats*, pp. 13 and 14; *Felix Farley's Bristol Journal*, 28 Sept. 1754.
61. Informations of Mary Rogers, Elizabeth Williams, Joseph King and Ann Doole, BRO JQS/P/8, 31 Oct. 1744.
62. BRO JQS/P/17, 8 April 1745.

63. Lamoine, ed., *Bristol Gaol Delivery Fiats*, p. 3, 8 April 1745, and 3 Sept. 1745.

64. *Felix Farley's Bristol Journal*, 30 May 1761.

65. BRO, JQS/P/89; JQS/S/47; SP/44/82/59; Lamoine, ed., *Bristol Gaol Delivery Fiats*, pp. 19–20.

66. PRO, Isabel Gross, ASSI 45/21/3/66; Jane Swan, ASSI 45/20/2/165; Margaret Cockburn, ASSI 45/28/2/17B; Alice Williamson, ASSI 45/26/2/116C; see Morgan and Rushton, *Rogues, Thieves*, pp. 121–2.

67. Peter King, 'Female Offenders, Work and Life Cycle Change in late Eighteenth-Century London', *Continuity and Change* 11 (1996), 61–90, p. 61; Morgan and Rushton, *Rogues, Thieves*, p. 237, n. 19; figures for Northumberland: single 54.5 per cent, married 28.9 per cent and widows 12.4 per cent.

68. Morgan and Rushton, *Rogues, Thieves*, p. 104.

69. DRO, Q/S/OB 12, pp. 39 and 48, 1760; PRO DURH 17/8.

70. *Virginia Gazette* (Purdie and Dixon), 25 April 1766 (Captain Thomas Blagdon); *Newcastle Courant*, 16 Aug. 1766; *Virginia Gazette* (Purdie and Dixon), 24 Oct. 1766 (Captain Sissons); for contrasting numbers, Coldham, *King's Passengers, passim*.

71. Captain John Smith, to 'South Potomack', *Virginia Gazette* (Purdie and Dixon), 8 Jan. 1767.

72. 'The Life of Elizabeth Ashbridge', in Daniel B. Shea (ed.), *Journeys in New Worlds: Early American Women's Narratives* (Madison: University of Wisconsin Press, 1990), pp. 150–1; report from Belfast: the occupation of soul-driving was described as 'very reputable' in the colonies, *Cumberland Pacquet*, 19 Oct. 1775.

73. Two ships, *William and Mary* and *George* taking 270 to Nova Scotia, *Newcastle Journal*, 5 March and 9 April 1774 (reference to 'the land of freedom'), and 16 April 1774; *Newcastle Courant*, 9 April and 20 Aug. 1774 – *Adventure*, Captain Wharton Wilson to Virginia, with 'emigrants and goods', safely arrived and servants sold within ten days; emigrant voyages of this period from northern England are analysed in Bernard Bailyn, *Voyagers to the West: a Passage in the Peopling of America on the Eve of the Revolution* (New York: Knopf, 1986), pp. 338, 373, 408 and 420.

74. On the wreck of the *Elizabeth* off the Welsh coast, a vessel used in the convict trade, with thirty-seven passengers on board, of whom only eleven were saved (but the captain and mate were lost), see *Felix Farley's Bristol Journal*, 10 Sept. 1774.

75. *Felix Farley's Bristol's Journal*, 28 Feb. 1761.

76. *Newcastle Journal*, 21 June 1766, announces the safe arrival of the *Jenny*, after eleven weeks, 'having some Days before she arrived been put to short allowance'; *Newcastle Courant*, 24 July 1773, 'the Adventure, Captain Wharton Wilson, of this port, which sailed from hence the 17th March, with servants and convicts, arrived at Baltimore town, in Maryland, on the 24th May last, all well'. On the average length of the voyage, I. K. Steele, *The Atlantic Community, 1675–1740: an Exploration of Communication and Community* (New York: Oxford University Press, 1986), p. 299, Table 4.9, and p. 301, Table 4.13.

77. *Virginia Gazette*, 14 April 1768; see experience of Adam Cunningham, 4 April to 29 Sept. (it took another two weeks to get to Virginia), Whitfield

J. Bell Jr, 'Adam Cunningham's Atlantic Crossing, 1728', *Maryland Histori-cal Magazine* 50 (1955), 195–202, pp. 196, 199 and 200; William Moraley, *The Infortunate: the Voyage and Adventures of William Moraley, an Indentured Servant*, ed. Susan E. Klepp and Billy G. Smith (University Park, PA: Penn-sylvania State University Press, 1992), pp. 54, 60 and 62, on a voyage of two months, three weeks; other passages included: nine weeks – Elizabeth Ashbridge, 'Some Account', p. 151; three months from London to York-town, Edward Miles Riley, ed., *The Journal of John Harrower: an Indentured Servant in the Colony of Virginia, 1773–6*, (Colonial Williamsburg and New York: Holt, Rinehart and Winston, 1963), 19–24; for the experience of Goronwy Owen going to Virginia in 1757-8, see Bedwyr Lewis Jones, 'Life aboard an Eighteenth-Century Convict Ship', *Maritime Wales* 2 (1977), pp. 16 and 18, two months and a few weeks; Harrower and Moraley sailed from London, Cunningham from Scotland and Ashbridge from Ireland.

78. John Duffy, 'The Passage to the Colonies', *Mississippi Valley Historical Review* 38 (1) (1951), 21–38, pp. 2, 5 and 38.

79. Farley Grubb, 'Morbidity and Mortality on the North Atlantic Passage: Eighteenth-Century German Immigration', *Journal of Interdisciplinary History* 17 (3) (1987), 565–85, pp. 567–8 and 571–2.

80. James C. Riley, 'Mortality on Long-Distance Voyages in the Eighteenth Century', *Journal of Economic History* 41 (3) (1981), 651–6, for summaries of slave death rates in note, p. 653. Ekirch, *Bound for America*, p. 105, Table 9.

81. Duffy, 'Passage to the Colonies', p. 25.

82. *Maryland Gazette*, 26 June 1751; 8 Nov. 1753; 9 July 1767, advertisement from Jonathan Plowman, imported on the *Success*, under Captain James Morrison from London, at the NW branch of the Patapsco, 'a parcel of healthy country servants for seven years'.

83. *Virginia Gazette* (Rind), 23 July 1767, dateline Annapolis 9 July; 27 Feb. 1752 – in discussing the hard labour bill for the second time; Maryland enacted legislation for quarantine, but in Virginia both attempts at a similar law were rejected by the London authorities, the April 1767 law being quashed in Aug. 1768: see *Virginia Gazette* (Rind), 3 Nov. 1768, and (Purdie and Dixon) 23 April 1772, and (Rind) 24 June 1773 (passed in April 1772); Kenneth Morgan points out that the 1767 account provoked a 'newspaper war' in the two colonies as to who exactly was responsible for disease, and whether convicts were worth importing, 'English and American Attitudes towards Convict Transportation, 1718–75', *History* 72 (224) (1984), 416–31, pp. 427–8.

84. Harry Piper Letterbook, microfilm, John D. Rockefeller Library, Colonial Williamsburg, 24 Oct. 1767.

85. Riley, ed., *Journal of John Harrower*, pp. 25 and 38–9; Bell, 'Andrew Cun-ningham's Atlantic Crossing', pp. 196–7.

86. Bedwyr Lewis Jones, 'Life Aboard on Eighteenth-Century Convict Ship', pp. 17–18; the letter was written in Welsh to Owen's friend Richard Morris at the Navy Office London, 12 Dec. 1757; *Oxford Companion to the Literature of Wales* (Oxford: Oxford University Press, 1986), entry by Bedwyr Lewis Jones, says his wife and youngest of three children died on the voyage. After teaching at the grammar school of the College of William and Mary,

Owen became minister of St Andrew's parish Brunswick County, Virginia, and was buried on his plantation near Dolphin to the north of Lawrenceville; on Welsh identity in America, see Boyd Stanley Schlenther, ' "The English is Swallowing up their Language": Welsh Ethnic Ambivalence in Colonial Pennsylvania and the Experience of David Evans', *Pennsylvania Magazine of History and Biography* 11 (2) (1990), 201–28.

87. Harry Piper Letter Book, 24 Oct. 1767; for a popular account, see Siân Rees, *The Floating Brothel: the Extraordinary True Story of an Eighteenth-Century Ship and its Cargo of Female Convicts* (London: Hodder Headline, 2001).

88. *Felix Farley's Bristol Journal*, 16 April 1774.

Chapter 4   Gangs, gentlemen and gypsies: Narratives of transportation

1. *Maryland Gazette*, 20 Aug. 1752, despatch from Bristol, England 2 May; *Sherborne Mercury*, 25 March 1751 and 8 April 1751 (quotation of quarrel) and report of reprieve, 25 Nov. 1751; *Felix Farley's Bristol Journal*, 2 May 1752; see also *Bristol Weekly Intelligencer*, 9 March 1751, and particularly 31 Aug. 1751 for sympathetic advertisement on Bishop's behalf.

2. *Felix Farley's Bristol Journal*, 17 March 1753.

3. See Chapter 5 for more of this kind of pattern of escape; *Virginia Gazette*, 6 July 1739, running away from William Walker, Westmoreland County on 2 July.

4. *Old Bailey Sessions Papers*, 1739, guilty of stealing three hats and 50 yards of linen, value 4s 10d, 12 February; *Gentleman's Magazine* 13 (1743), p. 442, execution on Kennington Common (Surrey), 'who was five times transported, for returning from transportation'; Richard Kibble, *A Genuine Account of the Behaviour, Confessions and Dying Words of Malefactors etc.* (London: for J. Nicholson, in the Old Bailey, 1743), 'He went to the Place of Execution seemingly unconcerned, and dy'd without speaking a word to any person whatever', pp. 7–8; A. Roger Ekirch, *Bound for America: the Transportation of British Convicts to the Colonies, 1718–75* (Oxford: Clarendon Press, 1987), pp. 148–9.

5. Ian K. Steele, *The English Atlantic, 1675–1740: an Exploration of Communication and Community* (New York and Oxford: Oxford University Press, 1986), p. 119.

6. Charles Coleman Sellers, *The Artist of the Revolution: the Early Life of Charles Willson Peale* (Hebron, CT: Feather and Good, 1939), p. 37.

7. William David Sloan and Julie Hedgepeth Williams, *The Early American Press, 1690–1783* (Westport, CT: Greenwood Press, 1994), p. 99; C. Y. Ferdinand, *Benjamin Collins and the Provincial Newspaper Trade in the Eighteenth Century* (Oxford: Clarendon Press, 1997), p. 13; and Steele, *English Atlantic*, p. 138.

8. C. John Summerville, *The News Revolution in England: Cultural Dynamics of Daily Information* (New York: Oxford University Press, 1996), p. 125, who makes the point that British newspapers began their promises with 'distant news', and only moved to local matters with great caution; on seaports, Steele, *English Atlantic*, p. 142; on colonial shipping and news distribution,

David A. Copeland, *Colonial American Newspapers: Character and Content* (Newark, DE: University of Delaware Press, 1997), Chapter 1, and appendices for content analysis of newspapers over time; Charles E. Clark and Charles Weatherall, 'The Measure of Maturity: the *Pennsylvania Gazette, 1728–65'*, *William and Mary Quarterly*, 3rd ser. 46 (1989), 279–303, Table IV, p. 293.

9. *London Evening Post*, 30 Sept. 1736, p. 2; *OBSP*, 24 May 1735, p. 88; reprieved in June – *Gentleman's Magazine* 5 (1735), p. 330; the complex story of the crime is told by Sellers, *Artist of the Revolution*, pp. 21–4; *Virginia Gazette*, 28 July 1738, advertisement for Charles Peale's *An Essay towards rendering the Rudiments of the Latin tongue more easy and agreeable to the Capacities of Children*; *The Selected Papers of Charles Willson Peale and his Family*: Vol. 5 *The Autobiography of Charles Willson Peale*, ed. Lillian B. Miller (New Haven, CT: Yale University Press, 2000); Peale senior had worked for Postmaster General Alexander Spotswood (Sellers, *Artist of the Revolution*, p. 25), another of whose white-collar criminals also gave him difficulty – London forger Joshua Dean, *Pennsylvania Gazette*, 15 June 1738, transported for life for forging paper stamps.

10. Charles E. Clark, *The Public Prints: the Newspaper in Anglo-American Culture, 1665–1740* (New York and Oxford: Oxford University Press, 1994), p. 239.

11. Malcolm Gaskill, 'Reporting Murder: Fiction in the Archives in Early Modern England', *Social History* 23 (1998), 1–30; Peter Lake, 'Deeds against Nature: Cheap Print, Protestantism and Murder in Early Seventeenth-Century England', in K. Sharpe and P. Lake (eds), *Culture and Politics in Early Stuart England* (Basingstoke: Macmillan Press [now Palgrave Macmillan], 1994), 257–83; Andrea Mackenzie, 'Making Crime Pay: Motives, Marketing Strategies, and the Printed Literature of Crime in England, 1670–1770', in Greg T. Smith, Allyson N. May, and Simon Devereaux (eds), *Criminal Justice in the Old World and the New: Essays in Honour of J. M. Beattie* (Toronto: Centre for Criminology, 1998), 235–69, p. 249; Michael Harris, 'Trials and Criminal Biographies: a Case Study in Distribution', in Robin Myers and Michael Harris (eds), *Sale and Distribution of Books from 1700* (Oxford: Oxford Polytechnic Press, 1982), 1–36; J. A. Sharpe, '"Last Dying Speeches": Religion, Ideology and Public Execution in Seventeenth-Century England', *Past and Present* 107 (1985), 144–67; Hal Gladfelder, *Criminality and Narrative in Eighteenth-Century England: Beyond the Law* (Baltimore, MD: Johns Hopkins University Press, 2001).

12. Daniel E. Williams, '"Behold a Tragic Scene Strangely Changed into a Theater of Mercy": the Structure and Significance of Criminal Conversion Narratives in Early New England', *American Quarterly* 38 (1986), 827–47; Ronald A. Bosco, 'Lectures at the Pillory: the Early American Execution Sermon', *American Quarterly* 30 (1978), 156–76; Daniel A. Cohen, *Pillars of Salt, Monuments of Grace: New England Crime Literature and the Origins of American Popular Culture, 1674–1860* (New York: Oxford University Press, 1993); Karen Halttunen, 'Early American Murder Narratives: the Birth of Horror', in Richard Wightman Fox and T. J. Jackson Lears (eds), *The Power of Culture: Critical Essays in American History* (Chicago: Chicago University Press, 1993).

13. *Pennsylvania Gazette*, 13 May 1730 (Kelsey), and 7 July 1737 (Smith).

14. Frank Luther Mott, *American Journalism: a History of Newspapers in the United States Through 250 Years, 1690–1940*, 6 vols (New York: Macmillan and Co., 1941, reprinted London: Routledge/Thoemmes Press, 2000), vol. 1, p. 56, passage written in 1728, p. 26.

15. Halttunen, 'Early American Murder Narratives', p. 78 for reprints in the colonies; *Virtue Triumphant, or Elizabeth Canning in America, being a circumstantial narrative of her adventures from her setting sail for transportation to the present time etc.* (Boston, 1757, reprinted for J. Cooke in London); *The Newgate Calendar*, introduction by Clive Emsley (London: Wordsworth Editions, 1997), pp. 244–8, note on p. 248, 'she was afterwards reputably married in America'.

16. James S. Amelang, *The Flight of Icarus: Artisan Autobiography in Early Modern Europe* (Stanford, CA: Stanford University Press, 1998), p. 3.

17. *Newcastle Journal*, 25 April 1767; identical versions in *Newcastle Courant*, 25 April 1767, and *York Courant*, 14 April 1767; he had been committed to Northumberland gaol in 1764 (*Newcastle Courant*, 2 June 1764) when it was said, 'he writes a remarkably fine hand', and reported that he had served as a sailor since his parents' transportation. See Coldham *Complete Book of Emigrants*, York, Lent 1759, where he was suspected of being a deserter from the 66th Regiment, and 1765, Cumberland.

18. Morgan and Rushton, *Rogues, Thieves*, pp. 88–91.

19. PRO ASSI 45/28/1/14B-D, Richard Clark, 1765.

20. *A Journal of the Proceedings of J. Hewitt, Coventry, one of his Majesty's Justices of the Peace for the said City and County in his Duty as a Magistrate, during a period of twenty years . . .* (London: for the author, T. W. Pasham, 1779), pp. 64–5.

21. *Newcastle Courant*, 21 April 1764.

22. Hewitt, *Journal*, p. 132; Tyne and Wear Archive Service, MF135 f.69v, for correspondence between the town clerk of Newcastle-upon-Tyne with John Hewitt.

23. Hewitt, *Journal*, pp. 163 and 202.

24. *The Life, Travels, Exploits, Frauds and Robberies of Charles Speckman alias Brown . . .* (London, 1763), in Rawlings, *Drunks, Whores and Idle Apprentices*, pp. 202 and 208 (quotation).

25. Ruth Paley, 'Thief-Takers in London in the Age of the McDaniel Gang, c.1745–54', in Douglas Hay and Francis Snyder (eds) *Policing and Prosecution in Britain 1750–1850*, (Oxford: Clarendon Press, 1989), pp. 331–4.

26. John Bender, *Imagining the Penitentiary: Fiction and the Architecture of Mind in Eighteenth-Century England* (Chicago: University of Chicago Press, 1987), p. 98–100; see Sir John Fielding's attempt to prevent David Garrick from putting it on, *Annual Register*, 15 Sept. 1773.

27. *London Evening Post*, 4 Nov. 1738; *Virginia Gazette*, 23 March 1739.

28. *London Evening Post*, 11 May 1736, p. 1; *OBSP*, 5 and 11 May 1736.

29. Philip Gaskell, 'Henry Justice, a Cambridge Book Thief', *Trans actions of the Cambridge Bibliographical Society* 1 (1952), 348–57, p. 353; OBSP, 11 May 1736; *London Evening Post*, 13 May 1736, p. 1; *London Evening Post*, 15 May 1736, p. 2 (quotation).

30. *London Evening Post*, 20 May 1736, p. 2; *Gentleman's Magazine* 6 (1736), p. 290; *OBSP*, Dec. 1735, for the trial of William Wreathock, Peter Chamberlain, James Ruffett alias Rufhead, George Bird the Younger, and Gilbert Campbell for highway robbery of Dr Nathaniel Lancaster the previous June; also trial of Thomas Cray or MacCray or MacCreagh, OBSP, 3 July 1735.

31. *Virgina Gazette*, 26 Nov. 1737; 28 Jan. 1737; Justice was on the *Patapsco Merchant*, under Captain Lux, in May 1736, Coldham, *King's Passengers*, p. 68; PRO T53/38/337.

32. *London Evening Post*, 11 Nov. 1736, p. 2; *London Evening Post*, 11 Dec. 1736 p. 2; J. M. Beattie, *Policing and Punishment in London, 1660–1750: Urban Crime and the Limits of Terror* (Oxford: Oxford University Press, 2001), p. 443; *OBSP*, 16 Oct. 1735 for his trial; PRO SP 36/38 Part 2, piece 1–2.

33. PRO SP 44/83/267, 7 Dec. 1738.

34. *London Evening Post*, 12 June 1739, and previous reports 14 and 24 May, 6 Sept. 1737; 2 Nov. 1738; 16 and 20 Jan., 10 April and 5 May 1739; *Gentleman's Magazine* 9 (1739), June, p. 325.

35. *London Evening Post*, 24 May 1737.

36. *Virginia Gazette*, 13 July 1739, story datelined London 10 April.

37. *Bibliothèque universelle, choisie, ancienne et moderne, contenant une très curieuse collection de livres ... recueillis ... par feu Monsieur Henri Justice de Rufforth* (The Hague: Nicolaas van Daalen, 31 Oct. 1763), and *Catalogue d'un très bel assortiment de livres en feuilles* (13 Aug. 1764), and *Catalogue d'une très belle collection de livres* (30 Nov. 1767) – traceable through the CD-Rom of Book Sales Catalogues of the Dutch Republic, 1599–1800; see also John Van der Zee, *Bound Over: Indentured Servitude and American Conscience* (New York: Simon and Schuster, 1985), pp. 170–8 and 369–70.

38. Gaskell, 'Henry Justice', p. 357, n. 6.

39. Michael Mascuch, *The Origins of the Individualist Self: Autobiography and Self-Identity in England, 1591–1791* (Cambridge: Polity Press, 1997), pp. 188–90.

40. *Amelia or the Distressed Wife: a History Founded on Real Circumstances, by a Private Gentlewoman* [i.e. Elizabeth Justice] (London: the Authoress, 1751), pp. 61–3, quotation p. 61.

41. Elizabeth Justice, *A Voyage to Russia, Describing the Laws, Manners, and Customs of that Great Empire ...* 2nd edn (London: G. Smith, 1746), p. viii, 48, 50, 62; she spent much of her time there reading the *Spectator*.

42. See James Patterson, 'An Examination of *A Voyage to Russia*: the First Travel Account Published by an Englishwoman', in Kim Wells (ed.), *Women Writers: a Zine*, Online Journal, 14 May 2001, at http://www.womenwriters.net/may2001/justicessay.htm.

43. See Elizabeth Kraft, 'The Two Amelias: Henry Fielding and Elizabeth Justice', *English Literary History (ELH)* 62 (2) (1995), 313–28: she is particularly strong on the theme of the prostitution of wives in both *Amelia* novels, pp. 318–19; R. Ballaster, 'Women and the Rise of the Novel: Sexual Prescripts', in Vivien Jones, (ed.) *Women and Literature in Britain, 1700–1800* (Cambridge: Cambridge University Press, 2000), 197–216.

44. *London Evening Post*, 28 Feb. 1736.

45. *Newcastle Courant*, 23 July 1768, James Johnson and William Simpson transported for seven years by quarter sessions at Hexham.

46. See the introduction to Edward Kimber, *Itinerant Observations in America*, ed. Kevin J. Hayes (Newark, DE: University of Delaware Press, 1998), pp. 13–15; the account attracted interest among earlier historians: see the edition of 1878 (Savannah, GA: J. H. Estill) in the US Library of Congress.

47. 'Eighteenth-Century Maryland as Portrayed in the "Itinerant Observations" of Edward Kimber', *Maryland Historical Magazine* 51 (1956), 315–36, p. 315, for the remark about a 'hack-writer who flourished in silence', and extracts from the *Itinerant Observations*.

48. Kimber, *Itinerant Observations*, Hayes edn, pp. 50–1; Jenny Uglow, *Hogarth: a Life and a World* (London: Faber and Faber, 1997), p. 438–45.

49. *The History of the Life and Adventures of Mr Anderson, containing his strange varieties of fortune in Europe and America, compiled from his own papers* (London: W. Owen, 1754, photographic reprint by Garland Publishing Inc, 1975); see W. Gordon Milne, 'A Glimpse of Colonial America as Seen in an English Novel of 1754', *Maryland Historical Magazine* 42 (1947), 239–52, who regards the novel as fairly accurate, and draws upon Kimber's own notebook to confirm the attribution; note that Kimber uses the word 'savannah' at one point to describe the Maryland landscape, *Mr Anderson*, p. 232.

50. *Memoirs of an Unfortunate Young Nobleman Return'd from a Thirteen Years Slavery in America, where he had been sent by the wicked contrivances of his Cruel Uncle*, 2 vols (London: printed for J. Freeman in Fleet St, 1743); the newspapers followed the Annesley legal case eagerly, and at length, in England.

51. The British Library has at least fifteen eighteenth-century editions, and about twenty more of various kinds, including the play. See A. Roger Ekirch, *Bound for America: the Transportation of British Convicts to the Colonies, 1718–75* (Oxford: Clarendon Press, 1987), pp. 62 and 162; Kenneth Morgan, 'Convict Runaways in Maryland, 1745–75', *Journal of American Studies* 23 (1989), 253–68, but see pp. 266–7 particularly; Stephen C. Bullock, 'A Mumper among the Gentle: Tom Bell, Colonial Confidence Man', *William and Mary Quarterly*, 3rd ser. 55 (1998), 231–58, see p. 236 where Bullock notes the use 'mumper' and 'mumping' in the Carew story; it meant either cheater or beggar (*OED* definition).

52. Hal Gladfelder, *Criminality and Narrative in Eighteenth-Century England: Beyond the Law* (Baltimore: Johns Hopkins University Press, 2001), p. 34; Peter Linebaugh, *The London Hanged: Crime and Civil Society in the Eighteenth Century* (Harmondsworth, Middlesex: Penguin, 1991), p. 125.

53. *The Life and Adventures of Bampfylde-Moore Carew, the noted Devonshire Stroler and Dog-Stealer, as related by himself during his passage to the Plantations of America* (Exeter: the Farleys, for Joseph Drew, opposite Castle Lane, 1745), 2 shillings; C. Y. Ferdinand, *Benjamin Collins and the Provincial Newspaper Trade in the Eighteenth Century* (Oxford: Clarendon Press, 1997), for the Farleys, p. 32, n. 19: 'our knowledge of the provincial press would benefit from a close study of the numerous Farley family of Bristol, Exeter and, for a short time, Salisbury. It is unclear if there were one or two Samuel Farleys at work in the early part of the century'.

54. *An Apology for the Life of Bampfylde-Moore Carew, (son of the Rev. Mr Carew, of Bickley), commonly known throughout the West of England, by the Title of King of the Beggars, and Dog Merchant-General*, 'The Whole Taken from his own Mouth' (London: printed by R. Goadby, and sold by W. Owen, at Temple-Bar, 1749); both this and the *Life and Adventures* were reprinted in *The King of the Beggars: Bampfylde-Moore Carew*, edited by C. H.Wilkinson (Oxford: Clarendon Press, 1931) whose notes trace many of the original sources, particularly of descriptions of America.

55. *Bristol Weekly Intelligencer*, 4 Nov. 1749; *Sherborne Mercury* or *Western Flying Post or Sherborne and Yeovil Mercury*, 15 Jan. 1750, advertisement for *An Apology for the Life*, with threat from R. Goadby of prosecuting plundered editions.

56. *Bath Journal*, 4 March 1754; *Sherborne Mercury*, 25 March 1751; later prices were 2 shillings.

57. Carlisle Public Library, Bibliotheca Jacksoniana, (14) NP, p. 42 in M176, Chapbooks, vol. 1, *The Adventures of Mr Bampfylde Moor Carew*, undated, frontispiece missing, 20 pages, with 11–14 absent, date uncertain; the British Library catalogue has many early nineteenth-century chapbooks, of about twenty-four pages, one of them by W. and T. Fordyce of Newcastle-upon-Tyne.

58. Advertisement, *Pennsylvania Gazette*, 21 April 1773, published by Bell.

59. *Gentleman's Magazine* 30 (Aug. 1750), pp. 339–400, with portrait engraving on p. 340 and four columns giving some of the stories.

60. Devon RO, QS 1/16 Order Book 1718–25, unpaginated at this point, work-house calendar, Easter 1724; QS 1/17 Order Book 1725–34, p. 139, Feb. 1727–8, proved to be a deserter on the oath of Sergeant John Williams of Lieutenant Colonel Handyside's Company of Colonel Henry Harrison's Regiment of Foot. This was one incident which was subsequently recorded in the *Life and Adventures*, though placed at a much later date, in the 1730s – see Wilkinson edn, p. 122.

61. QS 1/17 Order Book 1725–34, unpaginated, Easter 1730, Michaelmas 1730, and Epiphany 1730–1, in the workhouse calendars.

62. Wilkinson, *King of the Beggars*, pp. 101–2, and notes p. 302 – this is probably an eye-witness account of the 1735 expedition, in his view.

63. Wilkinson, *King of the Beggars*, pp. 132 and 149.

64. Wilkinson, *King of the Beggars*, p. 135.

65. Devon RO, QS 1/18 Order Book 1734–45, Easter 1739, pp. 105–7 and 113; QS 129/21 Transportation Bonds and Contracts, 18 July 1739.

66. Wilkinson, *King of the Beggars*, pp. 150–1; 'Griffy' cannot be confidently identified among the West Country transportees; see F. H. Schmidt, 'British Convict Servant Labor in Colonial Virginia' (unpublished PhD diss., College of William and Mary, 1976), p. 156, letter from William Barker Jr, 1758, giving similar details of selling convicts.

67. Wilkinson, *King of the Beggars*, p. 166–7.

68. Wilkinson, *King of the Beggars*, pp. 167 and 170–1, 171–2, and 186–93; for use of iron collars for servants, see the 1726 law in Virginia, an iron collar was to be placed around the inmate of a gaol (if a slave or runaway under arrest) hired out from the gaol, with PG (public gaol) stamped on it, *Statutes at Large: Being a Collection of All the Laws of Virginia from the First Session*

of the Year 1619, 13 vols, ed. Williaṁ W. Hening (Richmond, VA, and Philadelphia, 1809–23), vol. 4, p. 171, and vol. 5, p. 554 (1748); examples in *Chronicles of the Scotch-Irish Settlement in Virginia, Extracted from the Original Court Records of Augusta County, 1745–1800*, 3 vols, ed. Lyman Chalkley (Baltimore MD: Genealogical Publishing Co., 1965, 3rd printing 1966), p. 37 (1748).

69. Wilkinson, *King of the Beggars*, pp. 204, 206 and 210–13; Peter Linebaugh and Marcus Rediker, *The Many-Headed Hydra: Sailors, Slaves, Commoners and the Hidden History of the Revolutionary Atlantic* (London: Verso, 2000), Chapter 6, and particularly pp. 174–7.

70. PRO ASSI 23/5; Wilkinson, *King of the Beggars*, pp. 214, 240–1 (quotation p. 240), 247–9 and 256.

71. *Devon Notes and Queries* 12 (1922–3), Part 6, pp. 276–7, drawing upon Bridgwater Corporation manuscripts; Devon RO, QS 1/19 Devon County QS 1745–58, f.56, and discharged, f.61, Christmas adjournment 1747/8.

72. Robert Goadby, Wade's Passage, Bath, 1740–45, then The Hague 1745–48, then London, died in 1778, aged 57; see *The Dictionary of Printers, Booksellers . . . in England, Scotland and Ireland, 1726–75*, H. R. Plomer, G. H. Bushnell, E. R. Mc Dix (Oxford: Oxford Uuniversity Press, 1930, published 1932 for 1930), p. 104; see *Sherborne Mercury*, 13 May 1751, Goadby also advertised *The Unhappy Voyage and Long Captivity in Barbary of Thomas Pellow of the Borough of Penrynn in the County of Cornwall* and 19 Dec. 1768, advertisement for the eighth edition of the *Apology*, by R. Goadby, and W. Owen at Temple-Bar, and R. Baldwin, Pater-Noster Row (back page).

73. *Notes and Queries*, 2nd ser. 3 (1857), p. 4; 2nd ser. 4 (1857), p. 522 and 8th ser. 1 (1892), p. 393, where an edition of the *Weekly Entertainer and West of England Miscellany* (established by Robert Goadby in 1773) of 3 Jan. 1820 is cited as attributing the 1749 edition to Mrs Goadby; Rev. Thomas Moore, *The History of Devonshire from the Earliest Period to the Present*, 2 vols (London: Robert Jennings, 1829), vol. 1, pp. 700 and 717; *Gentleman's Magazine* 29 (1759), p. 442.

74. *Sherborne Mercury*, 12 Aug. 1751, p. 3.

75. Ekirch, *Bound for America*, pp. 201–2.

76. *South Carolina Gazette*, 15 Feb. 1773.

77. *Rivington's New York Gazetteer*, 13 May 1773.

78. *Pennsylvania Gazette*, 19 May 1773; *Boston Evening Post*, 31 May 1773 (minus the advertisement); *Virginia Gazette*, 3 June 1773.

79. *London Magazine or Gentleman's Monthly Intelligencer*, June 1773, p. 311, datelined New York, 13 May; *Gentleman's Magazine* 43 (July 1773), p. 357; *Annual Register*, 26 June 1773, pp. 113–14.

80. Michael Zuckerman, 'Tocqueville, Turner, and Turds: Four Stories of Manners in Early America,' *Journal of American History* 85 (1998), pp. 13–42, with Wilson on p. 24 where the story is used as proof of the failure of hier-archical social relations in the colonies; for a fanciful account, see Egon Larsen, *The Deceivers: Lives of the Great Imposters* (London: John Baker, 1966), pp. 52–7, Willie Donaldson ed., *Brewer's Rogues, Villains and Eccentrics*, (London: Cassell, 2002), also has an entry on Sarah Wilson, apparently based on Larsen.

81. *London Evening Post*, 3 July 1766, dated 28 June on p. 3; also reproduced in the *Annual Register*, 1766, pp. 119–20.

82. *York Courant*, 28 Oct. 1766; this was copied in the *London Evening Post*, 30 Oct. 1766.

83. Alderman J. Hewitt, *Memoirs of the Celebrated Lady Viscountess Wilbrihammon alias Mollineux, alias Irving, Countess of Normandy, and Baroness Wilmington, the greatest Impostress of the Present Age* (Birmingham: printed by C. Earl for the author, undated – the British Library suggests 1778), pp. 4 and 18–20; an introductory letter by Hewitt is dated at Coventry May 1778; *Felix Farley's Bristol Journal* and *London Evening Post*, 12 Sept. 1767; she may have been active in Swaledale, Yorkshire, in October 1768 – see the story of a fraudster claiming to be a relative of Lord Bute, reprinted in *The Boston Post-Boy and Advertiser*, 13 Feb. 1769, datelined Reeth, Swaledale, 12 Oct. 1768.

84. 'The Poor Unhappy Transported Felon's Sorrowful Account of the Fourteen Years Transportation at Virginia in America', reprinted with introductory notes by John Melville Jennings, *Virginia Magazine of History and Biography* 56 (1948), 180–94; argument about dating on p. 182, using an undated edition from Dublin, printed by B. Corcoran on the Inns-Quay near the Cloysters; the current University of Virginia website reproduces one printed in London and sold in Stonecutter Street, Fleet Market, also undated: http://uvawise.edu/history/runaways/lit/revel.htm.

85. Linebaugh and Rediker, *Many-Headed Hydra*, pp. 58–9; Revel is reprinted with commentary in Paul Lauter (ed.), *The Heath Anthology of American Literature*, 2 vols, 4th edn (Boston: Houghton Mifflin, 2002), vol. 1, pp. 267–75, and in Susan Castillo and Ivy Schweitzer (eds), *The Literatures of Colonial America: an Anthology* (Oxford: Blackwell, 2001), pp. 230–5, with the same version derived from Jennings.

86. Jennings, 'The Poor Unhappy Transported', p. 188; John Lauson, *The Felon's Account of his Transportation at Virginia in America*, rep. and ed. J. Stevens Cox (St Peter Port, Guernsey: Toucan Press, Mount Durand, 1969), 'from an original copy' of a mid-eighteenth-century pamphlet printed and sold by A. and J. Pile of Norton Fitzwarren, near Taunton in Somerset; we are grateful to Dr Farley Grubb, University of Delaware, for bringing the Lauson account to our attention.

87. *The Poor Unhappy Transported Felon's Sorrowful Account of his Fourteen Years Transportation at Virginia in America . . .* J. Revel, 'the Unhappy Sufferer', (London: ? *c*.1800); also another (London: printed J. Pitts, *c*.1816) both in the British Library which also has James Ruel, with the same title (Dublin: 'sold by The Hawkers', *c*.1820).

88. Anne Conlon, ' "Mine is a Sad Yet True Story": Convict Narratives, 1818–1850', *Journal of the Royal Australian Historical Society* 55 (1), 1969, 43–82, p. 61; she notes James Revell, *The Unhappy Transport, Giving a Sorrowful Account of his Fourteen Years' Transportation to Botany Bay, in New South Wales, in August 1810, and his return to London, 1824* (York: 1824); his story was published in York, Edinburgh and Gateshead, 'all in the same year'; There were two men of this name transported, from Ireland in 1817 and 1818, as well as one called Michael (p. 61). Also see John Jackson, 1825, *A Remarkable Narrative, or the Punishment of Transportation Explained, through*

*the return of a merchant's son to London after suffering fourteen years' extreme
cruelty* (London, 1825) (listed in Conlon, p. 76), is also telling the story of
James Revel, as is the story of William Dale, *The Unhappy Transport or the
Sufferings of William Dale* (London: c.1820), published by 'James Revel'.

89. Jennings, 'The Poor Unhappy Transported', p. 189, and also Lauson, *The
Felon's Account*, p. 7.
90. Jennings 'The Poor Unhappy Transported', pp. 191 and 193.
91. James Ruel, *The Unhappy Transport*, Part VI.
92. William Green, the unhappy sufferer, *The Sufferings of William Green, being
a sorrowful account of his seven years transportation, wherein is set forth the
various hardships he underwent with his parting and meeting again in that
Country with his intimate Friend Anthony Atkinson with their joyful arrival in
England, after being absent ten years. Likewise an Account of their manner of
Living; the Climate of the Country, and in what it principally abounds*
(Whitechapel, London: J. Long, undated, but after June 1774), two pence,
p. 7; Schmidt, 'British Convict Servant Labor', p. 156, claims that this is an
alias for William Barker Jr, from the late 1750s, though 'Green' says he was
transported in 1762.
93. Green, *The Sufferings*, pp. 5–6 – the text says 'are' but clearly means 'ever';
note that Edward Kimber wrote in verse, but it is hard to compare with the
Revel style.
94. *Literatures of Colonial America*, ed. Susan Castillo and Ivy Schweitzer, p. 230.
95. Jennings, 'The Poor Unhappy Transported', pp. 185 and 188; 'Death and
the Lady' had a long broadsheet history, appearing in the *Cobler's Opera*
(L. Ryan) of 1728.
96. Dave Harker, *Fakesong: the Manufacture of British 'Folksong': 1700 to the
Present Day* (Milton Keynes: Open University Press, 1985).
97. Roy Palmer, ed., *A Touch on the Times: Songs of Social Change, 1770 to 1914*
(Harmondsworth, Middlesex: Penguin, 1974), p. 242, for 'Botany Bay', and
p. 244 for the bushranging song 'Jim Jones'; also, Dave Harker, ed., *Songs
and Verse of the North-East Pitmen, c.1780–1844* (Gateshead: Athenaeum
Press, 1999), Surtees Society vol. 204, pp. 167 and 288.
98. See the larger printed version 'The Lads of Virginia', in Roy Palmer, *A Ballad
History of England from 1588 to the Present Day* (London: Batsford, 1979), pp.
66–7, and for original sources, p. 184; 'Virginny' was sung by Martin Carthy
on the album *Crown of Thorns* (1976), whose sleeve notes say that it was
collected from a Mrs Goodyear of Axford, near Basingstoke, Hampshire, by
Charles Gamblin, a helper of George Gardiner, in 1907, and also independ-
ently from Bob Hart (East Anglia) where the location is Australia and the
crime is highway robbery; see also website on singer Cyril Poacher which
notes he called his version *Australia*: see his CD *Plenty of Thyme* MTCD 303,
reviewed on http://www.mustrad.org.uk/article/poacher.htm.
99. Peter Buchan, *Ancient Ballads and Songs of the North of Scotland, hitherto
unpublished, with explanatory notes*, 2 vols (Edinburgh: W. and D. Laing,
J. Stevenson, 1828), vol. 2, p. 215, and devotes his notes to the Peter
Williamson story 'too notorious to require any illustration here'; for
Buchan's sources and editorial methods, see Harker, *Fakesong*, pp. 56–7, 68
and 75–6; much of this is noted on the website of David Kilpatrick of Kelso:
http://www.maxwellplace.demon.co.uk/pandemonium/scotslaves.htm.

100. Robert Reiner, 'Media-Made Criminality: the Representation of Crime in the Mass Media', in Mike Maguire, Rod Morgan and Robert Reiner (eds), *The Oxford Handbook of Criminology*, 2nd edn (Oxford: Oxford University Press, 1997), p. 194.

101. Certainly Daniel Defoe derived many of his characters and their experiences from such sources – see Robert R. Singleton, 'Defoe, Moll Flanders and the Ordinary of Newgate', *Harvard Literary Bulletin* 24 (1976), 407–13; Gladfelder, *Criminality and Narrative in Eighteenth-Century England*; Andrea Mackenzie, 'Making Crime Pay', p. 256.

102. Philip Rawlings, 'True Crime', in Jon Vagg and Tim Newburn (eds), *The British Criminology Conferences: Selected Proceedings*, Vol. 1: *Emerging Themes in Criminology* (British Society of Criminology, 1998, Internet publication).

103. *Maryland Gazette*, 24 Sept. 1767: three gypsies, convicts, Joseph Smith, 'an old man', William his brother and John, Joseph's son, run away from Thomas Samuel and John Snowden, Patuxent Ironworks, brought in on the *Thornton*, under Captain Read, 'lately'.

104. See the essays in Ian Duffield and James Bradley (eds), *Representing Convicts: New Perspectives on Convict Forced Labour Migration*, (London: Leicester University Press, 1997), particularly Ian Duffield, 'Problematic Passages: "Jack Bushman's" Convict Narrative', 29–42, and Toni Johnson Wood, 'Virtual Reality', 43–61.

105. Paul Lauter, ed, *Heath Anthology of American Literature*, 2nd edn (Boston: Houghton Mifflin, 1994), vol. 1, pp. 631–49, pp. 633–5 particularly.

106. *House of Commons Sessional Papers of the Eighteenth Century*, ed. S. Lambert, (Wilmington, DE: Scholarly Resources Inc., 1975), vol. 9, p. 358; see Robert Webber who asked to be hanged rather than transported at Maidstone assizes, *Annual Register* 1766, p. 135.

Chapter 5 Flight, escape and return

1. *Sherborne Mercury*, 26 March 1753; the precise date of the first edition of *The Discoveries of John Poulter, alias Baxter* is not known but it was probably late 1753.

2. These notices gave R. Goadby of Sherborne as the printer and 'W. Owen, Temple Bar, and J Palmer, Wine St, Bristol' as the booksellers. *Felix Farley's Bristol Journal*, 19 Jan. 1754, 2 Feb. 1754; for an excellent discussion on the wide market for such publications, see Philip Rawlings, *Drunks, Whores and Idle Apprentices: Criminal Biographies of the Eighteenth Century* (London: Routledge, 1992), introduction.

3. Advertisements for the 11th and 12th editions appeared in *Felix Farley's Bristol Journal*, 18 May and 22 June 1754; for Poulter's short-lived escape from 'Ivelchester' (Ilchester) gaol and speedy execution, see *Bath Journal*, 25 Feb. and 4 March 1754; *Felix Farley's Bristol Journal*, 2 March 1754.

4. R. Goadby, *The Discoveries of John Poulter, alias Baxter*, 14th edn (Sherborne, 1769), p. 28.

5. *Sherborne Mercury*, 9 April 1753, and 16 April 1753; this was also published separately and distributed widely; Pieter Spierenburg, *The Spectacle of Suffering: Executions and the Evolution of Repression: from a Preindustrial*

Metropolis to the European Experience (Cambridge: Cambridge University Press, 1984), p. 101.

6. Sydney Stafford Smythe to the Earl of Holdernesse, 28 Sept. 1753, PRO SP 36/123, Part 2, 94–5; Poulter's petition and 'The further Information, Examination, and Confession of John Poulter, otherwise Baxter', 127–8, 129.

7. *Old Bailey Sessions Proceedings, City of London and Middlesex*, 5–9 Dec. 1746 (J. Hinton, King's Arms, 1746); Coldham, *King's Passengers*, p. 113; Ruth Paley, 'Thief-takers in London in the Age of the McDaniel Gang, c. 1745–54', in Douglas Hay and Francis Snyder (eds), *Policing and Prosecution in Britain 1750–1850* (Oxford: Clarendon Press, 1989), 301–41, pp. 309–10, n. 28.

8. William Moraley, *The Infortunate: the Voyages and Adventures of William Moraley, an Indentured Servant*, ed. S. E. Klapp and B. G. Smith (University Park, PA: Pennsylvania State University Press, 1992), pp. 96–7.

9. Moraley, *The Infortunate*, pp. 111–13.

10. 'The Life and Actions of James Dalton (The noted Street-Robber)' in Rawlings, *Drunks, Whores and Idle Apprentices*, pp. 85–109, p. 96.

11. 'Life and Actions of James Dalton', p. 97.

12. Charles Speckman, 'The Life, Travels, Exploits, Frauds and Robberies, of Charles Speckman' (1763), in Rawlings, *Drunks, Whores and Idle Apprentices*, 194–200, pp. 194–5.

13. Alison Games, *Migration and the Origins of the English Atlantic World* (Cambridge, MA, and London: Harvard University Press, 1999), p. 105.

14. *Travels Through the Middle Settlements in North-America in the Years 1759 and 1760 with Observations upon the State of the Colonies by the Rev. Andrew Burnaby*, 2nd ed. (Ithaca, NY: Cornell University Press, 1960) pp. 13, 27 and 48.

15. Bernard Bailyn, *Voyagers to the West: a Passage in the Peopling of America on the Eve of the Revolution* (New York: Knopf, 1986), p. 344.

16. Richard S. Dunn, *Sugar and Slaves: the Rise of the Planter Class in the English West Indies, 1624–1713* (Chapel Hill, NC: University of North Carolina Press, 1972); Edmund S. Morgan, *American Slavery, American Freedom: the Ordeal of Colonial Virginia* (New York: W. W. Norton, 1975).

17. Farley Grubb, 'Does Bound Labour Have to be Coerced Labour?: the Case of Colonial Immigrant Servitude Versus Craft Apprenticeship and Life-Cycle Servitude-in-Husbandry', *Itinerario* 21 (1997), 28–51, p. 29; David W. Galenson, *White Servitude in Colonial America* (Cambridge: Cambridge University Press, 1981), pp. 5–15. By contrast, Christine Daniels regards English and American practices towards servants as comparable, and notes the numbers of successful petitions by servants in the Maryland courts; see Christine Daniels, '"Liberty to Complaine": Servant Petitions in Maryland, 1652–1797', in Christopher L. Tomlins and Bruce H. Mann (eds), *The Many Legalities of Early America* (Chapel Hill, NC: University of North Carolina Press, 2001), 219–49.

18. Grubb, 'Does Bound Labour Have to be Coerced Labour?', pp. 32 and 41–5.

19. Farley Grubb, 'The Statutory Regulation of Colonial Servitude: an Incomplete Contract Approach', *Explorations in Economic History* 37 (2000), 42–75, p. 60; on the basis of the sales of convicts shipped out of Bristol by Cheston and Stevenson between 1767 and 1775, Grubb argues that the sale of convicts was conducted under conditions resembling a 'spot' market

where the price of the convict was not fixed but negotiated allowing not only for age, gender, skill and length of sentence but for the specific crime for which individuals had been convicted. Farley Grubb, 'The Market Evaluation of Criminality: Evidence from the Auction of British Convict Labor in America, 1767–1775', *American Economic Review* 91 (1) (2001), 295–304; see also the same author's 'The Transatlantic Market for British Convict Labor', *Journal of Economic History* 60 (1) (2001), 94–122.

20. For the transformation of colonial Virginia into a slave society, Morgan, *American Slavery, American Freedom*, remains unsurpassed, but see also T. H. Breen, 'A Changing Labor Force and Race Relations in Virginia, 1660–1710', *Journal of Social History* 7 (1973), 3–15; for the impact of these changes on the role and status of women, Kathleen M. Brown, *Good Wives, Nasty Wenches, and Anxious Patriarchs: Gender, Race, and Power in Colonial Virginia* (Chapel Hill, NC: University of North Carolina Press, 1996).

21. David Waldstreicher, 'Reading the Runaways: Self-Fashioning, Print Culture, and Confidence in Slavery in the Eighteenth-Century Mid-Atlantic', *William and Mary Quarterly*, 3rd ser., 56 (1999), 243–72, pp. 249–50.

22. Grubb, 'Does Bound Labour Have to be Coerced Labour?', p. 31.

23. John Styles, 'Print and Policing: Crime Advertising in Eighteenth-Century Provincial England', in D. Hay and F. Snyder (eds), *Policing and Prosecution in England, 1750–1850* (Oxford: Oxford University Press, 1989), pp. 55–111.

24. See Landau on the control of mobility: Norma Landau, 'The Laws of Settlement and the Surveillance of Immigration in Eighteenth-Century Kent', *Continuity and Change* 3 (1988), 391–420.

25. G. Morgan and P. Rushton, 'The Magistrate, the Community and the Maintenance of an Orderly Society in Eighteenth-Century England', *Historical Research* 76 (2003), 54–77, pp. 61–5; for the general context of servanthood, see A. Kussmaul, *Servants in Husbandry in Early Modern England* (Cambridge: Cambridge University Press, 1981).

26. *Felix Farley's Bristol Journal*, 26 Jan. 1765, advertisement dated 24 Jan.

27. John Styles, 'Sir John Fielding and the Problem of Criminal Investigation in Eighteenth-Century England', *Transactions of the Royal Historical Society*, 5th ser. 33 (1983), 127–49; *Newcastle Courant*, 19 Dec. 1772, the town's quarter sessions receive the 'letter from Sir John Fielding'; he had earlier reported the escape of London's criminals to the country, *Newcastle Courant*, 12 Nov. 1763.

28. *Felix Farley's Bristol Journal*, 22 Oct. 1763, Letter to the Printer etc, on crime.

29. *Newcastle Journal*, 19 Feb. 1774; *Newcastle Courant*, 14 Sept. 1776.

30. Bailyn, *Voyagers to the West*, pp. 245–54; Kenneth Morgan, 'Convict Runaways in Maryland', *Journal of American Studies* 23, 253–68, p. 257; David C. Skaggs, *The Roots of Maryland Democracy* (Westport, CT: Greenwood Press, 1973), pp. 57–8.

31. *Virginia Gazette*, 2 Sept. 1757, *Virginia Gazette* (Purdie), 12 July 1776.

32. William Moraley, *The Infortunate*, p. 97; Poulter, *Discoveries*, pp. 28 and 44.

33. Ekirch's figure of 993 is based on fugitive notices for Maryland convicts appearing in the *Maryland Gazette* 1746–75 and supplemented by Maryland runaways found in the *Virginia* and *Pennsylvania Gazettes* while the figure of 816 used by Kenneth Morgan in his study of runaways for 1745 to 1775

is taken from the *Maryland Gazette* and the *Maryland Journal and Baltimore Advertiser*. A. Roger Ekirch, *Bound for America: the Transportation of British Convicts to the Colonies 1718–75* (Oxford: Clarendon Press, 1987), p. 195; Kenneth Morgan, 'Convict Runaways in Maryland', p. 254.

34. William Eddis, *Letters from America*, ed. Land, p. 38; Ekirch, *Bound for America* p. 202; Morgan, 'Convict Runaways in Maryland', p. 265.

35. Our figures are from 1739, but for reasons of comparability with Ekirch and Kenneth Morgan, we have excluded those few before 1745.

36. On convict bodies, see Gwenda Morgan and Peter Rushton, 'Running Away and Returning Home: the Fate of English Convicts in the American Colonies', *Crime, Histoire & Sociétés*, forthcoming.

37. Ekirch, *Bound for America*, p. 198.

38. Waldstreicher, 'Reading the Runaways', p. 247.

39. Bailyn, *Voyagers to the West*, p. 351.

40. DRO Q S OB 13, p. 54.

41. *Newcastle Courant*, 25 Jan. 1766; Tony Barrow, *The Whaling Trade of North-East England* (Sunderland: University of Sunderland Press, 2001), p. 11.

42. F. H. Schmidt, 'British Convict Servant Labor in Colonial Virginia' (unpublished Ph.D. diss, College of William and Mary, 1976), p. 162.

43. Schmidt, 'British Convict Servant Labor, pp. 144–5; Lyman Chalkley, ed., *Chronicles of the Scotch-Irish Settlement in Virginia, Extracted from the Original Court Records of Augusta County, 1745–1800*, 3 vols, (Baltimore MD: Genealogical Publishing Co., 1965, 3rd printing 1966), pp. 149 and 173.

44. For these circuits, see Schmidt, 'British Convict Servant Labor', p. 86; Bailyn, *Voyagers to the West*, pp. 344–50.

45. *Virginia Gazette* (Purdie & Dixon), 17 Oct. 1766.

46. For the distinction between 'Convicts of Distinction' and 'convicts of the common sort', see *Gentleman's Magazine*, 17 May 1736, discussed in Chapter 4.

47. Jonathan Prude, 'To Look upon the "Lower Sort": Runaway Ads and the Appearance of Unfree Laborers in America, 1750–1800', *Journal of American History* 78 (1) (1991), 124–59, pp. 141–3.

48. Bailyn, *Voyagers to the West*, p. 346.

49. *Virginia Gazette* (Pinkney), 4 May 1775; *Virginia Gazette* (Purdie), 12 May 1775.

50. *Newcastle Courant*, 16 Oct. 1773.

51. *Newcastle Journal*, 4 Dec. 1774, records the departure of *The Swift*.

52. William McGaughen to George Washington, 13 March 1774, *Papers of George Washington*, Colonial Series, v. 9, Jan. 1772–March 1774, ed. W. W. Abbot (Charlottesville and London: University Press of Virginia, 1994), p. 519.

53. W. W. Abbot and D. Twohig, eds, *Papers of George Washington*, Colonial Series, vol. 10, pp. 341–2.

54. *Virginia Gazette* (Purdie and Dixon), 21 June 1770.

55. Grubb, 'The Transatlantic Market for British Convict Labor', pp. 112–13; Kenneth Morgan, 'Convict Runaways in Maryland', p. 255; Shane White, *Somewhat More Independent: The End of Slavery in New York City, 1770–1810* (Athens, GA, and London: University of Georgia Press, 1991), pp. 134–9.

56. PRO ASSI 24/25; *Maryland Gazette*, 19 July 1753.
57. PRO ASSI 24/25; *Maryland Gazette* 28 Aug.–18 Sept. 1755. Pearce was again advertised in the *Maryland Gazette*, 15 Jan.–4 March 1756.
58. PRO ASSI 23/7; 24/25; *Maryland Gazette* 28 July 1768. Thomas Moore was transported from Surrey quarter sessions in 1766. Coldham, *King's Passengers*, p. 190.
59. *Maryland Gazette*, 2 Nov.–21 Dec. 1775; *Pennsylvania Gazette*, 8 Nov. 1775. Braddock advertised for Manley again *Pennsylvania Gazette*, 15 May 1776.
60. PRO ASSI/41/3, 42/5 (unpaginated, 1750); *Virginia Gazette*, 3 July 1752; *Pennsylvania Gazette*, 20 Feb. 1753.
61. James Bradley and Hamish Maxwell-Stewart, 'Embodied Explorations: Investigating Convict Tattoos and the Transportation System' in Ian Duffield and James Bradley (eds), *Representing Convicts: New Perspectives on Convict Forced Labour Migration* (Leicester: Leicester University Press, 1997), p. 198; 1,179 physical descriptions of Scottish convicts (1840–53) were studied, of which 308 or 26 per cent sported some form of tattoo (p. 184); Clare Anderson, 'The Genealogy of the Modern Subject: Indian Convicts in Mauritius, 1814–53', in Duffield and Bradley (eds) *Representing Convicts*, pp. 169 and 174.
62. *Pennsylvania Gazette*, 17 April 1760; *Maryland Gazette*, 28 May 1767; *Virginia Gazette* (Purdie and Dixon), 24 Nov. 1774; *Maryland Gazette*, 11 Sept. 1755; *Maryland Gazette*, 28 Aug. 1755.
63. *Maryland Gazette*, 18 April 1750, 21 Dec. 1769 and 1 Jan. 1763; *Pennsylvania Gazette*, 27 Jan. 1763.
64. *Virginia Gazette*, 17 Oct. 1766, (Pinkney), 4 May 1775.
65. *Pennsylvania Gazette*, 13 Aug. 1767; *Virginia Gazette* (Rind), 24 June 1773.
66. *Pennsylvania Gazette*, 21 Aug. 1766; *Maryland Gazette*, 27 June 1771; *Virginia Gazette* (Purdie and Dixon), 24 Nov. 1774.
67. *Virginia Gazette*, 1 June, 1775, (Rind), 24 June 1773.
68. *Maryland Gazette*, 17 Aug. 1748.
69. *Pennsylvania Gazette*, 31 July 1760; *Maryland Gazette*, 21 Dec. 1769, 15 March 1759.
70. *Maryand Gazette*, 11 Sept. 1755.
71. *Maryland Gazette*, 9 Nov. 1758; *Pennsylvania Gazette*, 7 Dec. 1758.
72. *Pennsylvania Gazette*, 26 April 1764; *Maryland Gazette*, 19 March 1767.
73. G. Lamoine, *Bristol Gaol Delivery Fiats 1741–99* (Bristol: Bristol Record Society, vol. 40, 1989), p. 20.
74. *Maryland Gazette*, 20 Sept. 1749; *Virginia Gazette* (Purdie and Dixon), 24 Nov. 1774, 16 May 1766, 21 June 1770.
75. *Virginia Gazette* (Purdie), 16 May 1766; *Pennsylvania Gazette*, 16 July 1769.
76. *Maryland Gazette*, 15 July 1762, *Pennsyvania Gazette*, 21 Aug. 1766; *Maryland Gazette*, 4 May 1769, 1 Jan. 1763 and 18 June 1767; *Pennsylvania Gazette*, 27 Jan. 1763 and 11 Nov. 1772; *Maryland Gazette*, 11 Nov. 1747.
77. *Pennsylvania Gazette*, 11 Nov. 1747.
78. *Maryland Gazette*, 28 Aug. 1755, 28 July 1768.
79. *Maryland Gazette*, 29 Aug. 1757, 18 April 1750; 28 Aug. 1755, 28 May 1767, 15 July 1762; *Virginia Gazette* (Purdie and Dixon), 16 May 1766.
80. *Maryland Gazette*, 20 Sept. 1749, 21 Dec. 1769, 29 Sept. 1767.

81. *Maryland Gazette*, 17 Aug. 1758; *Pennsylvania Gazette*, 21 Oct. 1758. *Virginia Gazette* (Purdie & Dixon), 24 Nov. 1774; Morgan, 'Convict Runaways in Maryland', pp. 255–8; on the demeaning of servant skills by masters, Waldstreicher, 'Reading the Runaways', p. 255.

82. Devon Record Office, QS 1/20, p. 220.

83. *Maryland Gazette* and *Pennsylvania Gazette*, 17 April–22 May 1766; Coldham, *King's Passengers*, p. 282.

84. Ekirch, *Bound for America*, p. 220.

85. *Exeter Flying Post*, 21 Aug. 1767; PRO ASSI 23/7.

86. *Exeter Flying Post*, 4 Sept. 1767.

87. Runaway advertisement for Elliott and Usher, *Virginia Gazette* (Purdie & Dixon), 9 July 1772, gives 15 June as the date of their flight; Braithwaite Atkinson, gaoler, claims that the date on which Elliott was delivered to the Cumberland contractor responsible for transporting convicts to the colonies was 'about the tenth or eleventh of Mar. last'. Information of Braithwaite Atkinson gaoler, 8 March 1773, ASSI 45/31/1/84.

88. It was reported in the *Newcastle Courant* that her gang spared no pains or cost to effect her return 'knowing that in six months time she'll pickpocket enough to pay all charges', *Newcastle Courant*, 26 May 1738.

89. Morgan and Rushton, *Rogues, Thieves*, Chapter 4, for gangs and their careers.

90. Beattie, *Crime and the Courts*, p. 503.

91. Ekirch, *Bound for America*, p. 215.

92. Deposition of Mathias Gyles, 13 Jan. 1743, PRO ASSI 45/22/3/15, (William Brown); *Felix Farley's Bristol Journal*, 14 May 1768 (David Thomas); Certificate signed by John Ridout, Naval Officer Port of Annapolis in Maryland, 4 March 1767, BRO JQS/P/49 (David Thomas); Information of Braithwaite Atkinson, gaoler, 8 March 1773, PRO ASSI 45/31/1/84 (William Elliott).

93. *Bristol Weekly Intelligencer*, 6 April 1752.

94. The Dying Declaration of Samuel Drayton, alias D–, who was executed at Dorchester, April the 8th, for returning from Transportation', Extract from Thomas Molland, *Special Grace Uninterrupted. in its Egress* (1775), p. 23; Coldham, *King's Passengers*, p. 239.

95. Elliott's first conviction and death sentence at the Carlisle assizes were reported in the *London Evening Post*, 13 Aug. 1771.

96. *Virginia Gazette*, 9 July 1772; PRO ASSI 30/1/42-4; information of Robert Walters, 16 Dec. 1772, ASSI 45/31/1/81; examination of William Elliott, 16 Dec. 1772, ASSI 45/31/1/82; ASSI 41/3. In reporting his second death sentence the *Newcastle Courant* 5056, 21 Aug. 1773 identified his crime as 'returning from transportation' but the consideration of his appeal points to horse-stealing though evidence that he was a returned transportee was submitted with the appeal.

97. *Felix Farley's Bristol Journal*, 23 Sept. 1775.

98. Ekirch, *Bound for America*, p. 214.

99. *Gloucester Journal*, 8 April 1740.

100. Lamoine, ed., *Bristol Gaol Delivery Fiats*, p. 1; *Gloucester Journal*, 20 Oct. 1741.

101. *Gloucester Journal*, 6 and 20 April 1742.

102. It was reported in the *Sherborne Mercury* that Matthew Cudmore 'in his last moments insisted in being innocent of the crime for which he suffers', *Sherborne Mercury*, 21 Aug. 1749; *Bristol Weekly Intelligencer*, 6 April 1752.
103. *Bristol Weekly Intelligencer* 18 and 25 April 1752.
104. P. W. Coldham, The *Complete Book of Emigrants in Bondage, 1614–1775* (Baltimore MD: Genealogical Publishing Co. Inc., 1988), p. 241.
105. *The Dying Declaration of Samuel Drayton, alias D–*, p. 23.
106. *Newcastle Courant*, 13 Aug. 1743; Morgan and Rushton, *Rogues, Thieves*, p. 143.
107. *Newcastle Courant*, 13 Aug. 1743.
108. ASSI23/7; Coldham, *Complete Book of Emigrants in Bondage*, p. 567; Coldham, *King's Passengers*, p. 211.
109. PRO PL 28/13, p. 164; Coldham, *Complete Book of Emigrants in Bondage*, p. 562.
110. SP 44/87/226, 5 March 1765.
111. Coldham, *King's Passengers*, p. 273; *Maryland Gazette*, 4–25 Oct. 1764.
112. 29 Aug. 1767, PRO PL 28/14, Order Book 2, p. 60.
113. PRO PL 28/14, Order Book 2, p. 83; Coldham, *Complete Book of Emigrants in Bondage*, p. 182.
114. C15/60/3, 26 July 1751 and 10 Aug. 1751.
115. Lamoine, ed., *Bristol Gaol Delivery Fiats*, 7 May 1761, p. 18, 19 Oct. 1761, pp. 19–20. For a south-western breakout, see *Sherborne Mercury*, 29 April 1754.
116. *Felix Farley's Bristol Journal*, 9 and 16 May, and 20 June 1761.
117. *Newcastle Courant*, 2 Aug. 1766; DURH 17/9; SP 44/89/9, 24.
118. Morgan and Rushton, *Rogues, Thieves*, pp. 106, and 166.
119. PRO SP 44/85/45, 10 Apr. 1748; cited in Ekirch, *Bound for America*, p. 65, n. 2.
120. Poulter, *Discoveries*, p. 28.
121. *Newcastle Courant*, 1 June 1745; see Chapter 3, pp. 27–9.
122. *Felix Farley's Bristol Journal*, 16 May and 27 June 1761; Coldham, *King's Passengers*, pp. 174–5.
123. PRO SP 44/91/53, Bilton, 5 April 1771; Smith (p. 29), 7 Jan. 1771 on condition of entering HM service, and in SP 44/89/311, reprieved for his natural life, 3 Aug. 1769; SP 44/90/241, 14 Dec. 1770; SP 44/90/246, 1 Feb. 1771 (William Marshall, Charles Mackenzie).
124. 'The Life and Actions of James Dalton', pp. 94–6; Coldham, *King's Passengers*, p. 7; Schmidt, 'British Convict Servant Labor', pp. 55–7 for shipboard risings.
125. *Felix Farley's Bristol Journal*, 2 June 1764.
126. *Virginia Gazette* (Purdie & Dixon), 21 Nov. 1769; Cheston Galloway Papers, Box 7, 17 Nov. 1769, and 14 March 1770, Maryland Historical Society microfilm; *Felix Farley's Bristol Journal*, 19 May 1764.
127. Poulter, *Discoveries*, p. 28.

Chapter 6 Panics and recriminations: Convergence and divergence and the criminal Atlantic

1. B. Bailyn, *Voyagers to the West: A Passage in the Peopling of America on the Eve of the Revolution* (New York: Knopf, 1986), pp. 293–4 – a coffle is a line of people; on p. 295 he talks rather exaggeratedly of the transportation of 'hardened criminals'.
2. See comments of Father Joseph Mosley, in 'Letters of Father Joseph Mosley, 1757–86', *Woodstock Letters* 35 (1906) p. 54: ships' captains allegedly flogged Catholics into taking the oath and denying their faith.
3. R. Beverly, *The History and Present State of Virginia* (London, 1722), p. 249; *American Weekly Mercury*, 14 Feb. 1721.
4. Farley Grubb, 'The Market Evaluation of Criminality: Evidence from the Auction of British Convict Labor in America, 1767–75', *The American Economic Review* 91 (1) (2001), 295–304, p. 303.
5. Malachy Postlethwayt, *The Universal Dictionary of Trade and Commerce, translated from the French of the Celebrated Monsieur Savary, . . . with large additions and improvements etc.*, 2nd edn, 2 vols (London: 1758), vol. 1, p. 534.
6. See Henry T. Tuckerman, *America and her Commentators* (New York: Augustus M. Kelley, 1970; first published New York, 1864), Chapter 7, 'English Abuse of America'.
7. J. M. Beattie, *Crime and the Courts in England, 1660–1800* (Princeton, NJ: Princeton University Press, 1986), pp. 188–9 and 253.
8. PRO SP 44/81, 530–5.
9. PRO SP 36/50, f.308 (Somerset), Thomas Pope, arrested for burglary 1740, reprieved for transportation for life; Henry Fielding, 'An Inquiry into the Late Increase in Robbers' in *The Works of Henry Fielding Esquire*, 10 vols (London: Smith Elder, 1882), vol. 7, p. 265.
10. J. M. Beattie, *Policing and Punishment in London 1660–1750: Urban Crime and the Limits of Terror* (Oxford: Oxford University Press, 2001), p. 473; Timothy Pitkin, *A Political and Civil History of the United States of America from the Year 1763 etc.*, 2 vols (New Haven, CT: Hezekiah Howe, Durrie and Peck, 1828), vol. 1, p. 133.
11. Kent County Court (Bonds and Indentures) 1715–20, f.50v–52v, the Transportation Act; A. Roger Ekirch, *Bound for America: the Transportation of British Convicts to the Colonies, 1718–75* (Oxford: Clarendon Press, 1987) pp. 138–9.
12. Waverly K. Winfree, comp., *The Laws of Virginia Being a Supplement to Hening's The Statutes at Large, 1700–50* (Richmond: Virginia State Library, 1971), pp. 212–22; Ekirch, *Bound for America*, p. 139; Gwenda Morgan, *The Hegemony of the Law: Richmond County, Virginia, 1692–1776* (New York and London: Garland, 1989), p. 144.
13. Winfree, *Laws of Virginia*, p. 217.
14. Winfree, *Laws of Virginia*, pp. 217–18 and 219.
15. Winfree, *Laws of Virginia*, p. 222.
16. Morgan. *Hegemony of the Law*, p. 145; Richard Morton, *Colonial Virginia*, 2 vols (Chapel Hill, NC: University of North Carolina Press, 1960), vol. 2, p. 526.
17. Ekirch, *Bound for America*, p. 138.

18. Alan Atkinson, 'The Free-born Englishman Transported: Convict Rights as a Measure of Eighteenth-century Empire', *Past and Present* 144 (1994), 88–115, pp. 100 and 106. Atkinson's ambitious article aims among other things 'to contribute to the thesis which would argue that for the period of Britain's "imperial meridian" – the late eighteenth and early nineteenth centuries – it may be misleading to think of the British empire merely as an appendage of the British state. In some ways Britain itself can be seen as merely the central dominion, the first among equals, so that parts of its home government can be properly understood only within the imperial context' (p. 91).

19. Cited in Morton, *Colonial Virginia*, vol. 2, pp. 525–6; Ekirch, *Bound for America*, pp. 141 and 173–4.

20. Ekirch, *Bound for America*, pp. 174–5, n. 2; Morton, *Colonial Virginia*, vol. 2, p. 512.

21. Richmond County Order Book 9, 18 May 1730, p. 519; J. P. Kennedy and H. R. McIlwaine, eds, *Journal of the House of Burgesses, 1727–40*, pp. 71, 87 and 123; on the destruction of Lee's house, Gooch to the Board of Trade, 26 March 1729, PRO CO 5/1321/110–11; Ekirch, *Bound for America*, p. 167; Morgan, *Hegemony of the Law*, pp. 153–4; Morton, *Colonial Virginia*, vol. 2, pp. 525–7; Fairfax Harrison, 'When the Convicts Came', *Virginia Magazine of History and Biography* 30 (1922), pp. 250–60.

22. *Maryland Gazette*, 4 Feb. and 18 March 1729.

23. Gooch to Board of Trade, CO /5/1323/12–13; Ekirch, *Bound for America*, pp. 174–5; Lee received £300 compensation for his losses.

24. Morgan, *Hegemony of the Law*, p. 153 .

25. Peter C. Hoffer and William B. Scott, eds., *Criminal Proceedings in Colonial Virginia: Record of Fines, Examinations of Criminals, Trials of Slaves, etc., from March 1710 to [1754]* [Richmond County Virginia], American Legal Records, vol. 10 (Athens, GA: University of Georgia Press, 1984), pp. xliv–lii; Philip J. Schwartz, *Twice Condemned: Slaves and the Criminal Laws of Virginia* (Baton Rouge: Louisiana State University Press, 1988), pp. 16–25; Morgan, *Hegemony of the Law*, pp. 99–137.

26. 'An Act for altering the method of Trial of certain Criminals' (1738), Hening, *Statutes*, 5, pp. 24–5; this was repeated in 1748, Hening, *Statutes*, 5, p. 545.

27. Cited in Ekirch, *Bound for America*, p. 137.

28. 'Act directing the Tryal of Slaves committing Capital Crimes; And for the more effectual Punishing Conspiracies and Insurrections of them and for the better Government of Negroes Mullatoes, & Indians, Bond or Free', 1723: Hening, *Statutes*, 4, 126–34, p. 133.

29. Emory G. Evans, 'A Question of Complexion: Documents Concerning the Negro and the Franchise in Eighteenth-Century Virginia', *Virginia Magazine of History and Biography* 71 (1963), 411–15, pp. 414–15; Winthrop D. Jordan, *White Over Black: American Attitudes toward the Negro, 1550–1812* (Chapel Hill, NC: University of North Carolina Press, 1968), pp. 127–8; note the earlier ruling in 1717 by the attorney general, that a free Christian Negro should have the same rights as any freeman, *Calendar of State Papers, America and West Indies, 1716–17*, p. 282.

30. The best discussion of this right is Farley Grubb, 'The Statutory Regulation of Colonial Servitude: an Incomplete-Contract Approach', *Explorations in*

Economic History 37 (2000), 42–75, where he notes that the phrase 'except convicts' in the 1753 Act has often been ignored, p. 70; Hening, *Statutes*, 6, p. 359; Maryland State Archives, Ridgely Account Book 1781–2, end-paper; R. Kent Lancaster, 'Almost Chattel: the Lives of Indentured Servants at Hampton-Northampton, Baltimore County', *Maryland Historical Magazine* 94 (3), (1999), 341–62, pp. 361–2, n. 5; Atkinson, 'Free-Born Englishman Transported', pp. 101–2.

31. H. R. McIlwaine, ed., *Legislative Journals of the Council of Colonial Virginia*, 3 vols (Richmond, VA, 1918–19), vol. 2, pp. 1034–5.

32. See T. H. Breen, 'A Changing Labor Force and Race Relations in Virginia, 1660–1710', *Journal of Social History* 7 (1) (1973), 3–25, p. 13, on late-seventeenth-century fear of rebellion by servants.

33. Beattie, *Crime and the Courts in England*, pp. 519 and 540.

34. *Pennsylvania Gazette*, 11 April 1751, stated that six Liverpool convicts shot the captain and took control of the ship; *Pennsylvania Gazette*, 1 April 1754 letter from Annapolis, describing how the crew, including two convicts, seized a sloop, murdered the captain William Curtis, 'turning pyrates in the Bay'; 25 April 1754 edition reported their arrest.

35. Nicholas Rogers, 'Confronting the Crime Wave: the Debate over Social Reform and Regulation, 1749–53', in Lee Davison, Tim Hitchcock, Tim Keirn and R. B. Shoemaker (eds), *Stilling the Grumbling Hive: the Response to Social and Economic Problems in England, 1689–1750* (Stroud: Alan Sutton, 1992), p. 87.

36. William Byrd II to Philip Ludwell (31 Jan. 1717/18), and to Mr Smyth (6 Sept. 1740), in Marion Tinling, ed., *The Correspondence of the Three William Byrds of Westover, Virginia, 1684–1776* (Charlottesville, VA: University Press of Virginia, 1977), vol. 1, pp. 310 and 557; Georgia and North Carolina were rumoured to be full of escaped convicts.

37. John Beattie, 'London Crime and the making of the "Bloody Code", 1689–1718' in Lee Davison et al. (eds), *Stilling the Grumbling Hive*, 49–76, pp. 63 and 68 particularly; D. A. Kent, 'Ubiquitous but Invisible: Female Domestic Servants in Mid-Eighteenth-Century London', *History Workshop Journal* 28 (1989), 111–28; Paula Humfrey, 'Female Servants and Women's Criminality in Early Eighteenth-Century London', in Greg T. Smith, Allyson N. May and Simon Devereaux, (eds), *Criminal Justice in the Old World and the New: Essays in Honour of J. M. Beattie* (Toronto: Centre for Criminology, 1998), 58–84.

38. Mark J. Stegmaier, 'Maryland's Fear of Insurrection at the Time of Braddock's Defeat', *Maryland Historical Magazine* 71 (1976), 467–83.

39. D. A. Kent, 'Ubiquitous but Invisible'; Rawlings, *Drunks, Whores and Idle Apprentices*, p. 17; Beattie, *Crime and the Courts*, Chapter 10, 521–45, on the paradox of the 1750s' search for both substitutes for transportation such as hard labour, and 'additional torments' for serious crimes.

40. Nicholas Rogers, 'Confronting the Crime Wave', p. 79; Ruth Paley, 'Thief-takers in London in the age of the McDaniel Gang c.1745–54', in D. Hay and F. Snyder (eds), *Policing and Prosecution in Britain, 1750–1850* (Oxford: Clarendon Press, 1989), 301–41; 'The Discoveries of John Poulter', published probably in 1753, reprinted in Rawlings, *Drunks, Whores and Idle Apprentices*, 137–77.

41. David A. Copeland, *Colonial Newspapers: Character and Content* (Newark, DE: University of Delaware Press, 1997), pp. 97 and 106, statistics pp. 288–99 and Table 7 on p. 294 particularly; Charles E. Clark, *The Public Prints: the Newspaper in Anglo-American Culture, 1665–1740* (New York and Oxford: Oxford University Press, 1994), p. 239ff.

42. See Rogers, 'Confronting the Crime Wave', and Peter King, 'Newspaper Reporting, Prosecution Practice and Perceptions of Urban Crime: the Colchester Crime Wave of 1765', *Continuity and Change* 2 (1987), 423–54, for an English case study. For a modern context, P. Schlesinger and H. Tumber, *Reporting Crime: the Media Politics of Criminal Justice* (Oxford: Clarendon Press, 1994).

43. *Maryland Gazette*, 20 March 1751; 3 April 1751; 10 April 1751 (the question asked); 17 April 1751; 24 April 1751 (account of his life and of the chains); *Pennsylvania Gazette*, 11 April 1751. See Maryland State Archives, Provincial Court Judgment Record, pp. 466 and 483; Coldham, *The Complete Book of Emmigrants in Bondage*, p. 777; Coldham, *King's Passengers*, p. 123. A disturbed servant, Patience Boston, who killed her master's young grandson was the subject of a 1735 pamphlet: see Daniel A. Cohen, *Pillars of Salt, Monuments of Grace. New England Crime Literature and the Origins of American Popular Culture, 1694–1860* (New York: Oxford University Press, 1993), pp. 72–5.

44. *Maryland Gazette*, 3 and 10 April 1751; 17 April 1751 (execution); ran away from Joseph Wood and Adam Vanberber, though 'lately come into the country', 10s reward, *Maryland Gazette*, 14 Nov. 1750, and also *Pennsylvania Gazette*, 11 Oct. 1750. Maryland State Archives, Provincial Court Judgment Record, p. 491 (killing Donald Mackenzie by hitting him with a club on the back of his head).

45. *Maryland Gazette*, 12 June 1751. At the same time in Annapolis two convict servants were also sentenced – Thomas Poney branded, and Onesipherous Lucas sentenced to death for burglary.

46. *Maryland Gazette*, 12 June 1751 (new law passed by assembly); 17 July 1751 (editorial and Mr Cole's robbery); 14 Aug. 1751; 6 Nov. 1751.

47. *Maryland Gazette*, 21 Aug. 1751.

48. *Virginia Gazette*, 27 June 1751; note Faller, *Turned to Account*, p. 320; *A Genuine and Authentick Account of the Life and Transactions of William Parsons Esq. . . . etc.* (London 1751): there were several editions in that year alone (see University of London Library, special collections – 3rd edn, 1751).

49. See the classic study of youth cultures and the media, Stanley Cohen, *Folk Devils and Moral Panics: the Creation of the Mods and Rockers* (London: Paladin, 1973).

50. *The Independent Reflector . . . by William Livingston and Others*, ed. Milton M. Klein (Cambridge, MA: Belknap Press of Harvard University Press, 1963), pp. 165–6 and pp. 168–9, dated 15 March 1753; Clark, *The Public Prints*, p. 240, for the case of 'Suss the Jew' from the London press.

51. *Virginia Gazette* 24 and 30 May 1751; *Pennsylvania Gazette*, 11 April, 9 May, 13 June and 5 Sept. 1751.

52. *Pennsylvania Magazine*, 11 April and 9 May 1751.

53. According to Kevin Hayes, Franklin's essay was reprinted in the *New York Evening-Post*, 15 April 1751, the *Maryland Gazette* 17 April; and both the

Boston Gazette and the *Boston Evening Post* on 23 April; it appeared in part in the *Virginia Gazette* on 2 May and in full on 24 May; Hayes also links the timing of Franklin's essay to the case of Jeremiah Swift; Kevin J. Hayes, 'The Board of Trade's "Cruel Sarcasm": a Neglected Franklin Source', *Early American Literature* 28 (1993), 171–6, pp. 174–5, n 2.

54. *Virginia Gazette*, 30 May 1751; there is a study to be done of the subsequent use of 'well peopling' in news, advertisements and commentaries in colonial and British newspapers: it is almost certainly used with satirical or ironic intent after Franklin; see Hayes, 'The Board of Trade's "Cruel Sarcasm"'.

55. *Sherborne Mercury*, 17 June 1751 – carrying a New York dateline of 27 March and the other two Philadelphia datelines of 11 and 13 April; 22 July 1751; *Gloucester Journal*, 18 June and 16 July 1751.

56. *Gentleman's Magazine* 21, June 1751; *London Magazine* 20, July 1751.

57. *Gloucester Journal*, 3 Sept. 1751.

58. Beattie, *Crime and the Courts*, p. 521.

59. *Virginia Gazette*, 13 and 27 Feb. 1752; Pennsylvania had tried to ban convicts entering in 1749. See 'A Bill to give power to change the punishment of felony in certain cases, and of certain other offences, to confinement and hard labour, in His Majesty's dockyards', in S. Lambert (ed.), *House of Commons Sessional Papers of the Eighteenth Century* (Wilmington, DE: Scholarly Resources, 1975), vol. 9. p. 358.

60. Beattie, *Crime and the Courts*, pp. 521–4, for criticisms of Radzinowicz's idea that the period marked a turning point in critiques of the bloody punishments, p. 522; and Rogers, 'Confronting the Crime Wave', p. 92. For executions under the Murder Act in north-east England, see Morgan and Rushton, *Rogues, Thieves*, pp. 118–23.

61. *Report from the Select Committee on Criminal Laws etc.* (House of Commons, ordered for printing, 8 July 1819): Appendix 4, pp. 146–51, execution rates were 52.8 per cent in the 1720s, and 53.4 per cent between 1749 and 1755, but only 37.5 per cent from 1730–48.

62. Beattie, *Crime and the Courts*, p. 547.

63. *Felix Farley's Bristol Journal*, 3–10 Aug. 1754.

64. *Virginia Gazette*, 2 April 1767, 'Extract of a Letter from an English Gentleman at Amsterdam to his friend in London, dated December 18'.

65. T. H. Breen, 'Ideology and Nationalism on the Eve of the American Revolution: Revisions *Once More* in Need of Revising', *Journal of American History* 84 (1997), 13–39, p. 19.

66. Breen, 'Ideology and Nationalism', p. 19; Linda Colley, *Britons: Forging the Nation, 1707–1837* (London: Pimlico/Random House, 1992); Colin Kidd, *British Identities Before Nationalism: Ethnicity and Nationhood in the Atlantic World, 1600–1800* (Cambridge: Cambridge University Press, 1999).

67. *Maryland Gazette*, 8 Aug. 1765, reprinted from the *Boston Gazette*, 15 July 1765, cited in Breen, 'Ideology and Nationalism', pp. 28–9.

68. Breen, 'Ideology and Nationalism', p. 31; on the radical whig tradition, see Bernard Bailyn, *The Ideological Origins of the American Revolution* (Cambridge, MA: Belknap Press of Harvard University Press, 1967) and Gordon S. Wood, 'Rhetoric and Reality in the American Revolution', *William and Mary Quarterly*, 3rd ser. 23 (1966), 3–32.

69. Stephen Conway, 'From Fellow-Nationals to Foreigners: British Perceptions of the Americans, c 1739–83', *William and Mary Quarterly* 59 (2002), 65–100, pp. 77–8, 81–2 and 94–5; see also his 'War and National Identity in the Mid-Eighteenth-Century British Isles', *English Historical Review* 116 (468) (2001), 863–93.

70. Tuckerman, *America and her Commentators*, p. 254, Colonel Barre, reporting to the elder Quincy, 'before the Revolutionary War'.

71. Breen, 'Ideology and Nationalism', pp. 29 and 32.

72. Adam Smith, *The Theory of Moral Sentiments*, ed. D. D. Raphael and A. L. Macfie (Oxford: Clarendon Press, 1976), p. 206.

73. Woody Holton, *Forced Founders: Indians, Debtors, Slaves, and the Making of the American Revolution in Virginia* (Chapel Hill, NC: University of North Carolina Press, 1999), p. 49.

74. George Birkbeck Hill and L. F. Powell, eds, *Boswell's Life of Johnson*, vol. 2 (Oxford: Clarendon Press, 1934), p. 312; Butler suggests the comment was made in 1769, see James Davie Butler, 'British Convicts shipped to American Colonies', *American Historical Review* 2 (1896), 12–33, p. 12; Boswell's *Life* was first published in 1791.

75. Breen, 'Ideology and Nationalism', pp. 29–30; *Pennsylvania Gazette*, 23 Nov. 1774, reprinted from the *London Chronicle*, 30 Aug. 1774, signed 'F.B.' i.e. Benjamin Franklin.

76. Cited in E. H. Gould, *The Persistence of Empire: British Political Culture in the Age of the American Revolution* (Chapel Hill, NC: University of North Carolina Press, 2000), p. 192.

77. 'Pathopoiea', *Felix Farley's Bristol Journal*, 16 April 1774.

78. 'Journal of a French Traveller in the Colonies, 1765', *American Historical Review* 26 (1921), 726–47, pp. 738 and 744.

79. Petition of Franklin to the House of Commons [12–15 April 1766], Leonard W. Labaree and William B. Willcox (eds), *The Papers of Benjamin Franklin* (New Haven, CT: Yale University Press, 1959–2001), 13, p. 24.

80. Ekirch, *Bound for America*, p. 227.

81. *Pennsylvania Gazette*, 23 Nov. 1774, citing the *London Chronicle*, 30 Aug. and 1 Sept. 1774, again calling the phrase a 'barbarous ill-placed sarcasm'; *Samuel Johnson: Political Writings*, vol. 10 of *The Works of Samuel Johnson*, ed. Donald. J. Greene (New Haven, CT: Yale University Press, 1977), p. 414, in the pamphlet 'Taxation no Tyranny'; George Birkbeck Hill, *Boswell's Life of Johnson*, vol. 2, p. 314, n. 3.

82. 'Letter from a gentleman at Boston to his friend in London', dateline 23 Dec., *Virginia Gazette* (Rind), 1 June 1769 (supplement).

83. Surry County, *Virginia Gazette* (Rind), 21 July 1774; Bruce A. Ragsdale, *A Planters' Republic: the Search for Economic Independence in Revolutionary Virginia* (Madison, WI: Madison House, 1996), p. 190.

84. *Virginia Gazette*, 22 Sept. 1775.

85. L. H. Butterfield et al. (eds), *Diary and Autobiography of John Adams*, vol. 2, Diary 1771–81, 23 Feb. 1777 (Cambridge, MA: Harvard University Press, 1961), p. 261.

86. *Gentleman's Magazine* 47, 1777, p. 608; *Old Bailey Sessions Papers*, Dec. 1777; *Pennsylvania Gazette*, 23 May 1778. There are some apparently genuine cases of mental distress where the defendant 'stood dumb' though brought out

to be charged at regular intervals over several years. *Newcastle Journal*, 10 Aug. 1754, Robert Swainston 'for standing mute on his arraignment in 1741'.

87. *Old Bailey Sessions Papers*, Feb. 1773.
88. Worcester, from Boston newspapers, *Virginia Gazette* (Dixon), 28 Oct. 1775 and (Pinkney), 26 Oct. 1775; *Pennsylvania Gazette*, 23 May 1778; for the abuse of prisoners in New York, see Barnet Schecter, *The Battle for New York: the City at the Heart of the American Revolution* (New York: Walker and Co., 2002), pp. 274–5, and p. 285 for Cresswell's account of the half-buried bodies of American prisoners; Holton, *Forced Founders*, p. 219.
89. *Journal of Nicholas Cresswell, 1774–77*, with a foreword by Samuel Thornley (New York: Lincoln Macveagh, Dial Press, 1924), p. 186.
90. 6–8 May 1787, quoted in Bob Reece, *The Origins of Irish Convict Transportation to New South Wales* (Basingstoke: Palgrave, 2001), p. 116; Michael Rozbicki, *The Complete Gentleman: Cultural Legitimacy in Plantation America* (Charlottesville and London: University Press of Virginia, 1998), pp. 92–6; Malachy Postlethwayt, *Dictionary of Commerce*, 3rd edn (London, 1766) cited in Scott Christianson, *With Liberty for Some: 500 Years of Imprisonment in America* (Boston, MA: Northeastern University Press, 1998), p. 49.
91. Jefferson's 'Observations on Demeunier's Manuscript [1786]', 'Observations on the article Etats-unis prepared for the Encyclopedie', *The Papers of Thomas Jefferson*, ed. Julian P. Boyd (Princeton, NJ: Princeton University Press, 1954), vol. 10, pp. 30 and 59–60. On Jefferson and population, see Daniel Scott Smith, 'Population and Political Ethics: Thomas Jefferson's Demography of Generations', *William and Mary Quarterly* 56 (1999), 591–612.
92. Edmund Randolph, *History of Virginia*, edited with an Introduction by Arthur H. Shaffer (Charlottesville: University Press of Virginia, 1970), pp. 37–8; William Stith, *The History of the First Discovery and Settlement of Virginia etc.* (Williamsburg, VA, 1747).
93. Fairfax Harrison, 'When the Convicts Came', pp. 250–60; Charles Edgar Gilliam, 'Jail Bird Immigrants to Virginia', *Virginia Magazine of History and Biography* 52 (1944), 180–2; Polly Cary Mason, 'More about "Jayle Birds" in Colonial Virginia', and Matthew Page Andrews, 'Additional Data on the Importation of Convicts', *Virginia Magazine of History and Biography* 53 (1945), pp. 37–41 and 41–2; Timothy Pitkin, *A Political and Civil History of the United States of America from the year 1763 etc.* 2 vols (New Haven, CT: Hezekiah Howe, Durrie and Peck, 1828); George Bancroft, *History of the United States of America* (New York: D. Appleton and Co., 1888); Butler, 'British Convicts shipped to American Colonies', 12–33.
94. Rawlings, *Drunks, Whores and Idle Apprentices*, p. 27.

Chapter 7 Conclusion

1. Wilfred Oldham, *British Convicts to the Colonies* ed. W. Hugh Oldham (Sydney: Australian National Library, 1990), p. 91.
2. *Virginia Gazette* (Rind), 9 March 1769.

3. *Virginia Gazette* (Purdie and Dixon), 30 April 1767; (Purdie and Dixon) 8 Oct. 1767; (Purdie and Dixon) 3 March 1768 for petition; (Purdie) 23 June 1775.

4. *Virginia Gazette* (Purdie and Dixon), 2 Sept. 1773.

5. *Maryland Gazette*, 13 Nov. 1783.

6. A. Roger Ekirch, *Bound for America: The Transportation of British Convicts to the Colonies, 1718–1775* (Oxford: Clarendon Press, 1987), p. 233, and generally pp. 233–7; A. Roger Ekirch, 'Great Britain's Secret Convict Trade to America, 1783–1784', *American Historical Review* 89 (1984), 1285–91; Bob Reece, *The Origins of Irish Convict Transportation to New South Wales* (Basingstoke: Palgrave, 2001), p. xv.

7. Reece, *Origins of Irish Convict Transportation*, pp. 67 and 101–2; note that company records only show sixteen men and one woman, not the full 122 of the cargo, pp. 113–14 and 115–16.

8. Jed Martin, 'Convict Transportation to Newfoundland in 1789', *Acadiensis* 5 (1) (1975), pp. 84–99; 102 men and twelve women, p. 88; pp. 89 and 90–3; note PRO HO42/4/158–9 Reading gaol calendar, with several sentenced to be transported to Nova Scotia 20 April 1784; see Jerry Bannister, 'Convict Transportation and the Colonial State in Newfoundland, 1789', *Acadiensis* 27 (2) (1998), 95–123, p. 118; for discussions concerning British Columbia, see Richard H. Dillon, 'A Plan for Convict Colonies in Canada', *Americas* 13 (2) (1956), 187–98.

9. PRO HO42/4/44–45 22 Jan. 1784; HO42/6/69, Lancaster Castle, 9 Feb. 1785, twenty-seven awaiting transportation.

10. PRO HO42/6/449 onwards, particularly pp. 451 and 453; HO 42/6/203 Shrewsbury, 20 April 1785, forty-six convicts, thirty-two under sentence of transportation; HO42/14/88 Warwick pleads for transportation to be carried out to relieve the gaol 'being crowded with prisoners, so as to give harm for their health and safety', 22 April 1789; HO 42/19/748, the county gaol in Cumberland is full and inadequate – plea to transport nine men, 31 Dec. 1791; HO 47/2, 27 Oct. 1785, John Parsons; HO 42/6/335, 26 April 1785, Edward Thompson; Mollie Gillen, 'The Botany Bay Decision, 1786: Convicts, not Empire', *English Historical Review* 97 (385) (1982), 740–66.

11. *Newcastle Courant*, 25 April 1789.

12. Timothy Pitkin, *A Political and Civil History of the United States of America from the year 1763 etc.*, 2 vols (New Haven, CT: Hezekiah Howe, Durrie and Peck, 1828), vol. 1, p. 133.

13. Gwenda Morgan, *The Hegemony of the Law: Richmond County, Virginia, 1692–1776* (New York and London: Garland, 1989), 13–50.

14. Philip J. Schwarz, *Twice Condemned: Slaves and the Criminal Laws of Virginia, 1705–1865* (Baton Rouge: Louisiana State University Press, 1988), p. 27–9; see p. 217 for women tried for theft.

15. Aaron S. Fogleman, 'From Slaves, Convicts, and Servants to Free Passengers: the Transformation of Immigration in the Era of the American Revolution', *Journal of American History* 85 (1998), 43–76, pp. 60 and 61.

16. David W. Galenson, *White Servitude in Colonial America: an Economic Analysis* (Cambridge: Cambridge University Press, 1981), p. 171.

17. Fogleman, 'From Slaves, Convicts, and Servants to Free Passengers', p. 65; he notes apprenticeship declined too (pp. 62–3), in part because courts

began to favour the apprentices in their complaints against their masters (p. 63).

18. Christopher Tomlins, 'Subordination, Authority, Law: Subjects in Labor History', *International Labor and Working-Class History* 47 (1995), 56–90, p. 63, referring to the US Supreme Court case, *Robertson v. Baldwin* (1896); Robert J. Steinfeld and Stanley L. Engerman, 'Labour – Free or Coerced? A Historical Reassessment of Differences and Similarities', in Tom Brass and Marcel van der Linden (eds), *Free and Unfree Labour: the Debate Continues* (Berne: Peter Lang, European Academic Publishers, 1997), 107–26, pp. ix and 108.

19. Robert J. Steinfeld, *The Invention of Free Labor: the Employment Relation in English and American Law and Culture, 1350–1870* (Chapel Hill, NC: University of North Carolina Press, 1991), pp. 114–16.

20. Christopher Tomlins, 'Reconsidering Indentured Servitude: European Migration and the Early American Labor Force, 1600–1775', *Labor History* 42 (1) (2001), 5–43, pp. 21–2; Bernard Bailyn, *Voyagers to the West: a Passage in the Peopling of America on the Eve of the Revolution* (New York: Knopf, 1986).

21. Introduction to Paul E. Lovejoy and Nicholas Rogers, eds, *Unfree Labour in the Development of the Atlantic World* (Ilford, Essex: Frank Cass, 1994), p. 3, and for estimates of about 28 million East India indentured servants, p. 7; and see Paul Craven and Douglas Hay, 'The Criminalization of "Free" Labour: Master and Servant in Comparative Perspective' in Lovejoy and Rogers (eds), *Unfree Labour*, pp. 71–101, for a comparative analysis of the development of unfree labour in British-controlled territories.

22. Tom Brass, 'Introduction: Free and Unfree Labour – the Debate Continues', in Tom Brass and Marcel van der Linden (eds), *Free and Unfree Labour: The Debate Continues* (Berne: Peter Lang, European Academic Publishers, 1997), p. 18; see Craven and Hay, 'Criminalization of "Free" Labour' for colonial redevelopments after 1800 in the British Empire.

23. Reece, *Origins of Irish Convict Transportation*, pp. 110–11; *Virginia Journal*, 10 Aug. 1786, cited in Reece, *Origins*; the New York press was becoming critical of the process, particularly as another shipload was being prepared.

24. Kenneth Morgan, 'English and American Attitudes towards Convict Transportation, 1718–1775', *History* 72 (1987), 416–31, p. 418.

25. *London Evening Post*, 13 Oct. 1737, copied to *Virginia Gazette*, 30 Dec. 1737.

26. Alan Atkinson, 'The Free-Born Englishman Transported: Convict Rights as a Measure of Eighteenth-Century Empire', *Past and Present* 144 (1994), 88–115, pp. 100 and 111 ('prisoners'); 'Letters of Father Joseph Mosley', *Woodstock Letters*, 35 (1906), p. 54.

27. Myra Glenn, *Campaigns against Corporal Punishment. Prisoners, Sailors, Women and Children in Antebellum America* (Albany, NY: State University of New York Press, 1984); V. A. C. Gatrell, *The Hanging Tree: Execution and the English People, 1770–1868* (Oxford: Oxford University Press, 1994); Cindy C. Burgoyne, 'Imprisonment the Best Punishment: the Transatlantic Exchange and Communication of Ideas in the Field of Penology, 1750–1820' (PhD diss., University of Sunderland, 1997).

Bibliography

Primary sources, United Kingdom

Bristol record office

JQS/D/7, 8, 9, 10, 11, Docket Books
JQS/P/3, 6, 8, 9, 13/3, 17, 20, 24, 25, 28, 30, 34, 36, 38, 40, 41, 45, 46, 49, 51,
    52, 54, 55, 56, 57, 58, 59, 67, 89, Informations, Recognizances
JQS/P/47, Transportation Bonds 1759–75

Cumberland record office

Carlisle:

CQ1/3, CQ1/4 Quarter Sessions Rough order book
CQ1/5, 6, 7, 8, 9, Quarter Sessions Minute Books
CQ2/2, 3, 4, 5, 6, Quarter Sessions Indictment Books
CQ4/1 Quarter Sessions Conviction Book
CQ6/1 and 2, Quarter Sessions Order Books
CQ8/1, 2 and 3, Quarter Sessions Private Order Books
Q11 Petitions
QF/5/7 Treasurer's Vouchers

Kendal:

WQ/O/2, 4, 5, 6, 7, 8, 9, Quarter Sessions Order Books
WQ/M/1 Quarter Sessions Rough Minute Book 1733–37
WQ/M/2, 3, 4, 5, 6, 7, Quarter Sessions Minute Books
WQ/SR/153 (Sessions Rolls)

Whitehaven: local studies library

YDX 79 Lutwidge Letterbooks

Devon record office (Exeter)

C 1/69, 1/70, 1/71, 1/72, 1/73a
ECA (Exeter City Archives) Quarter Sessions and Gaol Delivery Calendars, and
    Sessions 'Transportation Papers' Orders and Bonds
Miscellaneous Session Papers, Box 3 Bundle 19, and 'Ancient Letters 1703–1828'
ED/M/1482
QS 1/15, 1/16, 1/17, 1/18, 1/19, 1/20
QS 4
QS 10/1, 10/2
QS 129
R4/1/C/338 and 339

Durham record office (Durham)

Q/S/OB 8–16 Quarter Sessions Order Books
Q/S/OM Rough Order Books
Q/F/1–3 Treasurer's Accounts

Lancashire record office (Preston)

QSO/2 series of Order Books
QSR Sessions Rolls

Northumberland record office (Morpeth)

QSI 121 onwards, Quarter Sessions Indictments
QSB 48–91 Quarter Sessions Books
QSO 6–15 Quarter Sessions Order Books
Cook Papers ZCK3

Public record office (Kew)

ADM 2/489
ASSI 23
ASSI 24
ASSI 41
ASSI 43
ASSI 44
ASSI 45
CO5/1314-1327
DURH 16, 17
E370/39/8, E370/40/8
E190 Portbooks
HCA 30/258, High Court of Admiralty Papers
HO42
HO47
PL25/80–101
PL27/2
PL28/1–14
SP36
SP44

Tyne and Wear archive service (Newcastle)

540, 4–6 Quarter Sessions Books
592/1 (MF135) Town Clerk's Correspondence

Primary sources, United States of America

Maryland state archives (Annapolis)

Anne Arundel County Convict Record
Baltimore County Convict Record

Kent County Court (Bonds and Indentures) 1715–20, 1720–26, 1731–35, 1735–1740, 1743–46, 1746–56, 1754–58, 1759–67, 1767–72
Port Books
Provincial Court – Judgement Record

Maryland Historical Society (Baltimore)
Cheston-Galloway Papers, Microfilm
Ridgely Account Books, Microfilm

Virginia State Library, Richmond
Richmond County Criminal Trials 1710–54
Richmond County Order Books, 1–21

Newspapers and periodicals
Annual Register, London
Bath Journal, Bath
Boston Gazette, Boston
Boston Evening Post, Boston
Boston Post Boy and Advertiser, Boston
Bristol Weekly Intelligencer, Bristol
Cumberland Pacquet, Carlisle
Daily Advertiser, London
Dublin Evening Post, Dublin
Exeter Flying Post, Exeter
Felix Farley's Bristol Journal, Bristol
Gentleman's Magazine, London
Gloucester Journal, Gloucester
London Evening Post, London
London Magazine
Maryland Gazette, Annapolis
Newcastle Courant, Newcastle
Newcastle Journal, Newcastle
Pennsylvania Gazette, Philadelphia
Rivington's New York Gazeteer, New York
Sherborne Mercury, Sherborne
South Carolina Gazette, Charleston
Virginia Gazette, Williamsburg
Dixon & Hunter's *Virginia Gazette*, Williamsburg
Pinkney's *Virginia Gazette*, Williamsburg
Purdie's *Virginia Gazette*, Williamsburg
Purdie & Dixon's *Virginia Gazette*, Williamsburg
Rind's *Virginia Gazette*, Williamsburg
York Courant, York

Printed primary sources

Abbot, W.W., ed., *Papers of George Washington*, Colonial Series, v. 9, Jan. 1772–March 1774 (Charlottesville and London: University Press of Virginia, 1994)

Acts of the Privy Council (Colonial) (Hereford: 1910).

Adams, John, *Diary and Autobiography of John Adams*, L. H. Butterfield et al. eds (Cambridge, MA: Harvard University Press, 1961).

Annesley, James, *Memoirs of an Unfortunate Young Nobleman Return'd from a Thirteen Years Slavery in America, where he had been sent by the wicked contrivances of his Cruel Uncle*, 2 vols (London: printed for J. Freeman in Fleet St, 1743).

Ashbridge, Elizabeth, 'The Life of Elizabeth Ashbridge', in *Journeys in New Worlds: Early American Women's Narratives*, ed. Daniel B. Shea (Madison: University of Wisconsin Press, 1990).

Bell, Whitefield J., 'Adam Cunningham's Atlantic Crossing, 1728', *Maryland Historical Magazine* 50 (1955), 195–202.

Bentham, Jeremy, *An Introduction to the Principles of Morals and Legislation*, ed. J. H. Burns and H. L. A. Hart (London: Methuen, 1970).

Bibliothèque universelle, choisie, ancienne et moderne, contenant une très curieuse collection de livres . . . recueillis . . . par feu Monsieur Henri Justice de Rufforth (The Hague: Nicolaas van Daalen, 31 October 1763).

Burnaby, Andrew, *Travels through the Middle Settlements in North-America in the Years 1759 and 1760 by the Rev. Andrew Burnaby* (Ithaca, NY: Cornell University Press, 1960).

Calendar of State Papers Colonial, 1574–1660 (London: 1860).

Calendar of State Papers Colonial, America and West Indies, 1661–68 (London: 1880).

Calendar of State Papers, America and West Indies, 1716–17.

Carew, Bampfylde Moore, *The Life and Adventures of Bampfylde-Moore Carew, the noted Devonshire Stroler and Dog-Stealer, as related by himself during his passage to the Plantations of America* (Exeter: the Farleys, for Joseph Drew, opposite Castle-Lane, 1745).

Carew, Bampfylde Moore, *An Apology for the Life of Bampfylde-Moore Carew, (son of the Rev. Mr Carew, of Bickley), commonly known throughout the West of England, by the Title of King of the Beggars, and Dog Merchant-General*, 'The Whole Taken from his own Mouth' (London: printed by R. Goadby and sold by W. Owen, at Temple-Bar, 1749).

Carew, Bampfylde Moore, *The King of the Beggars: Bampfylde-Moore Carew*, ed. C. H. Wilkinson (Oxford: Clarendon Press, 1931).

Carter, Landon, *The Diary of Colonel Landon Carter of Sabine Hall, 1752–78*, ed. Jack P. Greene (Charlottesville, VA: University Press of Virginia for the Virginia Historical Society, 1965).

Catalogue d'un très bel assortiment de livres en feuilles (13 August 1764), and *Catalogue d'une très belle collection de livres* (30 November 1767).

Chronicles of the Scotch-Irish Settlement in Virginia, Extracted from the Original Court Records of Augusta County, 1745–1800, 3 vols, ed. Lyman Chalkley (Baltimore MD: Genealogical Publishing Co., 1965, 3rd printing 1966).

The Complete Newgate Calendar, 6 vols (London: Navarre Society, 1926).

Cowper, Dean Spencer, *Letters of Spencer Cowper, Dean of Durham, 1756–74*, ed. E. Hughes, Surtees Society, vol. 165 (Durham: Andrews, 1950).

Cresswell, Nicholas, *The Journal of Nicholas Cresswell, 1774–77*, with a foreword by Samuel Thornley (New York: Lincoln Macveagh, Dial Press, 1924).

Drayton, Samuel, *The Dying Declaration of Samuel Drayton . . . executed at Dorchester, April 8th 1775, for returning from Transportation* BL 1416 (1775).

Eddis, William, *Letters from America*, ed. Aubrey C. Land (originally published in London in 1792; Cambridge: Belknap Press of Harvard University Press, 1969).

Franklin, Benjamin, *The Papers of Benjamin Franklin*, ed. Leonard W. Labaree and William B. Willcox (New Haven, CT: Yale University Press, 1959–2001).

Gove, Philip Babcock, 'An Oxford Convict in Maryland', *Maryland Historical Magazine* 37 (1942), 193–98.

Green, William, the unhappy sufferer, *The Sufferings of William Green, being a sorrowful account of his seven years transportation, wherein is set forth the various hardships he underwent with his parting and meeting again in that Country with his intimate Friend Anthony Atkinson with their joyful arrival in England, after being absent ten years. Likewise an Account of their manner of Living; the Climate of the Country, and in what it principally abounds* (Whitechapel, London: J. Long, undated, but after the author 'returned on the second of June 1774').

Hainsworth D. R., ed., *The Correspondence of Sir John Lowther of Whitehaven, 1693–98: a Provincial Community in Wartime* (Oxford: Oxford University Press, 1983).

Hening, William Waller, ed., *The Statutes at Large, being a Collection of all the Laws of Virginia etc.*, 13 vols (Richmond, VA: Franklin Press, 1809–23).

Hewitt, John, *A Journal of the Proceedings of J. Hewitt, Coventry, one of his Majesty's Justices of the Peace for the said City and County in his Duty as a Magistrate, during a period of twenty years . . .* (London: for the author, T. W. Pasham, 1779).

Hewitt, Alderman J., *Memoirs of the Celebrated Lady Viscountess Wilbrihammon alias Mollineux, alias Irving, Countess of Normandy, and Baroness Wilmington, the greatest Impostress of the Present Age* (Birmingham: printed by C. Earl for the author, undated – prob. 1778).

Hoffer, Peter C. and Scott, William B., eds., *Criminal Proceedings in Colonial Virginia: Records of Fines, Examinations of Criminals, Trials of Slaves, etc., from March 1710 to [1754]* [Richmond County Virginia], American Legal Records, vol. 10 (Athens, GA: University of Georgia Press, 1984).

Jefferson, Thomas, *The Papers of Thomas Jefferson*, ed. Julian P. Boyd (Princeton, NJ: Princeton University Press, 1954–).

Jennings, John Melville, 'The Poor Unhappy Transported Felon's Sorrowful Account of his Fourteen Years Transportation at Virginia in America', *Virginia Magazine of History and Biography* 56 (1948), 180–94.

Johnson, Samuel, *Samuel Johnson: Political Writings*, vol. 10 of *The Works of Samuel Johnson*, ed. Donald. J. Greene (New Haven, CT: Yale University Press, 1977).

Joshua Johnson's Letterbook, 1771–74: Letters from a Merchant in London to his Partners in Maryland, ed. Jacob M. Price (London: London Record Society, 1979).

'Journal of a French Traveller in the Colonies, 1765', *American Historical Review*, 26 (1921), 726–47, 27 (1921), 70–89.

Kennedy, J. P., and McIlwaine, H. R., eds, *Journal of the House of Burgesses, 1619–1776*, 13 vols (Richmond, VA, 1905–15).

Kibble, Richard, *A Genuine Account of the Behaviour, Confessions and Dying Words of Malefactors etc.* (London: for J. Nicholson, in the Old Bailey, 1743).

Kimber, Edward, *Itinerant Observations in America*, ed. Kevin J. Hayes (Newark, DE: University of Delaware Press, 1998).

Kimber, Edward, *The History of the Life and Adventures of Mr Anderson, containing his strange varieties of fortune in Europe and America, compiled from his own papers* (London: W. Owen, 1754, photographic reprint by Garland Publishing Inc., 1975).

Lambert, S., ed., *House of Commons Sessional Papers of the Eighteenth Century* (Wilmington, DE: Scholarly Resources, 1975).

Lamoine, G., (ed.), *Bristol Gaol Delivery Fiats, 1741–99* (Bristol: Bristol Record Society, 1989, vol. 40).

Lauson, John, *The Felon's Account of his Transportation at Virginia in America*, rep. and ed. J. Stevens Cox (St Peter Port, Guernsey: Toucan Press, Mount Durand, 1969).

Livingston, William, *The Independent Reflector . . . by William Livingston and Others*, ed. Milton M. Klein (Cambridge, MA: Belknap Press of Harvard University Press, 1963).

McIlwaine, H. R., ed., *Legislative Journals of the Council of Colonial Virginia*, 3 vols (Richmond, VA: Virginia State Library, 1918–19).

Moraley, William, *The Infortunate: the Voyage and Adventures of William Moraley, an Indentured Servant*, ed. Susan E. Klepp and Billy G. Smith (University Park, PA: Pennsylvania State University Press, 1992).

Mosley, Father Joseph, SJ, 'Letters of Father Joseph Mosley, 1757–86', *Woodstock Letters* 35 (1906), 35–55 and 227–45.

The Newgate Calendar, introduction by Clive Emsley (London: Wordsworth Editions Ltd, 1997).

Parliamentary Papers, *Report from the Select Committee on Criminal Laws etc.* (House of Commons, ordered for printing, 8 July 1819).

Parsons, William, *Memoirs of the Life and Adventures of William Parsons, Esq etc.* (London: printed for F. Stamper, at Pope's Head, Cornhill, 1751).

Peale, Charles Willson, *The Selected Papers of Charles Willson Peale and his Family*: vol. 5 *The Autobiography of Charles Willson Peale*, ed. Lillian B. Miller (New Haven, CT: Yale University Press, 2000).

Poulter, John, *The Discoveries of John Poulter alias Baxter Who was Apprehended for Robbing Dr Hancock of Salisbury . . .* (Sherborne, Dorset, and London: R. Goadby and W. Owen, 1753).

Revel, James, *The Poor Unhappy Transported Felon's Sorrowful Account of his Fourteen Years Transportation at Virginia in America . . .* J. Revel, 'the Unhappy Sufferer', (London, c.1800).

Riley, Edward M., ed., *The Journal of John Harrower: an Indentured Servant in the Colony of Virginia, 1773–76* (New York: Holt, Rinehart & Winston, Inc., 1963).

Ruel, James, *James Ruel, the unhappy Sufferer* (Dublin: 'sold by The Hawkers', c.1820).

Quarter Sessions Records for the County of Somerset, 4 vols, ed. Rev. H. E. Bates (later H. E. Bates Harbin, from vol. 2) (Somerset Record Society, 1907–19).

Stokes, Anthony, *A View of the Constitution of the British Colonies . . .* (London, 1783).

Tinling, Marion (ed.), *The Correspondence of the Three William Byrds of Westover, Virginia, 1684–1776*, 2 vols (Charlottesville: University Press of Virginia, 1977).

'Washington Letters', *Archaeologia Aeliana*, new ser. 2 (1858), 120–6.

Winfree, Waverly K. comp., *The Laws of Virginia Being a Supplement to Hening's The Statutes at Large, 1700–50* (Richmond, VA: Virginia State Library, 1971).

Lists/profiles

Brewer's Rogues, Villains and Eccentrics, ed. Willie Donaldson (London: Cassell, 2002).

Cappon, Lester J. and Duff, Stella F., comps, *Virginia Gazette Index, 1736–80*, 2 vols (Williamsburg, VA: Institute of Early American History and Culture, 1950).

Cobley, John, *The Crimes of the Lady Juliana Convicts – 1790* (Sydney: Library of Australian History, 1989).

Coldham, Peter W., comp. and ed., *English Convicts in Colonial America*, vol. 1, Middlesex 1617–1775 (New Orleans: Polyanthos, 1974).

Coldham, Peter W., *The Complete Book of Emigrants in Bondage, 1614–1775* (Baltimore MD: Genealogical Publishing Co. Inc., 1988).

Coldham, Peter W., *The King's Passengers to Maryland and Virginia* (Westminster, MD: Willow Bend Books, 2000).

The Dictionary of Printers, Booksellers . . . in England, Scotland and Ireland, 1726–75, H. R. Plomer, G. H. Bushnell and E. R. McDix (Oxford: Oxford University Press, 1930, published 1932 for 1930).

Dobson, David, comp., *Directory of Scots Banished to the American Plantations, 1650–1775* (Baltimore, MD: Genealogical Publishing Company Inc., 1984).

Grubb, Farley, *Runaways, Servants, Convicts and Apprentices advertized in the Pennsylvania Gazette, 1728–96* (Baltimore, MD: Genealogical Publishing Company Inc., 1992).

Horowitz, Lois, *A Bibliography of Military Name Lists from Pre-1675 to 1900* (Metuchen, NJ and London: Scarecrow Press, Inc., 1990).

Kaminkow, Marion, and Kaminkow, Jack, eds, *Original Lists of Emigrants in Bondage from London to the American Colonies, 1719–44* (Baltimore, MD: Magna Carta Books, 1981).

Meaders, Daniel E., *Dead or Alive: Fugitive Slaves and White Indentured Servants before 1830* (New York and London: Garland, 1993).

Meaders, Daniel E., ed., *Advertisements for Runaway Slaves in Virginia, 1801–20* (New York: Garland, 1997).

Perry, J., ed., 'The Transportation of Felons to America, 1717–75: Some North Riding Quarter Sessions Records', *North Yorkshire County Record Office Journal* 8 (1981), 65–117.

Simmons, R. C., *British Imprints Relating to North America, 1621–1760: an Annotated Checklist* (London: British Library, 1996).

Simmons, R. C., 'Americana in British Books, 1621–1760', in Karen O. Kupperman (ed), *America in European Consciousness, 1743–50* (Chapel Hill, NC: University of North Carolina Press, 1995), 324–87.

Smith, Billy G., and Wojtowicz, Richard, *Blacks who Stole Themselves: Advertisements for Runaways in the Pennsylvania Gazette, 1728–90* (Philadelphia PA: University of Pennsylvania Press, 1989).

Secondary sources

Amelang, James S., *The Flight of Icarus: Artisan Autobiography in Early Modern Europe* (Stanford, CA: Stanford University Press, 1998).

Anderson, Clare, 'The Genealogy of the Modern Subject: Indian Convicts in Mauritius, 1814–53', in Ian Duffield and James Bradley (eds), *Representing Convicts: New Perspectives on Convict Forced Labour Migration* (Leicester: Leicester University Press, 1997), 164–82.

Andrews, Matthew Page, 'Additional Data on the Importation of Convicts', *Virginia Magazine of History and Biography* 53 (1945), 37–41.

Anon., 'Eighteenth-Century Maryland as Portrayed in the "Itinerant Observations" of Edward Kimber', *Maryland Historical Magazine* 51 (1956), 315–36.

Ariès, P., *The Hour of Our Death*, trans. H. Weaver (Harmondsworth, Middlesex: Penguin, 1983).

Armitage, David, 'Three Concepts of Atlantic History', in David Armitage and Michael J. Braddick (eds), *The British Atlantic World* (Basingstoke: Palgrave Macmillan, 2002), 11–27.

Atkinson, Alan, 'The Free-Born Englishman Transported: Convict Rights as a Measure of Eighteenth-Century Empire', *Past and Present* 144 (1994), 88–115.

Bailyn, Bernard, *Voyagers to the West: Passage to the Peopling of America on the Eve of the Revolution* (New York: Knopf, 1986).

Baine, Rodney M., 'Oglethorpe's Forty Irish Convicts', *Georgia Historical Quarterly* 78 (1994), 326–38.

Ballagh, James Curtis, *White Servitude in Colonial Virginia: a Study of the System of Indentured Labor in the American Colonies* (Baltimore, MD: Johns Hopkins University Press, 1895).

Ballaster, R., 'Women and the Rise of the Novel: Sexual Prescripts', in Vivien Jones (ed.), *Women and Literature in Britain, 1700–1800* (Cambridge: Cambridge University Press, 2000), 197–216.

Bancroft, George, *History of the United States of America*, vol. 1 (New York: D. Appleton and Company, 1888).

Bannister, Jerry, 'Convict Transportation and the Colonial State in Newfoundland, 1789', *Acadiensis* 27 (2) (1998), 95–123.

Barrow, Tony, *The Whaling Trade of North-East England* (Sunderland: University of Sunderland Press, 2001).

Barry, Jonathan, 'The Press and the Politics of Culture in Bristol 1660–1775', in Jeremy Black and Jeremy Gregory (eds), *Culture, Politics and Society in Britain, 1660–1800* (Manchester and New York: Manchester University Press, 1991).

Barry, Jonathan, 'Bristol Pride: Civic Identity in Bristol c1640–1775', in Madge Dresser and Philip Ollerenshaw (eds.), *The Making of Modern Bristol* (Tiverton, Devon: Redcliffe Press, 1996), 25–47.

Baseler, Marilyn, C., *'Asylum for Mankind': America 1607–1800* (Ithaca, NY: Cornell University Press, 1988).

Beard, Charles A., *An Economic Interpretation of the Constitution of the United States* (London: Macmillan Co., 1913).

Beattie, J. M., *Crime and the Courts in England, 1660–1800* (Princeton, NJ: Princeton University Press, 1986).

Beattie, J. M., 'London Crime and the Making of the "Bloody Code", 1689–1718', in L. Davison, T. Hitchcock, T. Keirn, R. B. Shoemaker (eds) *Stilling the Grum-*

bling Hive: the Response to Social and Economic Problems in England, 1660–1750 (Stroud, Glos.: Alan Sutton, 1992), 49–76.

Beattie, J. M., *Policing and Punishment in London, 1660–1750: Urban Crime and the Limits of Terror* (Oxford: Oxford University Press, 2001).

Beckett, J. V., *Coal and Tobacco: the Lowthers and the Economic Development of West Cumberland, 1660–1760* (Cambridge: Cambridge University Press, 1981).

Beckles, Hilary, 'A "Riotous and Unruly Lot": Irish Indentured Servants and Freemen in the English West Indies, 1644–1713', *William and Mary Quarterly*, 3rd. ser. 47 (1990), 503–22.

Beier, A. L., *Masterless Men: the Vagrancy Problem in England, 1560–1640* (London: Methuen, 1985).

Ben-Amos, I. K., 'Service and the Coming of Age of Young Men in Seventeenth-Century England', *Continuity and Change* 3 (1988), 41–64.

Ben-Amos, I. K., *Adolescence and Youth in Early Modern England* (New Haven, CT, and London: Yale University Press, 1994).

Bender, John, *Imagining the Penitentiary: Fiction and the Architecture of Mind in Eighteenth-Century England* (Chicago: University of Chicago Press, 1987).

Beverley, Robert, *The History and Present State of Virginia* (London, 1722).

Bezís-Selfa, John, 'Slavery and the Disciplining of Free Labor in the Colonial Mid-Atlantic Iron Industry', *Pennsylvania History*, 64 (1997), 270–86.

Black, Jeremy and Gregory, Jeremy, eds, *Culture, Politics and Society in Britain, 1660–1800* (Manchester and New York: Manchester University Press, 1991).

Blumer, G. A., 'The Washington and Colville Families', *Archaeologia Aeliana*, new series 19 (1897), 115–26.

Bosco, Ronald A., 'Lectures at the Pillory: the Early American Execution Sermon', *American Quarterly* 30 (1978), 156–76.

Bradley, James and Maxwell-Stewart, Hamish, 'Embodied Explorations: Investigating Convict Tattoos and the Transportation System', in Ian Duffield and James Bradley (eds), *Representing Convicts: New Perspectives on Convict Forced Labour Migration* (London: Cassell/Leicester University Press, 1997), 183–203.

Brass, Tom and van der Linden, Marcel (eds), *Free and Unfree Labour: the Debate Continues* (Berne: Peter Lang, European Academic Publishers, 1997).

Breen, T. H., A Changing Labor Force and Race Relations in Virginia, 1660–1710', *Journal of Social History* 7 (1973), 3–25.

Breen, T. H., 'An Empire of Goods: the Anglicization of Colonial America, 1690–1776', *Journal of British Studies* 25 (1986), 467–99.

Breen, T. H., 'Ideology and Nationalism on the Eve of the American Revolution: Revisions *Once More* in Need of Revising', *Journal of American History* 84 (1997), 13–39.

Brewer, John, *The Pleasures of the Imagination: English Culture in the Eighteenth Century* (New York: Farrar, Straus & Giroux, 1997).

Brown, Kathleen M., *Good Wives, Nasty Wenches, and Anxious Patriarchs: Gender, Race, and Power in Colonial Virginia* (Chapel Hill, NC: University of North Carolina Press, 1996).

Brown, W. Newman, 'The Receipt of Poor Relief and Family Situation: Aldenham, Hertfordshire, 1630–90', in R. M. Smith (ed), *Land, Kinship and Life-Cycle* (Cambridge: Cambridge University Press, 1984), 405–22.

Buchan, Peter, *Ancient Ballads and Songs of the North of Scotland, hitherto unpublished, with explanatory notes*, 2 vols (Edinburgh: W. and D. Laing, J. Stevenson, 1828).

Bullock, Stephen C., 'A Mumper among the Gentle: Tom Bell, Colonial Confidence Man', *William and Mary Quarterly*, 3rd. ser. 55 (1998), 231–58.

Burn, Richard, *The Justice of the Peace and Parish Officer*, 6th edn, 3 vols (London, 1758).

Burnard, Trevor, 'European Migration to Jamaica, 1655–1780', *William and Mary Quarterly*, 3rd ser. 53 (1996), 769–94.

Butler, James Davie, 'British Convicts shipped to American Colonies', *American Historical Review* 2 (1896), 12–33.

Carr, Lois Green, Morgan, Philip D., and Russo, Jean B., eds, *Colonial Chesapeake Society* (Chapel Hill, NC: University of North Carolina Press, 1988).

Carr, Lois Green, 'Emigration and the Standard of Living: the Eighteenth-Century Chesapeake', in John J. McCusker and Kenneth Morgan (eds), *The Early Modern Atlantic Economy* (Cambridge: Cambridge University Press, 2000), 319–43.

Castillo, Susan and Schweitzer, Ivy, eds, *The Literatures of Colonial America: an Anthology* (Oxford: Blackwell, 2001).

Charlesworth, Andrew, ed., *An Atlas of Rural Protest in Britain 1548–1900* (London: Croom Helm, 1983).

Christianson, Scott, *With Liberty for Some: 500 Years of Imprisonment in America* (Boston: Northeastern University Press, 1998).

Clark, Charles E., *The Public Prints: the Newspaper in Anglo-American Culture, 1665–1740* (New York: Oxford University Press, 1994).

Clark, Charles E., and Weatherall, Charles, 'The Measure of Maturity: the *Pennsylvania Gazette*, 1728–65', *William and Mary Quarterly*, 3rd ser. 46 (1989), 279–303.

Coates, Timothy J., 'Crime and Punishment in the Fifteenth-Century Portuguese World: the Transition from Internal to Imperial Exile', in Donald J. Kagay and L. J. Andrew Villalon (eds), *The Final Argument: the Imprint of Violence on Society in Medieval and Early Modern Europe* (Woodbridge: Boydell Press, 1998), 119–39.

Cogliano, Francis D., *Revolutionary America, 1763–1815* (London and New York: Routledge, 2000).

Cohen, Daniel A., *Pillars of Salt, Monuments of Grace: New England Crime Literature and the Origins of American Popular Culture, 1674–1860* (New York: Oxford University Press, 1993).

Cohen, Stanley, *Folk Devils and Moral Panics: the Creation of the Mods and Rockers* (London: Paladin, 1973).

Coldham, Peter Wilson, *Emigrants in Chains: a Social History of Forced Emigration to the Americas, 1607–1776* (Stroud, Gloucestershire: Alan Sutton, 1992).

Colley, Linda, *Britons: Forging the Nation, 1707–1837* (London: Pimlico/Random House, 1992).

Colley, Linda, *Captives: Britain, Empire and the World, 1600–1850* (London: Jonathan Cape, 2002).

Conlon, Anne, ' "Mine is a Sad Yet True Story": Convict Narratives, 1818–50', *Journal of the Royal Australian Historical Society* 55 (1) (1969), 43–82.

Conway, Stephen, 'War and National Identity in the Mid-Eighteenth-Century British Isles', *English Historical Review*, 116 (468) (2001), 863–93.

Conway, Stephen, 'From Fellow-Nationals to Foreigners: British Perceptions of the Americans, *c.*1739–1783', *William and Mary Quarterly*, 3rd. ser. 59 (2002), 65–100.

Copeland, David A., *Colonial American Newspapers: Character and Content* (Newark, DE: University of Delaware Press, 1997).

Craies, W. F. 'The Compulsion of Subjects to Leave the Realm', *Law Quarterly Review* 6 (1890), 388–409.

Craven, Paul and Hay, Douglas, 'The Criminalization of "Free" Labour: Master and Servant in Comparative Perspective', in Paul E. Lovejoy and Nicholas Rogers (eds), *Unfree Labour in the Development of the Atlantic World* (Ilford, Essex: Frank Cass, 1994), 71–101.

Damousi, Joy, ' "What Punishment Will Be Sufficient for These Rebellious Hussies?" Headshaving and the Convict Women in the Female Factories, 1820s–40s', in Ian Duffield and James Bradley (eds), *Representing Convicts: New Perspectives on Convict Forced Labour Migration* (London: Cassell/Leicester University Press, 1997), 204–14.

Daniels, Christine, ' "WANTED: A blacksmith who understands Plantation Work": Artisans in Maryland, 1700–1810', *William and Mary Quarterly*, 3rd. ser. 50 (1993), 743–67.

Daniels, Christine, ' "Liberty to complaine": Servant Petitions in Maryland, 1652–1797', in Christopher L. Tomlins and Bruce H. Mann (eds), *The Many Legalities of Early America* (Chapel Hill, NC: University of North Carolina Press, 2001), 219–49.

Davis, R., *The Rise of the English Shipping Industry in the Seventeenth and Eighteenth Centuries* (Newton Abbot, Devon: David and Charles, 1962).

Defoe, Daniel, *The Fortunes and Misfortunes of the Famous Moll Flanders*, ed. David Blewett (Harmondsworth: Penguin, 1989).

Devereaux, Simon, 'In Place of Death: Transportation, Penal Practices and the English State, 1770–1830', in Carolyn Strange (ed.), *Qualities of Mercy: Justice, Punishment and Discretion* (Vancouver: University of British Columbia Press, 1996), 52–76.

Dillon, Richard H., 'A Plan for Convict Colonies in Canada', *Americas* 13 (2) (1956), 187–98.

Dowdey, Clifford, *The Virginia Dynasties: the Emergence of 'King' Carter and the Golden Age* (Boston: Little, Brown and Company, 1969).

Dresser, Madge and Ollerenshaw, Philip, eds, *The Making of Modern Bristol* (Tiverton, Devon: Redcliffe Press, 1996).

Duffield, Ian, 'Problematic Passages: "Jack Bushman's" Convict Narrative', in Ian Duffield and James Bradley (eds), *Representing Convicts: New Perspectives on Convict Forced Labour Migration* (London: Cassell/Leicester University Press, 1997), 29–42.

Duffy, John, 'The Passage to the Colonies', *Mississippi Valley Historical Review* 38 (1951), 21–38.

Dunn, Richard S., *Sugar and Slaves: The Rise of the Planter Class in the English West Indies, 1624–1713* (Chapel Hill, NC: University of North Carolina Press, 1972).

Ekirch, A. Roger, 'Great Britain's Secret Convict Trade to America, 1783–84', *American Historical Review* 89 (1984), 1285–91.

Ekirch, A. Roger, 'Bound for America: a Profile of British Convicts Transported to the Colonies, 1718–75', *William and Mary Quarterly*, 3rd. ser. 42 (1985), 184–200.

Ekirch, A. Roger, 'The Transportation of Scottish Criminals to America during the Eighteenth Century', *Journal of British Studies* 24 (1985), 366–74.

Ekirch, A. Roger, *Bound for America: the Transportation of British Convicts to the Colonies, 1718–75* (Oxford: Clarendon Press, 1987).

Ellis, J. A., 'Urban Conflict and Popular Violence: the Guildhall Riots of 1740 in Newcastle upon Tyne', *International Review of Social History* 25 (1980), 333–49.

Ellis, Joyce, 'Regional and County Centres 1700–1840', in Peter Clark (ed.), *The Cambridge Urban History of Britain* (Cambridge: Cambridge University Press, 2000), vol. 2, 1540–1840, 673–704.

Emsley, Kenneth, 'A Circuit Judge in Northumberland', *Tyne and Tweed* 31 (1978), 13–18.

Evans, Emory G., 'A Question of Complexion: Documents Concerning the Negro and the Franchise in Eighteenth-Century Virginia', *Virginia Magazine of History and Biography* 71 (1963), 411–15.

Fabian, Ann, *The Unvarnished Truth: Personal Narratives in Nineteenth-Century America* (Berkeley, CA: University of California Press, 2000).

Faller, Lincoln B., *Turned to Account: the Forms and Functions of Criminal Biography in Late Seventeenth- and Early Eighteenth-Century England* (Cambridge: Cambridge University Press, 1987).

Ferdinand, C. Y., *Benjamin Collins and the Provincial Newspaper Trade in the Eighteenth Century* (Oxford: Clarendon Press, 1997).

Fielding, Henry, 'An Inquiry into the Late Increase in Robbers', in *The Works of Henry Fielding Esquire*, 10 vols (London: Smith Elder, 1882), vol. 7.

Fogleman, Aaron S., 'Migrations to the Thirteen British North American Colonies, 1700–75: New Estimates', *Journal of Interdisciplinary History* 22 (1992), 691–709.

Fogleman, Aaron S., 'From Slaves, Convicts, and Servants to Free Passengers: the Transformation of Immigration in the Era of the American Revolution', *Journal of American History* 85 (1998), 43–76.

Frank, Stephen P., *Crime, Cultural Conflict and Justice in Rural Russia, 1856–1914* (Berkeley, CA: University of California Press, 1999).

Fraser, A., *The Gypsies*, 2nd edn (Oxford: Blackwell, 1995).

Galenson, David W., *White Servitude in Colonial America: an Economic Analysis* (Cambridge: Cambridge University Press, 1981).

Games, Alison, *Migration and the Origins of the English Atlantic World* (Cambridge, MA, and London: Harvard University Press, 1999).

Games, Alison, 'Migration', in David Armitage and Michael J. Braddick (eds), *The British Atlantic World* (London: Palgrave Macmillan, 2002), 31–50.

Garnham, Neal, *The Courts, Crime and Criminal Law in Ireland, 1692–1760* (Dublin: Irish Academic Press, 1996)

Gaskell, Philip, 'Henry Justice, a Cambridge Book Thief', *Transactions of the Cambridge Bibliographical Society* 1 (1952), 348–57.

Gaskill, Malcolm, 'Reporting Murder: Fiction in the Archives in Early Modern England', *Social History*, 23 (1998), 1–30.

Gatrell, V. A. C., *The Hanging Tree: Execution and the English People, 1770–1868* (Oxford: Oxford University Press, 1994).

Gay, John, *The Beggar's Opera*, ed. Edgar V. Roberts (London: Edward Arnold, 1968, originally University of Nebraska Press, 1968).

Geertz, Clifford, *The Interpretation of Cultures: Selected Essays* (New York: Basic Books, 1973).

Gibson, Marion, *Reading Witchcraft: Stories of Early English Witchcraft* (London: Routledge, 1999).

Gillen, Mollie, 'The Botany Bay Decision, 1786: Convicts, not Empire', *English Historical Review* 97 (385) (1982), 740–66.

Gilliam, Charles Edgar, 'Jail Bird Immigrants to Virginia', *Virginia Magazine of History and Biography* 52 (1944), 180–82.

Gilroy, P., *The Black Atlantic: Modernity and Double Consciousness* (London: Verso, 1993).

Gladfelder, Hal, *Criminality and Narrative in Eighteenth-Century England: Beyond the Law* (Baltimore, MD: Johns Hopkins University Press, 2001).

Glenn, Myra, *Campaigns against Corporal Punishment: Prisoners, Sailors, Women and Children in Antebellum America* (Albany, NY: State University of New York Press, 1984).

Gould, E. H., *The Persistence of Empire: British Political Culture in the Age of the American Revolution* (Chapel Hill, NC: University of North Carolina Press, 2000).

Grant, Alison, 'Emigration from Devon in the Seventeenth Century', in Michael Duffy, Stephen Fisher, Basil Greenhill, David J. Starkey and Joyce Youings (eds), *The New Maritime History of Devon, Vol. I: From Early Times to the Late Eighteenth Century* (London: Conway Maritime Press and University of Exeter, 1992), 147–52.

Green, E.G., *Hanged for a Sheep: Crime in Bygone Derbyshire* (Cromford, Derbyshire: Scarthin Books, 1981).

Griffiths, Paul, 'Masterless Young People in Norwich, 1560–1645', in P. Griffiths, A. Fox and S. Hindle (eds), *The Experience of Authority in Early Modern England* (Basingstoke: Macmillan Press [now Palgrave Macmillan], 1996), 146–86.

Grubb, Farley, 'Morbidity and Mortality on the North Atlantic Passage: Eighteenth-Century German Immigration', *Journal of Interdisciplinary History* 17 (3) (1987), 565–85.

Grubb, Farley, 'Fatherless and Friendless: Factors Influencing the Flow of English Emigrant Servants', *Journal of Economic History* 52 (1992), 85–108 .

Grubb, Farley and Stitt, Tony, 'The Liverpool Servant Trade and the Transition to Slave Labor in the Chesapeake, 1697–1707: Market Adjustments to War', *Explorations in Economic History* 31 (1994), 376–405.

Grubb, Farley, 'Does Bound Labour Have to be Coerced Labour?: the Case of Colonial Immigrant Servitude Versus Craft Apprenticeship and Life-Cycle Servitude-in-Husbandry', *Itinerario* 21 (1997), 28–51.

Grubb, Farley, 'The Transatlantic Market for British Convict Labor', *Journal of Economic History* 60 (2000), 94–122.

Grubb, Farley, 'The Statutory Regulation of Colonial Servitude: an Incomplete-Contract Approach', *Explorations in Economic History* 37 (2000), 42–75.

Grubb, Farley, 'The Market Evaluation of Criminality: Evidence from the Auction of British Convict Labor in America, 1767–75', *American Economic Review* 91 (2001), 295–304.

Halttunen, Karen, 'Early American Murder Narratives: the Birth of Horror', in Richard Wightman Fox and T. J. Jackson Lears (eds), *The Power of Culture: Critical Essays in American History* (Chicago: Chicago University Press, 1993).

Hardy, James D., 'The Transportation of Convicts to Colonial Louisiana', *Louisiana History* 7 (1966), 207–20.

Harker, Dave, *Fakesong: the Manufacture of British 'Folksong': 1700 to the Present Day* (Milton Keynes: Open University Press,1985).

Harker, Dave, ed., *Songs and Verse of the North-East Pitmen, c.1780–1844* (Gateshead/Newcastle-upon-Tyne: Athenaeum Press, 1999), Surtees Society, vol. 204.

Harris, Michael, 'Trials and Criminal Biographies: a Case Study in Distribution', in Robin Myers and Michael Harris (eds), *Sale and Distribution of Books from 1700* (Oxford: Oxford Polytechnic Press, 1982), 1–36.

Harrison, Fairfax., 'When the Convicts Came', *Virginia Magazine of History and Biography* 30 (1922), 250–60.

Harrison, Fairfax, *Landmarks of Old Prince William: A Study of Origins in Northern Virginia*, 2 vols (Berryville, VA: Chesapeake Book Company, 1964).

Hay, Douglas, 'Property, Authority and the Criminal Law' in Douglas Hay et al. *Albion's Fatal Tree: Crime and Society in Eighteenth-Century England* (London: Allen Lane, 1975), 17–63.

Hayes, Kevin J., 'The Board of Trade's "Cruel Sarcasm": a Neglected Franklin Source', *Early American Literature* 28 (1993), 171–6.

Henry, Brian Henry, *The Dublin Hanged: Crime, Law Enforcement and Punishment in Late Eighteenth-Century Dublin* (Dublin: Irish Academy Press, 1994).

Herrick, Cheesman A., *White Servitude in Pennsylvania: Indentured and Redemption Labor in Colony and Commonwealth* (Philadelphia, 1926; New York: Negro Universities Press, 1969).

Guide to the Hertfordshire Record Office, Part 1: Quarter Sessions and Other Records in the Custody of the Officials of the County (Hertford: Hertfordshire County Council, 1961).

Hill, George Birkbeck, ed., *Boswell's Life of Johnson*, 6 vols, rev. L. F. Powell (Oxford: Clarendon Press, 1934).

Hodgson, J., 'Calendars of the Prisoners Confined in the High Castle in Newcastle upon Tyne, at the Assizes for Northumberland in the years 1628 and 1629', *Archaeologia Aeliana* 1 (1822), 149–63.

Holton, Woody, *Forced Founders: Indians, Debtors, Slaves and the Making of the Revolution in Virginia* (Chapel Hill, NC: University of North Carolina Press, 1999).

Horn, James P., 'The Letters of William Roberts of All Hallows Parish, Anne Arundel County, Maryland, 1756–1769', *Maryland Historical Magazine* 74 (1979), 117–32.

Howard, J., *An Account of the Principal Lazarettos in Europe* (Warrington: William Eyres, 1789).

Huggins, Nathan I., 'The Deforming Mirror of Truth: Slavery and the Master Narrative of American History', *Radical History Review* 49 (1991), 25–48.

Hughes, E., *North Country Life in the Eighteenth Century, Vol. 2: Cumberland and Westmorland* (London: Oxford University Press, 1965).

Humfrey, Paula, 'Female Servants and Women's Criminality in Early Eighteenth-Century London', in Greg T. Smith, Allyson N. May, and Simon Devereaux (eds), *Criminal Justice in the Old World and the New: Essays in Honour of J.M. Beattie* (Toronto: Centre for Criminology, 1998), 58–84.

Hussey, David, *Coastal and River Trade in Pre-Industrial England: Bristol and its Region, 1680–1730* (Exeter: Exeter University Press, 2000).

Ingram, M. J. 'Communities and Courts: Law and Disorder in Early Seventeenth-Century Wiltshire', in J. S. Cockburn (ed.), *Crime in England, 1550–1800* (London: Methuen, 1977), 110–34.

Innes, Joanna, 'The Role of Transportation in Seventeenth and Eighteenth-Century English Penal Practice', in Carl Bridge (ed.), *New Perspectives in Australian History* (London: Institute for Commonwealth Studies, Occasional Papers no. 5, 1990), 1–24.

Jackson, Gordon, 'Ports 1700–1840', in Peter Clark (ed.), *The Cambridge Urban History of Britain* (Cambridge: Cambridge University Press, 2000), vol. 2, 1540–1840, 705–731.

Jenkins, Philip, 'From Gallows to Prison? The Execution Rate in Early Modern England', *Criminal Justice History* 7 (1986), 51–71.

Johnson, Keach, 'The Baltimore Company Seeks English Markets: a Study of the Anglo-American Iron Trade, 1731–55', *William and Mary Quarterly*, 3rd ser. 16 (1959), 37–60.

Jones, Bedwyr Lewis, 'Life aboard an Eighteenth-Century Convict Ship', *Maritime Wales* 2 (1977), 16–18.

Jones, D. J. V. 'Life and Death in Eighteenth-Century Wales: a Note', *Welsh Historical Review* 10 (1981), 536–48.

Jordan, Winthrop D., *White Over Black: American Attitudes toward the Negro, 1550–1812* (Chapel Hill, NC: University of North Carolina Press, 1968).

Jordanova, L., 'Natural Facts: a Historical Perspective on Science and Sexuality', in C. P. MacCormack and M. Strathern (eds), *Nature, Culture and Gender* (Cambridge: Cambridge University Press, 1980), 42–69.

Jordanova, L., *Sexual Visions: Images of Gender in Science and Medicine between the Eighteenth and Twentieth Centuries* (Hemel Hempstead: Harvester Wheatsheaf, 1989).

Justice, Elizabeth, *Amelia or the Distressed Wife: a History Founded on Real Circumstances, by a Private Gentlewoman* [i.e. Elizabeth Justice] (London: the Authoress, 1751).

Justice, Elizabeth, *A Voyage to Russia, Describing the Laws, Manners, and Customs of that Great Empire . . .* , 2nd edn. (London: G. Smith, 1746).

Kay, Marvin L. Michael and Cary, Lorin Lee, 'Slave Runaways in Colonial North Carolina, 1748–75', *North Carolina Historical Review* 63 (1) (1986), 1–39.

Kellow, M. R. Margaret, 'Indentured Servitude in Eighteenth-Century Maryland', *Histoire Sociale/Social History* 17 (1984), 229–55.

Kent, D. A., 'Ubiquitous but Invisible: Female Domestic Servants in Mid-Eighteenth-Century London', *History Workshop Journal* 28 (1989), 111–28.

Kidd, Colin, *British Identities Before Nationalism: Ethnicity and Nationhood in the Atlantic World, 1600–1800* (Cambridge: Cambridge University Press, 1999).

King, Peter, 'Decision-makers and Decision-making in the English Criminal Law', *Historical Journal* 27 (1984), 25–58.

King, Peter, 'Newspaper Reporting, Prosecution Practice and Perceptions of Urban Crime: the Colchester Crime Wave of 1765', *Continuity and Change* 2 (1987), 423–54.

King, P. J. R., ' "Illiterate Plebian, Easily Misled": Jury Composition, Experience, and Behaviour in Essex, 1735–1815', in J. S. Cockburn and Thomas A. Green (eds), *Twelve Good Men and True: the Criminal Trial Jury in England, 1200–1800* (Princeton, NJ: Princeton University Press, 1988), 254–304.

King, Peter, 'Female Offenders, Work and Life Cycle Change in Late Eighteenth-Century London', *Continuity and Change*, 11 (1996), 61–90.

King, Peter, *Crime, Justice and Discretion in England 1740–1820* (Oxford: Oxford University Press, 2000).

Kraft, Elizabeth, 'The Two Amelias: Henry Fielding and Elizabeth Justice', *English Literary History* 62 (2) (1995), 313–28.

Kussmaul, A., *Servants in Husbandry in Early Modern England* (Cambridge: Cambridge University Press, 1981).

Lake, Peter, 'Deeds against Nature: Cheap Print, Protestantism and Murder in Early Seventeenth-Century England', in K. Sharpe and P. Lake (eds), *Culture and Politics in Early Stuart England* (Basingstoke: Macmillan Press [Now Palgrave Macmillan], 1994), 257–83.

Lancaster, R. Kent, 'Almost Chattel: the Lives of Indentured Servants at Hampton-Northampton, Baltimore County', *Maryland Historical Magazine* 94 (1999), 341–62.

Lancaster, R. Kent, 'Chattel Slavery at Hampton/Northampton, Baltimore County', *Maryland Historical Magazine* 95 (2000), 409–27.

Landau, Norma, 'The Laws of Settlement and the Surveillance of Immigration in Eighteenth-Century Kent', *Continuity and Change* 3 (1988), 391–420.

Laqueur, Thomas, 'Crowds, Carnivals and the State in English Executions, 1604–1800', in A. L. Beier, D. Cannadine and J. M. Rosenheim (eds), *The First Modern Society: Essays in Honour of Lawrence Stone* (Cambridge: Cambridge University Press, 1989), 305–55.

Larsen, Egon, *The Deceivers: Lives of the Great Imposters* (London: John Baker, 1966).

Latimer, John, *Annals of Bristol in the Eighteenth Century*, 4 vols (Bristol, 1893).

Lauter, Paul, ed., *The Heath Anthology of American Literature*, 2 vols, 4th edn (Boston: Houghton Mifflin, 2002).

Lee, Jeanne B., *The Price of Nationhood: the American Revolution in Charles County* (New York and London: Norton, 1994).

Linebaugh, Peter, 'The Ordinary of Newgate and His Account' in J. S. Cockburn (ed.), *Crime in England, 1550–1800* (London: Methuen, 1977), 246–69.

Linebaugh, Peter, *The London Hanged: Crime and Civil Society in the Eighteenth Century* (London: Allen Lane, 1991).

Linebaugh, Peter and Rediker, Marcus, *The Many-Headed Hydra: Sailors, Slaves, Commoners and the Hidden History of the Revolutionary Atlantic* (London: Verso, 2000).

Lovejoy, Paul E. and Rogers, Nicholas, eds, *Unfree Labour in the Development of the Atlantic World* (Ilford, Essex: Frank Cass, 1994).

Mackay, Lynn, 'Why They Stole: Women in the Old Bailey, 1779–1789', *Journal of Social History* 32 (1999), 623–40.

Mackenzie, Andrea, 'Making Crime Pay: Motives, Marketing Strategies, and the Printed Literature of Crime in England, 1670–1770', in Greg T. Smith, Allyson N. May, and Simon Devereaux (eds), *Criminal Justice in the Old World and the New: Essays in Honour of J. M. Beattie* (Toronto: Centre for Criminology, 1998), 235–69.

Martin, Jed, 'Convict Transportation to Newfoundland in 1789', *Acadiensis* 5 (1) (1975), 84–99.

Mascuch, Michael, *The Origins of the Individualist Self: Autobiography and Self-Identity in England, 1591–1791* (Cambridge: Polity Press, 1997).

Mason, Polly Cary, 'More about "Jayle Birds" in Colonial Virginia', *Virginia Magazine of History and Biography* 53 (1945), 37–41.

Mates, Julian, 'Some Early American Musical Stage Forms', *Popular Music and Society* 13 (1989), 67–75.

McGrath, Patrick and Williams, Mary E., *Bristol Inns and Alehouses in the Mid-Eighteenth Century* (Bristol: City of Bristol, 1979).

McMullan, John L., *The Canting Crew: London's Criminal Underworld, 1550–1700* (New Brunswick, NJ: Rutgers University Press, 1984).

Meaders, Daniel, 'South Carolina Fugitives as Viewed through Local Colonial Newspapers, with Emphasis on Runaway Notices, 1732–1800', *Journal of Negro History* 60 (April 1975), 288–319.

Mellish, Joanne Pope, *Disowning Slavery: Gradual Emancipation and 'Race' in New England, 1780–1860* (Ithaca, NY: Cornell University Press, 1998).

Meserve, Walter J., *An Emerging Entertainment – The Drama of the American People to 1828* (Bloomington: Indiana University Press, 1977).

Middleton, Arthur P., *Tobacco Coast: a Maritime History of Chesapeake Bay in the Colonial Era*, ed. George Carrington Mason (Newport News, VA: Mariners' Museum, 1953).

Milne, W. Gordon, 'A Glimpse of Colonial America as Seen in an English Novel of 1754', *Maryland Historical Magazine* 42 (1947), 239–52.

Moore, Rev. Thomas, *The History of Devonshire from the Earliest Period to the Present*, 2 vols (London: Robert Jennings, 1829).

Morgan, Edmund S., *American Slavery, American Freedom: the Ordeal of Colonial Virginia* (New York: Norton, 1975).

Morgan, Gwenda, *The Hegemony of the Law: Richmond County, Virginia, 1692–1776* (New York and London: Garland, 1989).

Morgan, Gwenda, '"One of the First Fruits of Liberty": Penal Reform in the Young Republic', in R. A. Burchill (ed.), *The End of Anglo-America: Historical Essays in the Study of Cultural Divergence* (Manchester: Manchester University Press, 1991), 87–112.

Morgan, Gwenda and Rushton, Peter, *Rogues, Thieves and the Rule of Law: the Problem of Law Enforcement in North-East England, 1718–1800* (London: UCL Press, 1998).

Morgan, Gwenda and Rushton, Peter, 'The Magistrate, the Community and the Maintenance of an Orderly Society in Eighteenth-Century England', *Historical Research* 76 (2003), 54–77.

Morgan, Kenneth, 'The Organization of the Convict Trade to Maryland: Stevenson, Randolph and Cheston, 1768–1775', *William and Mary Quarterly*, 3rd ser. 42 (1985), 201–27.

Morgan, Kenneth, 'English and American Attitudes towards Convict Transportation, 1718–1775', *History* 72 (1987), 416–31.

Morgan, Kenneth, 'Convict Runaways in Maryland, 1745–75', *Journal of American Studies* 23 (1989), 253–68.

Morgan, Kenneth, 'Convict Transportation to Colonial America', *Reviews in American History* 17 (1989), 29–34.

Morgan, Kenneth, 'Petitions against Convict Transportation', *English Historical Review* 104 (1989), 110–13.

Morgan, Kenneth, 'Shipping Patterns and the Atlantic Trade of Bristol, 1749–70', *William and Mary Quarterly*, 3rd ser. 46 (1989), 506–38.

Morgan, Kenneth, 'Convict Transportation from Devon', in Michael Duffy, Stephen Fisher, Basil Greenhill, David J. Starkey and Joyce Youings (eds), *The New Maritime History of Devon*, Vol. I: *From Early Times to the Late Eighteenth Century* (London: Conway Maritime Press and University of Exeter, 1992), 153–54.

Morgan, Kenneth, *Bristol and the Atlantic Trade in the Eighteenth Century* (Cambridge: Cambridge University Press, 1993).

Morgan, Kenneth, 'The Economic Development of Bristol, 1700–1850', in Madge Dresser and Philip Ollerenshaw (eds), *The Making of Modern Bristol* (Tiverton, Devon: Redcliffe Press, 1996), 48–75.

Morgan, Kenneth, *Slavery and Servitude in North America, 1607–1800* (Edinburgh: Edinburgh University Press, 2000).

Morgan, Kenneth, 'Business Networks in the British Export Trade to North America, 1750–1800', in John J. McCusker and Kenneth Morgan (eds), *The Early Modern Atlantic Economy* (Cambridge: Cambridge University Press, 2000), 16–62.

Morgan, Philip D., 'Colonial South Carolina Runaways: their Significance for Slave Culture', *Slavery and Abolition* 6 (1985), 57–78.

Morris, Richard B., *Government and Labor in Early America* (New York: Columbia University Press, 1946).

Morton, Richard L., *Colonial Virginia*, 2 vols (Chapel Hill, NC: University of North Carolina Press, 1960).

Mott, Frank Luther, *American Journalism: a History of Newspapers in the United States Through 250 Years, 1690–1940*, 6 vols (New York: Macmillan, 1941, reprinted London: Routledge/Thoemmes Press, 2000).

Mullin, G. W., *Flight and Rebellion: Slave Resistance in Eighteenth-Century Virginia* (New York: Oxford University Press, 1972).

Muskett, Paul, 'The Maidstone Prison Mutiny of 1765: Aspects of Eighteenth-Century Law Enforcement', *Southern History* 23 (2001), 30–51.

Myers, Robin and Michael Harris, eds, *Sale and Distribution of Books from 1700* (Oxford: Oxford Polytechnic Press, 1982).

Newton, James E. and Lewis, Ronald, *The Other Slaves: Mechanics, Artisans and Craftsmen* (Boston, MA: G. K. Hall Company, 1978).

Nokes, David, *John Gay: a Profession of Friendship. A Critical Biography* (Oxford: Oxford University Press, 1995).

Oldham, Wilfred, *British Convicts to the Colonies*, ed. W. Hugh Oldham (Sydney: Australian National Library, 1990).

Paley, Ruth, 'Thief-takers in London in the Age of the McDaniel Gang, *c*.1745–1754' in Douglas Hay and Francis Snyder (eds), *Policing and Prosecution in Britain 1750–1850* (Oxford: Clarendon Press, 1989), 301–41.

Palmer, Roy, *A Ballad History of England from 1588 to the Present Day* (London: Batsford, 1979).

Palmer, Roy, ed., *A Touch on the Times: Songs of Social Change, 1770 to 1914* (Harmondsworth: Penguin, 1974).

Patterson, James, 'An Examination of *A Voyage to Russia*: the First Travel Account Published by an Englishwoman', in Kim Wells, ed., *Women Writers: A Zine*,

Online Journal, 14 May 2001: http://www.womenwriters.net/may2001/justicessay.htm.

Pearson, G., *Hooligan: a History of Respectable Fears* (London: Macmillan, 1983).

Pitkin, Timothy, *A Political and Civil History of the United States of America from the year 1763 etc.*, 2 vols (New Haven, CT: Hezekiah Howe, Durrie and Peck, 1828).

Poole, Steve, 'To Be a Bristolian: Civic Identity and the Social Order, 1750–1850' in Madge Dresser and Philip Ollerenshaw (eds), *The Making of Modern Bristol*, (Tiverton, Devon: Redcliffe Press, 1996), pp. 76–95.

Postlethwayt, Malachy, *The Universal Dictionary of Trade and Commerce, translated from the French of the Celebrated Monsieur Savary, . . . with large additions and improvements etc.*, 2nd edn, 2 vols (London, 1758).

Price, Richard, *The Convict and the Colonel* (Boston, MA: Beacon Press, 1998).

Prude, Jonathan, 'To Look upon the "Lower Sort": Runaway Ads and the Appearance of Unfree Laborers in America, 1750–1800', *Journal of American History* 78 (1991), 124–59.

Purdue, A. W., *Merchants and Gentry in North-East England, 1650–1830: the Carrs and the Ellisons* (Sunderland: University of Sunderland Press, 1999).

Radzinowicz, L., *A History of English Criminal Law and its Administration from 1750*, 4 vols, vol. 1, *The Movement for Reform* (London: Stevens and Sons, 1948).

Ragsdale, Bruce A., *A Planters' Republic: the Search for Economic Independence in Revolutionary Virginia* (Madison, WI: Madison House, 1996).

Randolph, Edmund, *History of Virginia*, edited with an introduction by Arthur H. Shaffer (Charlottesville, VA: University Press of Virginia, 1970).

Rawlings, Philip, *Drunks, Whores and Idle Apprentices: Criminal Biographies of the Eighteenth Century* (London: Routledge, 1992).

Rawlings, Philip, 'True Crime', in the British Criminology Conferences: Selected Proceedings, Jon Vagg and Tim Newburn (eds) Vol. 1: *Emerging Themes in Criminology* (British Society of Criminology, 1998).

Rediker, Marcus, *Between the Devil and the Deep Blue Sea: Merchant Seamen, Pirates, and the Anglo-American Maritime World, 1700–50* (Cambridge: Cambridge University Press, 1997).

Reece, Bob, *The Origins of Irish Convict Transportation to New South Wales* (London: Palgrave, 2001).

Reiner, Robert, 'Media-Made Criminality: the Representation of Crime in the Mass Media', in Mike Maguire, Rod Morgan and Robert Reiner (eds), *The Oxford Handbook of Criminology*, 2nd edn (Oxford: Oxford University Press, 1997), 189–231.

Rice, J., ' "This Province, So Meanly and Thinly Inhabited": Punishing Maryland's Criminals, 1681–1850', *Journal of the Early Republic* 19 (1999), 15–42.

Richardson, D. and Schofield, M. M., 'Whitehaven and the Eighteenth-Century British Slave Trade', *Transactions of the Cumberland & Westmorland Archaeological and Antiquarian Society* 92 (1992), 83–204.

Rigg, A. N., *Cumbria, Slavery and the Textile Revolution* (Kirkby Stephen, Cumbria: Hewitson and Harker, 1994).

Riley, James C., 'Mortality on Long-Distance Voyages in the Eighteenth Century', *Journal of Economic History* 41 (1981), 651–6.

Roberts, Stephen K., 'Juries and the Middling Sort: Recruitment and Performance at Devon Quarter Sessions, 1649–70', in J. S. Cockburn and Thomas Green (eds), *Twelve Good Men and True: the Criminal Trial Jury in England, 1200–1800* (Princeton, NJ: Princeton University Press, 1987), 182–213.

Rogers, Nicholas, 'Confronting the Crime Wave: The Debate over Social Reform and Regulation', in Lee Davison, Tim Hitchcock, Tim Keirn and R. B. Shoemaker (eds), *Stilling the Grumbling Hive: The Response to Social and Economic Problems in England, 1660–1750*, (Stroud, Glos: Alan Sutton, 1992), 77–98.

Rogers, Nicholas, 'Vagrancy, Imprisonment and the Regulation of Labor in Eighteenth-Century Britain', *Slavery and Abolition* 15 (1994), 102–13.

Rowe, D. J., 'The North-East', in F. M. L. Thompson (ed.) *The Cambridge Social History of Britain, 1750–1950*, Vol. 1, *Regions and Communities* (Cambridge: Cambridge University Press, 1990), 415–70.

Rozbicki, Michael J., *The Complete Colonial Gentleman: Cultural Legitimacy in Plantation America* (Charlottesville, VA, and London: University Press of Virginia, 1998).

Rozbicki, Michael J., 'To Save Them from Themselves: Proposals to Enslave the British Poor, 1698–1755', *Slavery and Abolition* 22 (2) (2001), 29–50.

Ruff, Julius R., *Violence in Early Modern Europe* (Cambridge: Cambridge University Press, 2001).

Rule, John, *Albion's People: English Society, 1714–1815* (London: Longman, 1992).

Rule, John, 'Social Crime in the Rural South in the Eighteenth and Early Nineteenth Centuries', in John Rule and Roger Wells, *Crime, Protest and Popular Politics in Southern England, 1740–1850* (London: Hambledon Press, 1997), 153–68.

Rushton, Peter, 'Crazes and Quarrels: the Character of Witchcraft in the North East of England, 1649–80', *Durham County Local History Society Bulletin* 31 (1983), 2–40.

Rushton, Peter, '"The Matter of Variance": Adolescents and Domestic Conflict in the Pre-Industrial Economy of Northeast England, 1600–1800', *Journal of Social History* 25 (1991), 89–107.

Sacks, D. H., *The Widening Gate: Bristol and the Atlantic Economy, 1450–1700* (Berkeley, CA: University of California Press, 1991).

Salinger, Sharon V., *'To Serve Well and Faithfully': Labor and Indentured Servants in Pennsylvania, 1682–1800* (New York: Cambridge University Press, 1987).

Scharf, J. Thomas, *History of Maryland from the Earliest Period to the Present Day*, 3 vols (Hatboro, Pennsylvania: Tradition Press, 1967, originally 1879, with a new foreword by Morris L. Radoff).

Schlesinger, P. and Tumber, H., *Reporting Crime: the Media Politics of Criminal Justice* (Oxford: Clarendon Press, 1994).

Schmidt, F. H., 'Sold and Driven: Assignment of Convicts in Eighteenth-Century Virginia', *The Push from the Bush: a Bulletin of Social History* 23 (1986), 2–27.

Schwartz, Stuart B., 'The Formation of a Colonial Identity in Brazil', in Nicholas Canny and Anthony Pagden (eds), *Colonial Identity in the Atlantic World, 1500–1800* (Princeton, NJ: Princeton University Press, 1987), 15–50.

Schwarz, Philip J., *Twice Condemned: Slaves and the Criminal Laws of Virginia, 1705–1865* (Baton Rouge: Louisiana State University Press, 1988).

Sellers, Charles Coleman, *The Artist of the Revolution: the Early Life of Charles Willson Peale* (Hebron, CT: Feather and Good, 1939).

Sharpe, J. A., *Crime in Seventeenth-Century England: a County Study* (Cambridge: Cambridge University Press, 1983).

Sharpe, J. A., ' "Last Dying Speeches": Religion, Ideology and Public Execution in Seventeenth-Century England', *Past and Present* 107 (1985), 144–67.

Shaw, A. G. L., *Convicts and the Colonies: a Study of Penal Transportation from Great Britain and Ireland to Australia and Other Parts of the British Empire* (London: Faber and Faber, 1966, Irish Historical Press, 1998 2nd edn).

Singleton, Robert, 'Defoe, Moll Flanders, and the Ordinary of Newgate', *Harvard Library Bulletin* 24 (Oct 1976), 407–13.

Skaggs, David C., *The Roots of Maryland Democracy* (Westport, CT: Greenwood Press, 1973).

Slack, P., *Poverty and Policy in Tudor and Stuart England* (London: Longman, 1988).

Sloan, William David, and Williams, Julie Hedgepeth, *The Early American Press, 1690–1783* (Westport, CT: Greenwood Press, 1994).

Smith, Abbot E., *Colonists in Bondage: White Servitude and Convict Labor in America, 1607–1776* (Chapel Hill, NC: University of North Carolina Press, 1947; New York: Norton, 1971).

Smith, Adam, *The Theory of Moral Sentiments*, ed. D. D. Raphael and A. L. Macfie (Oxford: Clarendon Press, 1976).

Smith, Billy G., 'Runaway Slaves in the Mid-Atlantic Region during the Revolutionary Era' in Ronald Hoffman and Peter J. Albert (eds), *The Transforming Hand of Revolution: Reconsidering the American Revolution as a Social Movement* (Charlottesville, VA, and London: University Press of Virginia for the United States Capitol Historical Society, 1993), 199–230.

Smith, Daniel Scott, 'Population and Political Ethics: Thomas Jefferson's Demography of Generations', *William and Mary Quarterly*, 3rd. ser. 56 (1999), 591–612.

Smith, Warren B., *White Indentured Servitude in Colonial South Carolina* (Columbia, SC: University of South Carolina Press, 1961).

Sollars, Basil, 'Transported Convict Laborers in Maryland during the Colonial Period', *Maryland Historical Magazine* 2 (1907), 17–47.

Souden, David, ' "Rogues, Whores and Vagabonds?": Indentured Servant Emigrants to North America and the Case of Mid-Seventeenth Century Bristol', *Social History* 3 (1978), 23–41.

Speck, W. A., *Literature and Society in Eighteenth-Century England, 1680–1820: Ideology, Culture and Politics* (London: Longman, 1998).

Spierenburg, Pieter, *The Spectacle of Suffering. Executions and the Evolution of Repression: From a Preindustrial Metropolis to the European Experience* (Cambridge: Cambridge University Press, 1984).

Spierenburg, P., *The Prison Experience: Disciplinary Institutions and Their Inmates in Early Modern Europe* (New Brunswick and London: Rutgers University Press, 1991).

Stanard, Mary N., *Colonial Virginia: Its People and Customs* (Philadelphia and London: J. P. Lippencott, 1917).

Steele, Ian K., *The English Atlantic: 1675–1740: an Exploration of Communication and Community* (New York: Oxford University Press, 1986).

Stegmaier, Mark J., 'Maryland's Fear of Insurrection at the Time of Braddock's Defeat', *Maryland Historical Magazine* 71 (1976), 467–83.

Steinfeld, Robert J., *The Invention of Free Labor: the Employment Relation in English and American Law and Culture, 1350–1870* (Chapel Hill, NC: University of North Carolina Press, 1991).

Steinfeld, Robert J. and Engerman, Stanley L., 'Labour – Free or Coerced? A Historical Reassessment of Differences and Similarities', in Tom Brass and Marcel
van der Linden (eds), *Free and Unfree Labour: the Debate Continues* (Berne: Peter
Lang, European Academic Publishers, 1997), 107–26.

Stevenson, John, 'The "Moral Economy" of the English Crowd: Myth and
Reality', in A. Fletcher and J. Stevenson (eds), *Order and Disorder in Early Modern
England* (Cambridge: Cambridge University Press, 1987), 218–38.

Stevenson, John, *Popular Disturbances in England 1700–1832*, 2nd edn (London
and New York: Longman, 1992).

Stith, William, *The History of the First Discovery and Settlement of Virginia etc.*
(Williamsburg, VA, 1747).

Stretton, Tim, *Women Waging Law in Elizabethan England* (Cambridge: Cambridge
University Press, 1998).

Styles, John, 'Sir John Fielding and the Problem of Criminal Investigation in
Eighteenth-Century England', *Transactions of the Royal Historical Society*, 5th
ser. 33 (1983), 127–49

Styles, John, 'Print and Policing: Crime Advertising in Eighteenth-Century
Provincial England', in D. Hay and F. Snyder (eds), *Policing and Prosecution in
England, 1750–1850* (Oxford: Clarendon Press 1989), 55–111.

Summerville, C. John, *The News Revolution in England: Cultural Dynamics of Daily
Information* (New York: Oxford: University Press, 1996).

Szasz, Ferenc. M., 'Peter Williamson and the Eighteenth-Century Scottish-
American Connection', *Northern Scotland* 19 (1999), 47–61.

Tattersfield, N., *The Forgotten Trade, comprising the Log of the Daniel and Henry of
1700 and Accounts of the Slave Trade from the Minor Ports of England, 1698–1725*
(London: Pimlico, 1998).

Thompson, E. P., 'The Moral Economy and the English Crowd in the Eighteenth
Century', *Past and Present* 50 (1971), 79–94.

Thompson, E. P., *Whigs and Hunters: the Origin of the Black Act* (London: Allen
Lane, 1975).

Thompson, E. P., *Customs in Common* (Harmondsworth: Penguin, 1993).

Tomalin, Claire, *Samuel Pepys: the Unequalled Self* (London: Viking/Penguin,
2002).

Tomlins, Christopher, 'Subordination, Authority, Law: Subjects in Labor History',
International Labor and Working-Class History 47 (1995), 56–90.

Tomlins, Christopher, 'Reconsidering Indentured Servitude: European Migration
and the Early American Labor Force, 1600–1775', *Labor History* 42 (1) (2001),
5–43.

Towner, Lawrence A., '"A Fondness for Freedom": Servant Protest in Puritan
Society', *William and Quarterly*, 3rd ser. 19 (1962), 201–19.

Tuckerman, Henry T., *America and her Commentators, with a Critical Sketch of Travel
in the United States* (New York: Augustus M. Kelley, 1970, originally New York:
1864).

Uglow, Jenny, *Hogarth: a Life and a World* (London: Faber and Faber, 1997).

Van Der Zee, John, *Bound Over: Indentured Servitude and American Conscience* (New
York: Simon and Shuster, 1985).

Ville, S., 'Total Factor Productivity in the English Shipping Industry: the North-East
Coal Trade, 1700–1850', *Economic History Review*, 2nd ser. 39 (1986), 355–
370.

Waldstreicher, David, 'Reading the Runaways: Self-Fashioning, Print Culture, and Confidence in Slavery in the Eighteenth-Century Mid-Atlantic', *William and Mary Quarterly*, 3rd ser. 56 (1999), 243–72.

Wales, Tim, 'Poverty, Poor Relief and the Life-Cycle: Some Evidence from Seventeenth-Century Norfolk', in R. M. Smith (ed.), *Land, Kinship and Life-Cycle* (Cambridge: Cambridge University Press, 1984), 351–404.

Wareing, John, ' "Violently Taken Away or Cheatingly Duckoyed": the Illicit Recruitment in London of Indentured Servants for the American Colonies, 1645–1718', *London Journal* 26 (2001) 1–22.

Wareing, John, 'Preventive and Punitive Regulation in Seventeenth-Century Social Policy: Conflicts of Interest and the Failure to Make "Stealing and Transporting Children and Other Persons" a Felony, 1645–73', *Social History* 27 (2002), 288–308.

Weber, Max, *Economy and Society*, 2 vols, trans. G. Roth and C. Wittich (Berkeley, CA: University of California Press, 1978).

Welford, Richard, *Men of Mark 'Twixt Tyne and Tweed*, vol. 3 (London and Newcastle-upon-Tyne: 1895).

Wells, R. A. E., 'Sheep-Rustling in Yorkshire in the Age of the Industrial and Agricultural Revolutions', *Northern History* 20 (1984), 127–45.

White, Shane, *Somewhat More Independent: The End of Slavery in New York City, 1770–1810* (Athens, GA, and London: University of Georgia Press, 1991).

Williams, Daniel E., ' "Behold a Tragic Scene Strangely Changed into a Theater of Mercy": the Structure and Significance of Criminal Conversion Narratives in Early New England', *American Quarterly* 38 (1986), 827–47.

Winslow, Cal., 'Sussex Smugglers', in D. Hay et al. (eds), *Albion's Fatal Tree: Crime and Society in Eighteenth-Century England* (London: Allen Lane, 1975), 119–66.

Wood, Peter, *Black Majority: Negroes in Colonial South Carolina: From 1670 through the Stono Rebellion* (New York: Knopf, 1974).

Wrightson, Keith *Earthly Necessities: Economic Lives in Early Modern Britain* (New Haven, CT, and London: Yale University Press, 2000)

Wyatt, J. W., 'Transportation from Gloucestershire, 1718–1773', *Gloucestershire Historical Studies* 3 (1969), 2–15.

Zuckerman, Michael, 'Tocqueville, Turner and Turds: Four Stories of Manners in Early America', *Journal of American History* 85 (1998), 13–42.

Unpublished sources

Burgoyne, Cindy C., 'Imprisonment the Best Punishment: the Transatlantic Exchange and Communication of Ideas in the Field of Penology, 1750–1820' (PhD diss., University of Sunderland, 1997).

Hay, Douglas, 'Crime, Authority and the Criminal Law: Staffordshire, 1750–1800' (PhD diss., University of Warwick, 1975).

Pole, S.C., 'Crime, Society and Law Enforcement in Hanoverian Somerset' (PhD diss., University of Cambridge, 1983).

Schmidt, F. H., 'British Convict Servant Labor in Colonial Virginia' (PhD diss., College of William and Mary, 1976).

Index

DATE DUE

APR 06 '09 S		
APR 2 1 2009		